The Man Who Would Be Jack

THE MAN WHO WOULD BE JACK

DAVID BULLOCK

LUME BOOKS

LUME BOOKS

First published in 2020 by Lume Books
30 Great Guildford Street,
Borough, SE1 0HS

ISBN 978-1-83901-237-2

Typeset using Atomik ePublisher from Easypress Technologies

www.lumebooks.co.uk

For
Benjamin and Samuel

Prologue

5 March 1891
Lambeth Infirmary

As if imitating death, the patient, who earlier had tried to slit his mother's throat, lay motionless upon an iron bed, his arms loose at his sides, his eyes wide staring passively ahead, the only sign of life being the small beads of sweat that prickled upon his forehead.

He was younger than most in the infirmary, tall and thin and from the quality of his clothing a man of means. Though he had the appearance of an imbecile the behaviour of the four orderlies who, armed with cudgels, surrounded his bed, indicated that he was anything but an average patient.

Earlier he had fought them, kicking out as the warders attempted to remove him from his home in Kennington. Arriving under the silence of dawn the guards believed that by catching the patient in a state of sleep he would present a far easier prospect. As the four orderlies, clad in white-belted coats, entered the darkness of his room, they found the patient awake, dressed and, to their surprise, ready to fight.

At first the sheer number of guards proved overwhelming, grabbing at the patient's ankles and arms as he crawled backwards on his bed. As he thrashed in a frenzy of kicks and blind punches the patient berated the guards with an onslaught of obscenities. One he bit, before striking another, the largest of the group who had half unbuckled his belt in order to strap the patient's feet.

i

Seizing his opportunity to escape, the patient bolted towards the door, only to be stopped by a stern blow to the face that not only subdued him but wrenched a tooth from his mouth.

In the time that had elapsed between leaving Kennington and reaching the Infirmary, the patient's mood had changed dramatically. Gone was the anger, the aggression, even his groans had ceased, with the only sound filling the near-empty ward being the heavy breaths of the four orderlies, reverberating against the grey walls.

Though the guards were vigilant, what they hadn't noticed, as they carried the lifeless man from the carriage to his bed, were his brilliant blue eyes taking note of the route. Making a mental map of his new environment: the small stone fireplace to his left, the large barred window to the rear of the ward, ablaze with March sunlight, and the door in the farthest corner that led to the main Infirmary corridor and importantly offered the only opportunity of escape.

For two hours he remained silent. Stripped of all clothing except a shirt, he lay quietly upon his bed under the gaze of his jailers, patiently waiting for his moment.

By noon it had arrived.

When he struck, he did so with such speed as to leave his warders reeling. With an animal ferocity he bolted from his bed, knocking two guards to the ground. Before they knew what had hit them the shoeless and trouserless patient was already through the ward doors, shirt-tails flying as he took off down the corridor.

The orderlies made chase and by the time the patient had reached the Laundry Block, two of them, the fittest of the four men, were almost upon him. It was only on entering the laundry room itself that he felt it, a cool breeze invading the warmth of the two wood-burning stoves used to heat irons.

Beyond a forest of washboards and mangles, of ceiling racks adorned with damp garments, a window had been left ajar. As the panicked voices neared, he eased the window frame upwards before stepping lightly onto the roof of the adjoining boiler house.

After a short drop the patient was out, running barefoot along the gravelled terrace. With no obstacles to block his route he reached the eight-foot boundary wall in no time and only then, as he stared at the wall looking for a foothold, did he hear the alarm being raised as shouts and whistles engulfed the infirmary yard behind him.

On looking back he could see that other warders were now in pursuit, those better positioned for such a chase. Two had come from the House Block, while another – a bear of a man – had emerged from the ground-floor Labour Ward.

What they saw would later be reported upon and used as a means of describing the agility and athleticism of a man who, according to his guards, managed to scale the boundary wall 'with the ease and nimbleness of a monkey'.

Once over, his feet hit the cobbles running. Although there were many strange and wonderful sights in the teeming streets of Lambeth, a man sprinting between over-laden carriages and market stalls wearing nothing but a shirt drew bemused and shocked attention. As the alert spread, first via shouts and then by policemen's whistles, constables ran to the scene.

In no time every police station in London was aware of the escape, with the patient's description having been wired from Lambeth Police Station along with a note indicating the need for his urgent capture.

Aware that a mob was starting to form behind him, the patient made for the first building he could see. A school. Bursting through the front doors he darted his gaze to each corner of the classroom, from the mighty blackboard that ran the length of the top wall and stood watch over rows of empty desks, to the back of the room.

Faint shrieks could be heard coming, not from the street but the rear of the school, the backyard where, being midday, the children were enjoying playtime.

As the semi-naked fugitive smashed through the back door the joyful cries soon turned to screams of panic. Some of the pupils ran, while others remained, frozen with fear, as the escapee frantically took in his surroundings.

The open front door of the school had allowed the screams to travel, alerting a patrolling constable who immediately followed the trail of cries. By the time he reached the yard the fugitive was gone, with only the extended arms of several older boys indicating his whereabouts. With trembling fingers, the boys pointed to the wall that separated the yard from a residential garden. Assuming incorrectly that the escapee had entered the adjoining garden in order to break into the house, the constable ran back to the street and after summoning two colleagues charged through the front door.

The fugitive, however, had other ideas. Instead of entering the house, he had vaulted over a series of garden walls before crashing into a randomly chosen property via the back door.

Fortunately for him it was empty. The residents, their curiosity pricked by the commotion outside, had taken to the street. Inside, his luck improved further as folded neatly upon a wooden chest lay a pair of striped trousers, as well as a check jacket and a brown overcoat next to a black felt hat and a pair of worn leather boots.

Losing no time he dressed, pulling the hat low over his brow in order to cover his eyes, before exiting smartly out of the front door. Only as he pulled the door to a close did the fugitive stop for the first time, pausing for the briefest of moments in order to take in the chaotic scene outside.

To his left, three constables were struggling to make entry into another property, believing he was inside. In front, a large crowd had gathered, a gaggle of women whispering excitedly under their breaths, gasping and pointing at the petrified school children who had formed a circle, enclosing their distraught teacher.

Next to them another group was forming: men and boys, some armed with clubs, ready to assist the police in bringing their quarry to justice. Standing quite still, the fugitive raised the collar of his newly acquired coat, before calmly walking past the excited crowd. Under the very noses of his pursuers he crossed the road, away from the whistles and cries, before vanishing into the teeming streets of Lambeth.

Thomas Hayne Cutbush, the most dangerous man in all of London, was free.[1]

ONE

The Scoop of the Century

The attic room in which Inspector Race stood was dark and sparsely furnished. Its walls, rafters and bare floorboards cloaked in dense, edgeless, shadow.

The scent of geraniums that lightly touched the remainder of the house was absent here. Replaced, instead, by damp and dust and the stench of perspiration. An unpleasant and oppressive place that for twenty-five years Thomas Cutbush had called home.

For four days Cutbush had remained at large and in that time he had attacked two women with a knife, the first assault far more vicious than the second. By 9 March he had become Scotland Yard's most wanted man.[1]

In setting Inspector Race the task of catching Thomas Cutbush, the Metropolitan Police had chosen well. A solid man with a full beard and a high intelligent forehead above a youthful face, 36-year-old William Race was a shrewd and dedicated officer who knew the dangerous streets of Kennington and east London all too well.

Since joining the Metropolitan Police in 1880, Race had ascended through the ranks, running criminals to ground in a fashion that drew attention not only from his colleagues but also the press. His adventures were often published in the local newspapers, in which he was applauded for his courage, a trait much needed for anyone willing to don the police uniform in such perilous times.[2]

Policing London in the 1880s was a tough and thankless task, with corruption and danger lurking around every corner. The first concern for new recruits was simply being able to fight. With over 2,000 assaults each year, the police had never been so unpopular, especially after the series of brutal Ripper murders that had occurred in 1888 in Whitechapel and three years later remained unsolved.

Though not initially engaged in that investigation, like so many officers posted in nearby districts, Race had been drafted into the East End from Kennington to assist in the hunt for the Ripper. Offering a level head, unclouded by the hysteria surrounding the case, for Inspector Race Jack the Ripper had simply been another criminal who, like Thomas Cutbush, needed to be stopped.[3]

Race wasted little time in getting to know his latest quarry. Interviewing Cutbush's aunt Clara, who lived with her sister and her strange son in Albert Street, he discovered that Cutbush was known for an evil temper. He learnt from the aunt that her nephew had the habit of walking the streets of London late at night and would return in the early hours covered in mud and blood.[4]

Cutbush, so she said, was obsessed with the study of medical books and made many anatomical drawings and sketches of mutilated women. He would also discuss, with anyone who would listen, the symptoms and cures of certain horrible diseases.[5]

As his aunt testified, prior to his arrest, Cutbush had once assaulted a servant girl, taking a knife to her throat before being disturbed.[6]

During a visit to the house Race took possession of the six-inch Bowie knife used by Cutbush in his previous attacks. Cutbush though had laid his hand on another weapon while he remained at large and during that time he would commit two knife attacks on women, one notable in its savagery.

When the Inspector discovered that the fugitive had an intimate knowledge of the area where the Whitechapel murders had occurred, he began to see in Cutbush far more than the weak-minded criminal as depicted by the newspapers.

As Race drew his net tight, and came face-to-face with his man on

9 March, apprehending Cutbush at the rear of his home in the early morning, his appearance could not fail to jolt a memory. Race knew that in catching Cutbush he had laid his hands on one of the most dangerous men he had ever encountered.

The trial held on 14 April 1891 at the South London County Sessions would come to a surprisingly premature conclusion, with Dr Gilbert (the medical officer at Holloway Prison where Cutbush was being held) finding him mentally unstable and while 'not absolutely insane' being sufficiently so as to 'not understand the charge brought against him'. With that, and much to the frustration of both the defence and Cutbush's own family, the jury passed their verdict.[7]

On 23 April Thomas Cutbush arrived in the village of Crowthorne in Berkshire with his hands and feet shackled, having been removed from Holloway by train. There he was placed in Broadmoor Asylum for the Criminally Insane, where he was due to remain at her Majesty's Pleasure.

And, though for some the story of Cutbush and his crimes ended as he entered through the towering gates of Britain's most secure asylum, for Inspector Race it had just begun.

In the months that followed he began to take an active, almost obsessive, interest in linking Cutbush to the Ripper case. Having ascertained that he had worked in Whitechapel during 1888 as a clerk with a tea importer, Race thought it odd that, when questioned, Cutbush chose to deny any knowledge of the East End. When the suspect excused his drawings as being part of his studies, to enable him to practise in the medical profession, Race became even more intrigued.

The Inspector looked back on the suspect profile compiled by doctors who in 1888 had worked on the Ripper case and found a direct resemblance to Cutbush. He returned to Albert Street and spoke once again to the family. Discovering the locations where Cutbush had worked and finding that he was repeatedly sacked from positions due to his poor timekeeping. He also discovered that his whereabouts on each of the nights when the Ripper murders occurred could not be confirmed.[8]

While searching Cutbush's room the Inspector found, stuffed up the chimney breast, clothing stained with blood and covered in turpentine as if in preparation to be burnt.[9]

As the year neared its end Race had compiled a wealth of information on Cutbush, discovering further evidence of his violent tendencies, including a previously undisclosed murder attempt on a colleague, as well as the brutal rape of a prostitute that had occurred prior to the start of the Ripper murders.[10] Race looked back upon witness statements from those who said they had seen the Ripper on the nights of the murders and couldn't fail to see a direct match with Cutbush.

By 1892, confident in his findings, the experienced Race took his suspicions to his superiors, namely Chief Inspector Chisholm and Chief Constable Macnaghten. He laid before them his findings, including his suggested motive that Cutbush had killed due to him suffering from homicidal mania brought on through a twisted fascination with anatomy and contempt for prostitutes.[11]

Much to the Inspector's surprise the case against Cutbush, one which he had worked tirelessly on for over a year, was rejected without explanation. Though Cutbush presented the most viable suspect put forward since the murders began in 1888, the senior officers of Scotland Yard were keen to let the mystery of the Ripper case simply rest.

Inspector Race was not of the same opinion.

Fleet Street – 'the street of ink' – was packed full of newspapers desperate for original crime stories.Dubbed the 'golden age' of newspaper publication, due to technical advances in printing and communication, distribution of local and national press was at its peak.[13]

The leading papers of the day included the *Morning Post, Evening News, Lloyd's Weekly* and *Reynolds's Weekly*, all with their own passionately held political allegiances and agendas. Competition was savage and one thing editors knew was that nothing shifted papers like a good murder.[14]

Investigative journalism, if still a somewhat unreliable and chaotic field, was well established by this time, from the tabloid approach of blackmailing celebrities of the day and hounding out scandals to unmasking political and international intrigue.

The police rarely gave information to the press and frustrated journalists desperate for a new titbit of information about the Jack the Ripper case had a tendency to get creative with the facts. Inspector Race, however, turned out to be a most reliable and forthcoming source.

In 1893 he approached *The Sun* newspaper,one of the nation's first and most lively tabloids, and told them the incredible story of Thomas Cutbush. Eager to seize such a unique opportunity the paper's chief editor, T. P. O'Connor, immediately assigned his top journalists to speak with Race and find out all they could. For the ailing newspaper, which although selling well struggled to meet its distribution costs, this was an unexpected and much needed lifeline.[16]

The first man chosen for the task of interviewing Inspector Race was news editor Kennedy Jones, known to most as 'KJ', who at the age of twenty-six had arrived in Fleet Street hungry for his fortune. A man of sharp imagination and guile, KJ, with his strong features and stiff black hair, was described by some as a 'rough diamond'[17] and by others as 'brutal'.[18].

Though his gruff demeanour drew a mixed reaction from his colleagues he was seen by most as an expert in the 'mechanics of journalism'.[19]. Yet, after three years the wealth KJ so desired had failed to materialise and he found himself living in a modest house in Brixton with his two young children and pregnant wife.[20]

T. P. O'Connor's second choice was the handsome Louis Tracy, who had only recently joined *The Sun* after achieving popularity with a number of other newspapers. Although only a young man Tracy had a thirst for adventure and in the preceding years had been lured overseas, leading to his 1892 biography: *What I saw in India: The Adventures of a Globetrotter.*[21]

Together the two journalists met Race, and were shown Cutbush's drawings and the Bowie knife which unbeknownst to Race's superiors he had kept, instead of booking it into the prisoner's property store. They would learn of the attic room, Cutbush's family history, how his physical appearance matched the descriptions of the most reliable witnesses who thought they had seen the Ripper, the strange way he talked, his odd night walks, his daring escape and the two attacks on the young women.

The Inspector would also recount a strange confession made by Cutbush shortly after his arrest. While alone with his prisoner in the police wagon, used to convey him to Kennington Lane Police Station, Cutbush began to speak. Eager to know what had led the police to his door, he asked whether his arrest was due to what he described as the 'Mile End job'.

Receiving little in the way of a reply he continued, informing Race that he had been mistaken as Jewish and had escaped capture. As the Inspector listened it became apparent that Cutbush was referring to a previous attempt, made by him, to accost a woman —a prostitute — who by his own admission he had 'just missed.'[22]

As Race admitted to KJ and Tracy in 1893, he knew nothing of any incident occurring in the area of Mile End. Unbeknownst to all three men this admission would later prove crucial to their investigation.

For KJ and Tracy, such cooperation from a Police Inspector was unheard of. Perhaps most tantalising of all, Thomas Cutbush was still alive, although incarcerated in Block One, a highly secure area of Broadmoor Asylum reserved for the nation's most dangerous lunatics.

If Race was right, then this would be the scoop of the century

TWO

The First Victim

Five years earlier, the summer of 1888 had been one of the wettest and coldest on record. Snow had fallen in July, cloaking London's skyline in a blanket of crisp white, before being washed away by freezing downpours the following month.[1]

On 30 August, 42-year-old Mary Ann Nichols was making her usual evening journey through the dark maze of Whitechapel in search of drink, clients and a bed for the night. With her missing teeth and greying hair, Mary could hardly be described as attractive, though she had little trouble finding clients. 'I'll soon get my doss money,' she had boasted to the keeper of a lodging house earlier that evening.[2]

For many women living in the East End, selling their bodies was a quick and easy way to stave off cold and starvation – a not uncommon death. Prostitution was an enormous industry.

Estimates of their numbers in London varied from 8,000 (the police) to 80,000 (the church), indicating no shortage of demand. All classes partook, though the Victorian moralists reserved their heaviest strictures for the working classes. Along with drink, prostitutes were the main vice for dockworkers, labourers and even policemen.[3]

Murder was considered an occupational hazard for Whitechapel's fallen women, residing en masse within the cheap lodging houses found on almost every street. These disproportionately tall buildings were crammed into tiny streets just ten to sixteen feet wide; Flower and Dean

Street alone boasted thirty-one lodging buildings with a total of 902 rooms – home to the largest concentration of criminals in all of London.[4]

Teeming with thousands of immigrants from Eastern Europe and beyond, so densely populated was Whitechapel that throughout the 1880's homelessness was rife, with men, women and in some cases entire families sleeping rough upon the festering streets or under railway bridges.

For Mary Nichols this was a life unexpected, a far cry from the world of respectability that she had left behind seven years earlier. Abandoned by her husband William Nichols, disowned by her five children, Mary now found herself alone in the most brutal quarter of England's great capital, a reeking labyrinth of alleys and narrow streets, where gangs of pickpockets and street robbers ruled and where survival came at a price.

Although Mary had been able to get off the streets in the April of 1888, when she found work as a domestic servant in Wandsworth, this would prove an all too brief interlude from prostitution in an otherwise bleak and perilous existence. And though swapping the streets of Whitechapel for a grand, newly decorated house should have appealed to Mary, with its trees and gardens filled with an air untarnished by the smog of east London, within two months she was gone, fleeing under the cover of darkness, having stolen various items that she would later pawn.

By mid-July Mary Nichols was back in Whitechapel, working her old haunts as a prostitute.

In little over a month she would be dead.

By 12.30 a.m. on Friday 31 August, under a starless sky alive with the red haze of a nearby dock fire, Mary left the Frying Pan pub on Brick Lane, alone. Rain had fallen in the two hours that she had spent drinking, leaving a wet film upon the cobbles outside.

By 1.30 a.m. she was ready for bed and came to Thrawl Street Lodging House, though without having the four pence required for a night's doss, her stay was brief. On being asked to leave Mary replied that she would soon return with her money and asked that a bed be kept for her.

From Thrawl Street Mary made her way to the Whitechapel Road where, with its many pubs and music halls, she hoped to find a client.

Having been unable to shelter from a short downpour, she presented a miserable and desperate sight to her old friend Emily Holland who was returning from Shadwell Dry Dock, where she had been to watch the fire. Staggering along the street, standing only with the aid of a shop wall, Mary barely registered who was talking to her, despite Emily being an old friend.

Worried that Mary should still be walking the streets in such poor conditions, Emily tried in vain to convince her to return to Thrawl Street, where the pair had once shared a room. Such pleas fell on deaf ears, with Mary's confident reply being that she would find her doss money and would then return.

As the Whitechapel Church clock struck two-thirty Emily caught a final glimpse of her friend, disappearing eastwards into the gloom of the Whitechapel Road.[5]

By 3.30 a.m. Mary had found another client. Coffee-stall keeper John Morgan was preparing to close his stall on Cambridge Heath Road when the two figures emerged under the haze of a nearby street lamp. Though eager to return to his lodgings and avoid the storm that had threatened for most of the previous evening, like so many of those working a trade in Whitechapel, Morgan was aware that every penny counted.

According to a statement given the next day, John Morgan confirmed that he had sold Mary a mug of tea, as well as stating that at that time she appeared to be in the company of a man. The couple looked as if they had had a quarrel. Standing a little away from Mary in the poorly lit road, Morgan could see little of her companion much beyond his dark hair and short beard. Eager to help the police and the press with their enquiries, Morgan also provided a name for Mary's client: he had heard her calling him 'Jim'.[6]

Before being disturbed by the screams, Sarah Colwell had been sleeping quite peacefully with her children in Honeys Mews on Brady Street; a long thoroughfare running parallel to Cambridge Heath Road. Until then the street had appeared silent, save for the gentle tread of the beat officers who regularly patrolled the area, keeping a watchful eye over its many dwellings, as well as the large Jewish Cemetery situated on its western side.

Sarah's children had been the first to wake, alerting their mother that a woman was trying to break into the house. As she gathered the youngsters into her bed and listened the first scream came; a woman's cry splitting the silence of the street, followed by several thuds as if someone was hitting the front door.[7]

Too afraid to move or even dare to look out of the bedroom window Sarah and her children listened as the screams faded down Brady Street. The woman was running, that much she could tell, in the direction of Buck's Row and strangely, though it sounded as if she was being struck as she ran, only one set of footsteps could be heard.

By 3.40 a.m. the footfalls and screams had ceased. Lying flat upon her back in the entrance to Brown's stable-yard on Buck's Row, Mary's body was discovered only moments later by a Carman named Charles Cross. Unbeknownst to him, while on his way to work, Cross had followed Mary's route from Cambridge Heath Road, where he lived on Doveton Street.

In the darkness of Buck's Row, illuminated by a single street lamp, Cross initially didn't see anything untoward. Walking at a brisk pace on the north side of the street, with tall warehouses casting deep shadows against the crowded tenements opposite, he eventually reached a three-storey office building named Essex Wharf. It was only then that he saw the shape of Mary's body.

At first he believed the dark object lying upon the ground was material, possibly tarpaulin. Intrigued, Cross decided to take a closer look only to be halted by the sound of footsteps walking towards him from the direction of Brady Street. Charles Cross was joined by Robert Paul, a fellow Carman who, like him, had been on his way to work and who it would appear was just as inquisitive. As the pair stepped closer to the stable-yard entrance they soon became aware that the form upon the ground was that of a woman.

On the street the darkness was so thick that both men saw nothing of the horrific wounds. Holding Mary's hands, Cross felt only cold skin, no warmth, no pulse and though he listened intently as he leant his head close to Mary's open mouth – no breaths. The men saw that Mary's skirts had been pulled up and rearranged them in an effort to protect her modesty.

On realising the enormity of their discovery both men ran, searching desperately for a police officer. Within minutes three constables, PCs Neil, Mizen and Thain, were staring at Mary's corpse.

With the light of morning still to come illumination was provided only by the dim glow of Neil's bull's-eye lantern. As the flames danced against the circular panel of glass held aloft by Neil the officers caught their first glimpse of the murderer's work: two deep gashes to Mary's neck.

By 4 a.m. the divisional surgeon, Dr Llewellyn , had arrived in Buck's Row after being awoken by PC Thain. Somewhat anxious to return to his bed, Dr Llewellyn's examination was nothing short of rudimentary. As later recalled, the doctor first checked Mary's hands and wrists, finding them cold. Although the body and legs had retained some warmth there was no heartbeat. Accordingly Dr Llewellyn pronounced life extinct and estimated that she had been dead no longer than half an hour.

In no time the narrow street, which only minutes earlier had been deserted, was filled. As police whistles carved through the morning air more officers arrived at the crime scene. They were joined by a throng of onlookers, all eager to catch a glimpse of Mary's body.

Preliminary enquiries were underway by the time Dr Llewellyn ordered the body to be removed to the mortuary, with residents questioned as to whether they had heard anything suspicious.[8]

Much to the surprise of PC Neil, Mr Purkiss, who lived closest to the spot where Mary had been killed, and who was the most likely to have heard the attack, claimed to have seen and heard nothing.

By 5.40 a.m. the length of Buck's Row and Queen Street had been searched by a team of constables and sergeants, summoned from neighbouring beats. Surrounding areas were also checked, with Inspector Spratling and Sergeant Godley examining the District Railway embankment and the deserted yard belonging to the Great Eastern Railway, looking for blood stains and weapons. However, none were found. [9]

Within a matter of hours the morning editions hit the newsstands, with the 125,000 readers of the *Star* treated to one of the first reports to cover the murder, with a headline designed to grab the attention of every reader, courtesy of editor Ernest Parke, one of Fleet Street's most skilled penmen: A REVOLTING MURDER/ANOTHER WOMAN FOUND HORRIBLY MUTILATED IN WHITECHAPEL/GHASTLY CRIME BY A MANIAC.[10]

As the papers were keen to confirm, after the body had been removed to the local mortuary Dr Llewellyn discovered that the injuries to Mary's neck were not the only wounds upon the body. On inspecting the victim's abdomen, the doctor found a jagged cut, described as being so deep as to have ripped through the tissues of the stomach.

There were also three or four similar cuts running downwards, on the right side of the abdomen, all of which had been inflicted with a long bladed knife.

With shafts of sunlight streaming through a moth-eaten curtain, Sarah Colwell awoke, oblivious to the chaos that had ensued just yards from her house. Only on stepping into the street to find breakfast did she notice the crowd. By 8 a.m. word of the murder had spread, with a mass of sightseers having descended upon the neighbourhood along with a horde of journalists.

Walking northwards down Brady Street in the direction of Buck's Row, Sarah was unaware that she was heading towards three such reporters, gathered together in a huddle around a particular spot on the junction. As she walked, Sarah recalled the events of the previous evening, remembering the screams, the panicked clatter of footsteps and the desperate cries for help that had gone unanswered. Instinctively she knew that the unusual activity in the street was somehow connected to what she had heard.

Passing two constables who appeared to be questioning a slaughterman that Sarah recognised as working at a nearby yard, she neared the junction of Brady Street and Buck's Row. Of the three well attired reporters, two were standing upright, feverishly making pencilled notes in small paper pads, while the third was knelt upon the ground.

Although a wave of excited voices streamed towards Sarah from the direction of Buck's Row, her attention remained steadfast, continuing to be drawn to the reporters, whose muffled voices seemed filled with an almost childish excitement. Intrigued, Sarah craned her neck, trying desperately to see what it was that had interested the journalists.

As she stepped closer, the large figure of a policeman came into view on her right. Inspector Helson, who moments earlier had returned to the area from the mortuary, walked with purpose as he headed towards Brady Street. As he reached the first reporter, the Inspector came to a halt.

It was as the third man, who had been kneeling and inspecting the ground, stood and began a battle of words with Helson, that Sarah caught sight of that which had fascinated the reporters and what the Inspector believed had already been washed away.

Helson would go on to confirm at the subsequent inquest that, although by the time he had returned to Buck's Row the blood that had surrounded the body had been washed from the ground, the smears of blood in Brady Street were still present.[11]

The bloody stains, of which there were several, were a shock to Sarah Colwell. An all too clear indication of what had become of the woman, the stranger, whose cries for help now reverberated within her conscience as clearly as they had done four hours earlier. When she caught sight of what appeared to be a bloody handprint, Sarah was sick.

After providing the police with a statement later that day, Sarah would discover that she had not been the only one to hear strange noises during the morning of the murder. A similar story to hers would be given by another resident of the neighbourhood, Mrs Harriet Lilley, who along with her husband lived on Buck's Row, only two doors away from where the body was discovered.

As later retold in numerous tabloid reports, for Harriet Lilley the night of 30 August had been a restless one. Staying in the front room of her house she had been unable to sleep, finding herself instead listening to the quiet drizzle outside. Only at 3.30 a.m. did she hear anything out of the ordinary, what she described as a painful moan. This was followed by two or three faint gasps coming from just below her bedroom window.

After that came the whispers and several breathless cries, stifled and unlike that of a normal brawl, of which Harriet had heard many since moving to the area. Edging herself closer to the window, she placed an ear against the thin glass pane in the hope of determining the source of the noise, only to be jolted from her bed as the roar of a goods train, passing on the East London Railway, rattled behind the house.

As the sound of the engine passed, diluting into nothing more than a vague drone, Harriet attempted once again to gauge the sound that had been present moments earlier. The cries, however, had stopped. And though, unlike Sarah Colwell, Mrs Lilley had dared to look outside, the darkness beyond her window was too dense to see anything other than her own startled reflection.[12]

By the time Harriet Lilley's story made the papers several days later, the press were already in a state of frenzy, covering every aspect of the case, from the discovery of the body and the severity of the mutilations to detailed coverage of the inquest, with testimonies of the police and witnesses being duplicated in almost every newspaper.

Held at the Whitechapel Working Lads' Institute on Whitechapel Road, the inquest opened on Saturday 1 September, under the control of Mr Wynne E. Baxter, Coroner for South-East Middlesex.

First to speak was Edward Walker, the father of Mary Nichols, who, after confirming her identity and stating that he hadn't seen his daughter for three years, felt the need to assure the Coroner that as far as he knew his daughter had not a single enemy.[13]

Next to take the stand was PC Neil, followed by the highly anticipated evidence of Dr Llewellyn, who drew a hushed silence from the gathered audience as he began his testimony.

Describing how he found the body, Dr Llewellyn painted a vivid image of the victim lying upon her back with her legs extended and her throat severed by two deep cuts. As well as eliminating the obvious fact that the wounds had not been self-inflicted, the doctor then explained that only when the body arrived at the mortuary were the extent of the mutilations realised.

After explaining the savagery with which the abdominal wounds had been inflicted, the doctor then elaborated on other injuries found to Mary's face: bruising on the right side running along the lower part of the jaw, caused by a powerful blow. Yet more bruising was found on the left side of the face, resulting from the pressure of fingers, the perception being that the killer had gripped Mary's chin with one hand before striking her with the other.[14]

The inquest covered the murder in great detail determining that the killer could have inflicted the wounds in four or five minutes, as well as establishing that in order for all the vital organs to have been attacked in the manner observed, the killer must have had a rough knowledge of anatomy. It also clearly showed that the police had very few leads from which to work.[15]

Although a thorough search had been made of the neighbourhood, the murder weapon, believed by Dr Llewellyn to have been a long bladed knife, had not been located. The blood found in the street was determined to belong solely to the victim and, beyond the statements of Sarah Colwell and Mrs Lilley, no further evidence was forthcoming that would in any way help determine the killer's identity.

While the newspapers revelled in the horrific details of the crime, with *Reynolds's* awarding Mary's murder the biggest splash, stating that the mutilations were too horrible to describe or even hint at – before describing them in great detail – there was one crucial piece of evidence of which the tabloids were not aware. An 'H' Division police constable had been patrolling Buck's Row at the time of the murder and had made a crucial observation. Had his testimony not been omitted from the inquest it would have provided the newspapers with an even more sensational headline: that the killer had actually been seen.

THREE

A New Suspect

As Louis Tracy and Kennedy Jones would discover, rumours of a sighting in Buck's Row had circulated within the lower ranks of Scotland Yard for some time. Although only officially being made public years after the Ripper case had closed, in a book written by a former Metropolitan police officer, its significance was still as powerful then as it had been on that fateful morning in the August of 1888.

According to a constable, who wished to remain anonymous, from 3.15 a.m. on the morning of the murder he had been patrolling Buck's Row. Having walked its length the officer had almost turned out of the street when he first caught sight of him, the figure of a tall man stepping out of the darkness, near to the spot where the body of Mary Nichols would later be discovered, crossing over the road as if surprised by the presence of the policeman. Due to the speed with which the unknown man turned and walked in the opposite direction, the constable felt unsettled and began to follow.

Momentarily distracted by a quarrelling couple in a nearby alley, when the constable looked back up the street the man had disappeared, leaving in his wake only the thick darkness from which he had emerged. Only after returning to Buck's Row half an hour later, in the immediate aftermath of the discovery of the body, did the constable realise the importance of his sighting. He was in no doubt that the man he had seen was her killer.

16

The constable was able to provide a description, stating that the suspect was tall and moved with the energy and swiftness of a young man. From his vantage point he could see that the man's clothes appeared of a good quality. He wore a tweed cap pulled low over his forehead and a coat, with the collar raised.

As for whether the suspect wore a beard, the constable could not say, though he believed the man had a moustache. It was the man's eyes that the constable remembered most clearly, appearing noticeably dark against his skin, even at a distance.

The fullest source of the information was writer and former detective Edwin T. Woodhall,[1] who joined the Metropolitan Police Force in 1906 and whose career had brought him into contact with many policemen who had actively worked on the Ripper investigation. For his book, entitled *Jack the Ripper; or When London Walked in Terror*, Woodhall interviewed many of the officers involved in the case and gained access to a wealth of sensitive information.

The constable (unnamed by Woodhall) appears to have kept the information pertaining to his sighting in Buck's Row largely to himself. For motives that remain opaque, he only spoke of it in full years after the Ripper case had gone cold. Albeit brief, the importance of the constable's evidence to the case being built by KJ and Louis Tracy was monumental. As far as the journalists were concerned, the description of the person seen in Buck's Row matched only one man.

For KJ and Tracy, the sighting offered more than they could have hoped; a glimpse of the man most likely to have been Mary's killer, who resembled in every way what they knew of Thomas Cutbush.

Armed with a significant clue, the two journalists began to delve deeper into their suspect's past. In the hope of understanding his motivation and importantly finding more evidence that could link him to the Ripper, KJ and Tracy looked to uncover every last detail of Cutbush's life prior to his arrest in 1891.

A month before the murder of Mary Nichols, on 24 July, 23-year-old Thomas Cutbush had taken a position as a clerk with a tea importer in

Whitechapel.[2] It was just a 45-minute walk from his home in Albert Street in Kennington. His daily commute took him north on Kennington Park Road, through Newington Butts, over London Bridge and then on to Whitechapel.

Due to his father abandoning him in the year he was born, fleeing to New Zealand where he would bigamously marry his second wife [3], Cutbush was raised by his mother and aunt, a nervous and excitable pair of women who fussed over him, the youngest male in the family.

From an early age he had appeared quiet and academically unremarkable and although his mother said he protected weaker boys from bullies, he was generally regarded by those who knew him as something of an eccentric.

After finding employment his odd behaviour immediately drew attention from his new colleagues. Desperate to cure an ailment that produced sores on his cheeks and forehead, Cutbush became obsessed with anointing his face, placing creams and lotions upon his skin and spending hours looking at his own reflection. For the most part his colleagues left him alone. Though his self-medication provoked comments Cutbush appeared oblivious to how his habits might appear to others.[4]

One day an elderly clerk watched perplexed as Cutbush fussed over his face in a mirror. 'I have known much better-looking men than you who did not spend half as much time in looking at themselves,' the man joked. Cutbush said nothing. A few minutes later the old man was found lying in a pool of his own blood at the foot of a long flight of stairs. As colleagues rushed to his aid, Cutbush, who was standing on the top step, sounding sincere, said: 'Poor gentleman, he has fallen downstairs.'

The man was left seriously injured and remained insensible for several weeks. When he eventually came to, Cutbush was gone, having been sacked shortly after the incident.[5]

Although several years had passed by the time Louis Tracy eventually sat down with the old man in the offices of *The Sun*, his recollection of the events was crystal clear. 'He was hidden by darkness,' the old man recalled as he took his seat opposite Tracy, his low voice quivering as he remembered the incident that had left a jagged scar above his temple.

After a short pause, which allowed Tracy time to pass his guest a tall glass of water, the elderly gentleman continued: 'As I walked up the flight of stairs I saw no one – not a soul. Only when I reached the top did I see him step from the shadows. I attempted to walk past him but …'

Eager to press the old man Tracy leant forward in his chair: 'But?' he said.

'Without a word he grabbed me by the shoulders. He was stronger than he looked. I felt his grip tighten and then – he pushed. The next I knew I was at the bottom of the stairs on the stone floor. I heard the others – my colleagues who were standing at my side – though their voices were distant.'

'And do you remember anything else?' quizzed Tracy.

After sipping the water the old man answered: 'Yes, as I lay on the ground, before the others came to my aid I had looked directly at him, at Thomas.'

'Yes?' asked Tracy.

'And though I might have been mistaken – in the blur of it all, the one thing I remember is the expression on his face. I thought he was grimacing at first, the way his cheeks raised and his eyes crinkled, but that was only until I realised – he was smiling at me.'

As *The Sun* journalists followed a growing trail, from one employer to another through the streets of Whitechapel, it became clear that Cutbush had been unable to hold down any job for more than a few weeks.

They were told the same story again and again. Of Cutbush's inability to keep time and his general lateness, his gruff demeanour and his peculiar eccentricities, such as his desire to advise everyone he met as to the treatment of horrible diseases.

Then there were the medicines, bottles of lotions kept in his pockets that after applying to his face would leave his fingers stained with a black substance. When at his desk Cutbush would spend much of his time either sleeping or sketching upon pieces of paper, revelling in the disgusted cries of his fellow workers as their eyes met with his graphic illustrations.

Although much had been gained from the interviews conducted between Louis Tracy and Cutbush's ex-colleagues, his last meeting, with a gentleman later referred to as 'SY', would prove the most revealing.

Dressed smartly in a black, high-buttoned, overcoat Tracy arrived at the final establishment in which Cutbush had been employed: a business directory located in the heart of London's East End.

Of the many men employed within the office only one had worked for the firm at the same time as Cutbush. Although he remembered Thomas, much to Tracy's surprise, the man initially appeared reluctant to speak openly and only after being assured of anonymity did

'SY' – as he would later be referred to – tell Tracy what he knew.

Much like the previous establishments visited by *The Sun* journalist, Cutbush had again left his mark. Although having worked at the firm longer than any other, Cutbush's attitude and behaviour had not improved, with his position only lasting as long as it had due to the leniency of his employer.

Unlike other firms, here Cutbush appeared to have been well liked, at least by 'SY' and for a time appeared happy in his work, seemingly enjoying his position as a travelling canvasser far more than the office-bound role of a clerk.

On a daily basis Cutbush would traverse the sprawling streets of east London selling advertising space to businesses, gaining knowledge of the geography of the East End that would aid him in more ways than one.

Although immersing himself in his new found position, eventually the old traits resurfaced: the sketching, the strange topics of conversation, and the one that would ultimately cost him his job – lateness.[6]

On being dismissed Cutbush vowed to stay in touch with several of his colleagues, including 'SY' who, at least initially, was keen to remain in contact. Most of the meetings that followed were unremarkable, with the pair having little to say to one another beyond a shared enjoyment of the music hall.

It was their last meeting, however, that remained at the forefront of 'SY's reminiscences, an occasion that would end their acquaintance once and for all.

'That's when he told me,' said 'SY', responding to Tracy's probing, having explained that until their last meeting he had only ever considered Cutbush to be a harmless eccentric.

'Told you what?' asked the reporter, his short pencil gripped tightly between index finger and thumb. After a considered pause in which 'SY' assured himself that he was not being watched or overheard, he answered: 'That he was going to kill his doctor.

FOUR

Cutbush and the Doctor

Of the many consultations held within the surgery of Dr Brooks in the bustling Westminster Bridge Road, none were more memorable than the frequent and often lengthy visits of Thomas Cutbush. As the doctor would confirm, this was not due to the nature of his patient's illness or method of treatment, but instead for the peculiarity of Cutbush's behaviour and his almost constant state of delusion.

Believing that he had contracted syphilis from a prostitute a year earlier, in the July of 1888 Cutbush began what would later become an obsessional search for a cure and in turn became a regular visitor to the family doctor.[1]

Like gonorrhoea and herpes, during the nineteenth century syphilis was common throughout London. Prostitution was rife and half of all outpatients in London's hospitals were suffering with sexually transmitted diseases, of which syphilis was one of the most common.[2]

For those who contracted the four-stage disease, the first sign of infection would usually appear after three months, at the point of contact, in the form of small sores, before progressing into a rash or in some cases wart-like lesions that would show upon the surface of the skin. The infection would usually be spread to sexual partners in the third or latent stage, with the disease lying dormant within the body.

If untreated, patients would develop the tertiary and most dangerous stage: spreading to every part of the body, causing an agonising array of symptoms including blindness, paralyses and insanity, followed, in some cases, by death.

Since the first case of the disease in 1494, syphilis had long been perceived as a consequence of immorality. The source of the infection was thought to be women, specifically prostitutes, who spread the infection among those men who sought their services without the use of protection.[3]

Although condoms were available in the nineteenth century, they were considered the possession of the middle and upper classes, being too expensive for the working-class man, who lacked the money and education to consider such an item to be an important purchase.[4]

So severe was the spread of venereal disease that in 1864, in order to assert some control, prostitution became regulated, with the Contagious Disease Act allowing police constables to arrest prostitutes in order to ascertain whether they were infected.

Its treatment varied wildly depending on the practices of individual doctors and though to some it was thought that to find a cure would lead to even greater promiscuity, tens of thousands of women underwent the most common method of treatment – confinement.

Women, of which the larger percentage were prostitutes, would be confined in a 'Lock Hospital' for thirty days until the primary sores passed, after which time it was assumed that they were cured and no longer contagious.

To hinder the progress of the disease mercury would be administered, the side effects of which would prove equally severe. Patients could expect loss of teeth, throat and lip ulcerations followed by acute kidney damage, all in the name of medicine.[5]

Having read of the symptoms Cutbush was convinced of his affliction and, though being informed by Dr Brooks many times that he was not infected, such was Cutbush's belief in his condition that he continued to pursue treatment, often arriving at the surgery without appointment and sometimes waiting for hours only to be given the same clear diagnosis.

'He complained that he was suffering from some constitutional disease of an aggravated type,' confirmed Dr Brooks during the first of two interviews conducted with KJ during December 1893.

'I examined him carefully, made every kind of necessary test, and came to the conclusion that he was suffering from nothing but a delusion and mental aberration.'[6]

According to his family, Cutbush wouldn't listen. Blinded by his own conviction, he began to believe that Dr Brooks had given an incorrect diagnosis and had failed to see his symptoms, leading to a contempt bordering on hatred.

To Thomas Cutbush, Dr Brooks was perceived to be like many medical men of the time: under-educated and overpaid, so-called professionals who conducted their duties with little regard for the integrity of their patients.

Only two years earlier the Medical Amendment Act had been passed, reforming medical education and practices, before which students were held with little regard. Young males who were more inclined to look upon their chosen studies as a means of benefiting their social status, rather than the world of medicine.

Until the reform, the dissection rooms were considered by many students as a playground, with serious study being overshadowed by the antics of young men who, more often than not, presented a more regular attendance at the local ale house than the lecture hall.[7]

Although, after studying at respected medical establishments, many doctors practised with a degree or medical certificate, others offered their services while having no legal sanction to do so.

As KJ and Tracy would learn, as they researched the history of the Ripper case, so poor was the public perception of doctors in the 1880s that after the murder of Mary Nichols many medical men were hailed, at least by the press, as the most likely perpetrator.

Due to the manner in which the killer had attacked Mary's internal organs, rumours began to surface on the streets of Whitechapel that a local doctor was responsible. Though beginning as nothing more than a whisper, within a matter of months such theories began to make the headlines.

One of the first stories, appearing in a number of newspapers at the time, related to an incident that occurred in the area of Commercial Street, in the very district where Mary Nichols had lost her life.

On 11 November 1888, as police constables arrived to make the arrest of a gentleman who had publicly proclaimed to be Jack the Ripper, they were greeted by a baying mob. To cries of 'lynch him' the suspect had been knocked to the ground, and had it not been for the quick thinking of the attending officers, the beating he received would have been far more serious.

After being taken to the nearby Leman Street Police Station the man was questioned and gave his name as Holt, as well as stating that he was a doctor from St George's Hospital. Though subsequently discharged, with his actions perceived as being nothing more than a prank, the incident received much coverage.[8]

Shortly after the arrest and later release of Dr Holt another story hit the papers, that of two Scotland Yard detectives in hot pursuit of a doctor from Birmingham, who was thought to be the Ripper. As he arrived at Euston Station from the Midlands the suspect was swiftly apprehended and removed to Scotland Yard for questioning.

Although giving a satisfactory account of his movements, which ultimately led to his release, to the reporters of the *Morning Advertiser*, the adventures of Detectives Leach and White were still worthy of much hype.[9]

As the months passed after the murder of Mary Nichols, the prospect of a doctor being responsible for her killing began to gather momentum, bringing the medical profession under the microscope. And though many professionals went on record to refute such claims, their efforts were greatly hindered when, during the autumn of 1888, a Kensington-based doctor named James Gloster was named as a killer, being charged with the wilful murder of dressmaker Eliza Jane Schumacher.

The case was followed avidly by the press. Speculation suggested that a death bed confession had lead police to believe Dr Gloster had performed an abortion upon Miss Schumacher of 'a bungling fashion'. Dr Gloster stated that he had not performed the operation nor had he been present when it had been conducted, however, it would take two days of cross examination before his acquittal was eventually granted. Although being discharged, the case of Dr Gloster left a lingering sense among the populace of London that doctors could not be trusted or indeed relied upon for their expertise.[10]

To Thomas Cutbush Dr Brooks was seen as equally unreliable, a mere amateur in a profession in which Cutbush believed he himself could excel.

As the days and months passed, Cutbush's routine of checking his face for signs of infection became obsessional; whether at home or work, he would carry a small mirror in his pocket and would spend hours staring at his own image. Convinced that only further treatment could aid his pains, his visits to Dr Brooks became relentless.

Though many people had passed through the surgery in Westminster Bridge Road, Dr Brooks couldn't fail to remember the strange young man from Kennington. As he recalled to KJ, Cutbush had attended his surgery for many months on a regular basis. 'He was an outpatient,' said Dr Brooks, and knowing little of him and nothing of his people it was virtually impossible to communicate with him outside of the appointments.

In order to humour his patient's whims Dr Brooks had dispensed a tonic combined with a sedative to calm the nerves. However, the treatment didn't go as planned. According to a letter written in Cutbush's hand and found in his room by Kennedy Jones, the medicine had an adverse reaction:

I thought no more of the matter until a day or so afterwards, when I came on very ill. All the nerves and bones in my head seemed dropping to pieces. The nerve muscles of my face and jaw were greatly agitated – spots with large, red irritant patches came out on my face, and a dreadful burning pain in my left side.[11]

Four days after receiving the medicine Cutbush returned to Westminster Bridge Road and complained of the doctor's incompetence. Only then did Dr Brooks sense the extent of his patient's delusions. Believing the red patches to be gummas, a non-cancerous growth and symptom of tertiary syphilis, Cutbush demanded nothing less than a specific treatment for the infection.

Seeing his patient enraged, Dr Brooks dispensed what would be Cutbush's last prescription of iron, strychnine and sarsaparilla, informing him that the latter could be used as a herbal remedy to fight syphilitic infection. Cutbush left the surgery and his visits ceased.[12]

As the side effects continued Cutbush became convinced that something far more sinister was at work than a simple misdiagnosis. With the medicine provided to fight the infection only worsening the fever and making the sores even more acute, he now not only believed that he was suffering from syphilis but also that his own doctor was trying to poison him.[13]

Although a year had passed since Cutbush had first journeyed to the surgery of Dr Brooks, his anger had failed to subside. After being left disfigured by his doctor's treatment, he gave up seeking medical assistance, choosing instead to self-medicate. Cutbush complained regularly that his face felt as if it was twisting within his skin, causing his features to contort, and as a result he became obsessed with his own appearance.[14] On leaving home he would routinely draw up his collar and lower his cap in order to hide his face, choosing the evenings to walk and using the darkness as a mask.

Bent on revenge, Cutbush wished to attack the doctor's professionalism and initially took his grievance to the authorities, communicating in the first instance with Scotland Yard. In a letter written to Dr Brooks, Cutbush explained that the doctor's career would soon be over, that he had contacted the police and laid before them certain information.[15] He waited patiently for a response and, though many more letters would be written, Scotland Yard never replied.

With his paranoia growing at a rapid rate Cutbush took his concerns higher, communicating with members of Parliament such as Lord Grimthorpe and Henry Labouchere, his suggestion being to pass a Bill to prevent doctors from dispensing their own medicines.[16]

Again, Cutbush was ignored. Now seething, he saw only one avenue left to pursue and resolved to take his grievance to court, wishing to discredit Dr Brooks in the most public of arenas. After much effort, Cutbush eventually found himself in the legal offices of a criminal prosecutor, who would later be referred to by *The Sun* as 'Mr D. G.'

After waiting in a small room that adjoined the main prosecutor's office, Cutbush was eventually shown through. The London office, sitting on the top floor of a six-storey block, was spacious yet cluttered, with the vast view of the city below intermittently obscured by piles of legal documents sitting aloft a desk of dark mahogany.

The prosecutor, a man of large build, dressed in an ill-fitting suit that reeked of cigar smoke, greeted Cutbush as he had done on previous occasions: with a seated handshake and a partial smile that struggled to lift the corners of his thick moustache.

As the prosecutor said to Kennedy Jones four years later, Cutbush came and went, much like many of his other clients, with their conversations remaining very much a one-sided affair. For longer than the appointed time Cutbush would speak of his grievances, explaining how disgraceful it was that doctors were allowed to dispense their own prescriptions, as well as citing Dr Brooks as a poisoner.

The prosecutor listened, allowing Cutbush to vent, while as a gesture of good manners making illegible notes upon his papers.

After explaining that he was unable to offer assistance, the prosecutor was surprised by the abrupt nature with which Cutbush left. On this occasion, unlike others, he offered no argument or criticism of his judgement and instead simply left the office without a word.

The prosecutor went to his window and looked down, expecting to see Cutbush eventually emerge from the street entrance below, but his want-to-be client failed to appear. Several hours passed and the prosecutor, feeling a pang that spoke of having spent too much time sitting awkwardly upon the edge of his seat, pushed his chair out from beneath his desk, checked his brass pocket watch and pondered whether he'd catch the next omnibus, which arrived at ten-minute intervals only two streets away.

All too aware of the many criminal types infesting the thoroughfares of London, such as the carriage thieves who needed little invitation to plunder a man of his wealth, the prosecutor preferred to take the more populated mode of transport. As he placed the watch in the pocket of his waistcoat and prepared to sort the last of his papers, only then did he hear it.

At first it sounded like a shift – a subtle noise, barely audible but present nonetheless. The sound of what seemed like a foot scuffing against the floor.

Looking to his right, the prosecutor stared through the windowed door of his office. It was shut – which was normal. Beyond the panel of glass, on which his name was embossed in bottle green, he could see the blond hair of his clerk, sitting diligently on the other side, which again was as it should be. Inside the office it felt different. As he heard the noise again, the hairs on his neck began to stand up. It was then that he realised – he wasn't alone.

Jolting to a standing position while at the same time turning himself around, he stood, his heart pounding like a train engine. For the briefest of moments the pair stood, inches away from each other. Arching his back as if to make space, the prosecutor momentarily froze, waiting for Cutbush to make a move.

He soon obliged.

As Cutbush's right hand, which until that moment had hung loosely by his side, inched towards his trouser pocket the prosecutor grabbed him by his shoulders. The next minute he was forcing him backwards away from the desk and had he not stumbled over a box of papers, he would have in all certainty put him through the door.

By the time he managed to get to his feet, Cutbush was gone, the office door clattering back on itself while the surprised clerk simply watched on from his desk. The prosecutor later spoke of his surprise as to how Cutbush was able to enter the office without being seen. On one particular point, however, he was certain: as he looked into the eyes of Cutbush, what he saw was an unwavering, unrelenting, malice.

In the course of his duties as a public prosecutor he had met many men, criminals and lunatics of all types, but never before had he ever felt such fear. During his interview with KJ, he impressed most strongly on the journalist his belief that Cutbush had intended to assault him, if not commit murder. And had he not ran him out, the solicitor believed that he would have undoubtedly succeeded.[17]

As Kennedy stood up to leave, aware that he was standing in the very spot where Cutbush had taken up his position, the prosecutor provided one final observation. Having read much of the coverage of the Ripper murders and being all too aware of the avenue being pursued by *The Sun* journalists, he stated that should his belief be correct and Cutbush had indeed meant to kill him, then surely he was attempting murder in the same fashion in which the women were killed in Whitechapel, creeping silently into a position behind his intended target, watching and waiting before making a move?

Intrigued by the solicitor's comments KJ left and returned to *The Sun*'s offices on Tudor Street, a small thoroughfare that ran parallel to Fleet Street on a site where the waters of the Thames menaced the lower steps at its highest tides.

As Kennedy Jones pushed open the door of *The Sun* buildings, keen to inform his partner of his findings, he was surprised to discover Tracy inside, having returned early from Whitechapel, where he too had concluded an interview, this time with Cutbush's old colleague – 'SY'.

After retreating to the rear office, passing the busy composing room along a bright corridor, the two men took their seats, separated by a desk comprising a typewriter and a bundle of letters that since he had left had toppled over. Kennedy Jones spoke first, informing Tracy of his discoveries. After a short pause, it was then KJ's turn to listen. Having himself received what he believed to be a crucial piece of evidence, Tracy, barely able to contain his enthusiasm, began to relay the recently acquired testimony of 'SY'.

With the autumn of 1890 drawing to a close, 'SY' had received an unexpected and unwelcome visit from Cutbush. His behaviour as well as his personality seemed by then to have adopted a darker edge.

According to 'SY', initially he had appeared tired, rambling on for a time, almost lost to his own confused state before suddenly snapping, as if awaking from a slumber. Only then did Cutbush come to the real reason for his visit, asking 'SY' in an almost flippant manner to lend him a pistol.[18]

Without any desire to hide the reason for his request, Cutbush openly admitted his intentions; he informed 'SY' of the poisoning, of his disfigurement and of his hatred for Dr Brooks. On being asked as to his intentions Cutbush responded excitedly, informing 'SY' that he intended to murder his doctor in cold blood.

To Louis Tracy, who had already begun to see in Thomas Cutbush a man more than capable of murder, 'SY's' evidence was proof positive.

FIVE

The Laying Out

8 September 1888
29 Hanbury Street, Whitechapel

It was 5.45 a.m. when John Davis awoke on a morning so cold that his breaths formed a mist in front of his face. Sitting on the edge of a narrow bed in a cramped room that he shared with his wife and three sons, Davis contemplated the day ahead.

Working as a Carman at Leadenhall Market meant a half-hour walk through Whitechapel, Bishopsgate and beyond. A journey that Davis, having had a particularly poor night's sleep, didn't relish.

The mug of tea, prepared by his wife, offered the only heat in what seemed the coldest of rooms. Cupping it in both hands, he lowered his head, allowing its steam to warm his face, while wearily placing his feet into a pair of black leather boots.

After dressing, with several layers disguising the slightness of his frame, Davis bid his wife farewell and pulled the door of their room to a close, before descending the three flights of stairs that sliced through the centre of their home.[1]

Although being a larger-than-average building that at one time had ably served the needs of the local cotton weavers, by 1888 29 Hanbury Street had followed a growing trend and had been converted into rented accommodation.

While the ground floor was used for business purposes, with Mrs Hardyman's Cat Meat shop doing a trade selling skewered meat for a farthing a time and the rear of the house being used as a packing case business by its owner, every other room in the property was used to accommodate residents, with a total of seventeen people inhabiting an assortment of small, decaying rooms.[2]

On reaching the ground floor of the house, every staircase acknowledging his tread with resonating creaks, John Davis found himself in need of relief. Instead of turning right and heading towards the front door, he turned left, walking along a dark passageway leading to the rear yard and privy.

Knowing the back door was never locked, Davis simply gripped the rusted handle and pushed, the door opening only as wide as the fence situated to its left would allow. As the morning sunlight spilled into the corridor it took a moment for Davis's eyes to adjust; when they eventually did the first thing he saw was the blood.

In one corner of the small yard a body of a woman had been 'laid out' upon the ground. Her left arm was lying bent across her breast, her legs drawn up and spread wide open, with her dress lifted up so that every last detail of her butchery was made clear.

Davis had seen carcasses before at Leadenhall: headless, limbless beasts dressed for market and hung out for sale, but nothing came close to this. Unable to remove his gaze, he attempted to comprehend the disjointed figure that lay before him. Beyond the swollen cheeks and lifeless eyes, the remainder of the woman's face was a blur of pale, colourless skin, blotted with flecks of red blood. Hanging awkwardly away from her neck, the woman's face rested to her right upon the grass and what appeared to be a mound of blood-stained rags.

Below the neck was a jumble. A confused mess of dishevelled clothing; once white petticoats now stained a bright crimson, raised high above the woman's knees, over which a black skirt had been pulled even higher. Through a ripped bodice, pockets of white flesh could be seen, no longer smooth, instead a ruin of cuts and slashes, exposing dark angular pieces of flesh.[3]

Stumbling backwards, almost unable to stand, the shocked Davis ran back into the passageway and out into the street, pleading for someone to help him.

And though the neighbourhood would soon reel in shock and horror at the news of another murder, Annie Chapman, for a moment at least, remained anonymous, before becoming known to the world – as the second victim of Jack the Ripper.

Annie, or 'Dark Annie' as she was often called, was well known in Whitechapel. A sociable, polite woman who only ever considered prostitution a last resort, she often attempted to make the few pennies required for her lodgings from needlework or selling matches on street corners.

Though appearing older than her years, in 1888 Annie was forty-seven. Being plump and short with a bulbous nose and missing teeth, she was by no means the beauty of Whitechapel, yet beyond the weathered skin and coarse brown hair, her attractive blue eyes offered a glimpse of her former self: a woman once of respectable means and who, for a time at least, had led a decent life.

Not having a pimp or a mistress or a brothel from which to work, when Annie resorted to soliciting she would do so in the open, against fences or forsaken carts in the alleys of Commercial Street, in some cases barely earning enough to purchase a stale loaf of bread or half a pint of ale.

Though something of an amateur street walker, she was nevertheless knowledgeable of her patch and her trade, of which the most common requirement was privacy. Getting caught by a patrolling constable was not good for business and would often, if not always, result in non-payment.[4]

Unlike the picturesque village of Clewer in Berkshire, where until 1884 Annie had lived with her husband, Whitechapel was a bustling neighbourhood. Day and night, a throng of police constables could be found patrolling the streets, as well as many being placed on static points, where they would remain from 9 p.m. until 1 a.m.[5]

With such a constant police presence, for the many prostitutes working the area, seclusion was considered a must, being a vital element to the success of a night's trade. As Annie was aware, 29 Hanbury Street offered the perfect location for soliciting, providing the darkness and solitude appreciated by paying clients.

So popular was it as a location that only a matter of hours prior to Annie Chapman's arrival at 5.30 a.m. another prostitute by the name of Emily Walter was found using its isolation as a means of increasing her funds.[6]

Three hours later Annie found herself following the same route as Emily Walter, entering through the second of two crumbling doors that adorned the front of the house, before being cast into darkness and having to negotiate the twenty-foot corridor that separated the street from the rear of the property.

After stepping down into the partly paved yard, with the cold air biting at her skin, Annie turned her back on her client, placing one hand upon the fence panel, while raising her skirts with the other.

As her head collided with the fence, its splintered panel catching on her skin, instinctively Annie grasped at the man's hands. In an attempt to strangle his victim, the killer had grabbed her by the neck, his grip so tight that, on the discovery of her body a half an hour later, Annie's tongue was left protruding between her front teeth.[7]

A second before losing consciousness, she would have heard a noise – a movement, the sound of a door opening only inches from her face, followed by the footsteps of a man walking parallel to her on the opposite side of the fence.

Next door, a young carpenter named Albert Cadoche was also in need of relief. A man who could – who should – have saved Annie's life.

As she fell upon the mudded ground, desperately fighting for breath, Annie mustered only a muffled cry of 'No!' before losing consciousness. Cadoche would later inform the police that he had indeed heard Annie's cries but thought nothing of it, such noises being all too common in the neighbourhood of Whitechapel. Being in a hurry to get to work, he simply left Hanbury Street and by 5.32 a.m. had reached the Spitalfields Church on Commercial Street, leaving Annie Chapman to meet her fate.[8]

By 6.30 a.m. the once quiet yard was alive with activity. Police constables, suited Inspectors from CID, as well as the Divisional Surgeon, Dr Phillips, had all been called to Hanbury Street by Inspector Joseph Chandler, the first officer to arrive on the scene.

Much to the annoyance of the many eager spectators who had taken up positions at the windows of several neighbouring properties, all that remained visible of Annie's corpse were her laced boots and striped stockings protruding beyond a large piece of sacking, placed over her body to protect any evidence.

Underneath, the corpse remained in the same horrific state as had greeted John Davis at 6 a.m. and subsequently Inspector Joseph Chandler, who on hearing Davis's pleas for help, ten minutes later, entered the backyard.

While Chandler's observations in large part tallied with those of John Davis, what the first witness had missed was the reason for the irregular positioning of Annie's face: her head had been virtually severed from her neck. Chandler noted the abdomen – that it had not only been attacked but ripped completely open and further, that what John Davis had assumed to be a pile of blood-stained rags next to the victim's head was in fact a mound of flesh and body parts.[9]

If that wasn't horrifying enough, one further discovery would shock the experienced Chandler and every other officer involved in the case. That beyond the brutality inflicted upon Annie Chapman's lifeless body, the attempted severance of her head and the frenzied assault upon her abdomen, the killer on this occasion had taken a trophy and removed the uterus, part of her vagina and two thirds of her bladder.

At around 6.40 a.m. Sergeant Badham placed what remained of Annie's body into an ambulance before removing it, on the request of Dr Phillips, to the mortuary on Eagle Street. It was there, in the cramped, poorly lit, shed, where the doctor would later conduct a more extensive examination and report his findings. Phillips discovered a jagged gash running from Annie's rectum to her breastbone as well as finding that her small intestines had been removed. The doctor also noted that the savage cuts to Annie's throat would have caused decapitation had it not been for the presence of a handkerchief tied around her neck.

As the police investigation began, headed by Inspector Frederick Abberline and using many of the same officers involved in the Mary Nichols's murder case, it became obvious that the police were now treading new ground and for the first time were hunting a serial killer. Due to the horrific nature of the Nichols's murder and the unparalleled press interest that followed, Scotland Yard were keen to place the investigation in the reliable hands of an Inspector who knew Whitechapel and its criminals all too well.

Having served in the police for twenty-five years, fourteen of them spent in Whitechapel, Inspector Abberline was the perfect choice. In his time up to the Ripper murders he had accumulated a wealth of experience and was ready for what would prove his greatest challenge. A stout, smartly presented man of a quiet demeanour, he was popular not only for his kind nature but for his meticulous working methods, for which he received countless commendations.[10]

With the discovery of Annie Chapman, aware that they were now under the gaze of the watching world, the police investigation stepped up a gear. Immediately after the removal of Annie's body to the mortuary a thorough search was made of the murder scene.

Led by Inspector Chandler, a detailed examination was made of the rear yard, resulting in numerous finds. Where Annie's body had fallen several items remained scattered upon the ground: a piece of coarse muslin, a small tooth comb and a pocket hair comb, along with a torn piece of envelope used by Annie to hold several pills.

Keen to widen their enquiries, the police conducted interviews with every lodger residing in 29 Hanbury Street, as well as making thorough searches of their rooms. They would also visit almost every house in the vicinity in an attempt to uncover a clue that might lead them to the killer, though on every occasion their efforts went unrewarded.[11]

The victim's identity was soon confirmed by Amelia Palmer, an old friend. Alongside the victim's name, she was able to provide the police with a great many details relating to Annie's life in Spitalfields, as well as Windsor, where she had once lived with her family.

When the telegram arrived in the offices of Superintendent Hayes of Windsor Police Station, bearing the stamp of Scotland Yard and the name Annie Chapman, the superintendent was somewhat surprised.[12] Hayes, an officer remembered in England for arresting Scottish assassin Roderick Maclean, who six years earlier had attempted to shoot Queen Victoria, was instantly intrigued.[13]

Far from being unfamiliar with the name printed upon the telegram, Hayes knew Annie Chapman well, as did a great many of the officers working in the town.

Checking his files, Hayes noted that Annie had been arrested on numerous occasions for drunkenness and subsequently informed Scotland Yard of his findings. The well-informed superintendent was also able to provide a glimpse into Annie's past, confirming that she had been married to a man named John Chapman, a head coachman in the service of a respectable gentleman living in the Royal Borough.

Together the couple had lived in the village of Clewer and for a while had seemed happy, with Annie appearing to have achieved the life she had always wished for, a stable relationship with a hardworking husband, with whom she had three children. However, Annie's polite and often kindly nature was regularly overshadowed by her need for drink. Her fondness for rum would prove too strong come the weekends, and often resulted in a change of personality, leading to arguments, raucous behaviour and the inevitable arrest.

Eventually in 1884 the marriage ended, John Chapman unable to cope with his wife's habitual drinking. Though the break-up with her husband was amicable, Annie could no longer bear to stay in Berkshire, choosing instead to return to her birthplace.

She deserted her children in the process. Arriving in London neatly attired in a fine cotton dress and unblemished boots, Annie had initially looked out of place in the squalid East End. Though for a time living relatively well on an allowance provided by her husband and the earnings of her new partner John Sivvey, by the January of 1887, owing to the cessation of the allowance on her husband's death and subsequent departure of her lover, Annie's appearance had changed.[14] Her once neat clothes, now a multitude of rags, clung to her bloated frame, while her hair appeared loose and unkempt.[15]

That which had sustained Annie's bleak existence had come to an end, leaving her in a state of desperation, with no choice other than to turn to history's oldest profession.

It was further discovered that in the week preceding her death Annie had complained to Amelia Palmer of feeling unwell and on several occasions had said that she was thinking of seeking help at a Casual Ward, an area of the workhouse that provided basic accommodation for those without funds and where the ill could be treated by a medical officer. Amelia had kindly lent Annie some money and told her that under no circumstances was she to spend it on liquor.

Three days later Annie's health had declined further. She told friends that she was much worse and feeling very ill. Only hours prior to her death, having spent what money she had on rum, Annie had managed to gain entry to Crossingham's Lodging House on Dorset Street and was found warming herself in the small kitchen.

Timothy Donovan, the deputy of the lodging house and a man known for his uncharitable nature, demanded that should she wish to stay then she must pay up – alternatively, she could leave. The latter was her only option.

At 1.45 a.m. Annie took to the streets: desperate, unwell and in need of money. As she left, unsteadily, from Dorset Street and headed towards Spitalfields Church, she was heard to tell the night watchmen of Crossingham's to keep a bed for her as she would soon be back.

She would never return.

The investigating officers were quick to concur that the same hand that had brutally slain Mary Nichols a week earlier had taken the life of another woman. Two unsolved murders, both by the same perpetrator, was a precedent for Whitechapel. And though initially the officers leading the case seemed devoid of clues, by the time of Annie Chapman's inquest on 10 September, they were able to determine that, as with the Nichols case, the killer had again been seen. It was a remarkable chance.

At around 5.30 a.m., only minutes prior to the murder, a resident of Church Row named Elizabeth Darrell was making her usual journey to the Spitalfields Market via Hanbury Street. As she reached Mrs Hardyman's Cat Meat Shop at number 29, she spotted Annie standing outside. As confirmed by Darrell, she was not alone and appeared to be in conversation with a man. Aware that Annie was a prostitute and believing that the man was in all certainty a client, Darrell took little notice of his appearance other than to observe that he bore a dark complexion and appeared to be Jewish.

Darrell could only add that he was taller than Annie and was wearing dark clothing.

As she passed, Darrell heard the man talk, asking Annie 'Will you?' and then hearing her reply of: 'Yes'.[16]

In no time Fleet Street realised that it had now had a major murder mystery on its hands. *The Times* took the view that the abdominal mutilations were 'too shocking to be described', but readers of *The Star* were not spared. Parke's subhead roared: 'HORROR UPON HORROR. THE HEART AND LIVER WERE OVER HER HEAD! WHITECHAPEL IS PANIC-STRICKEN AT ANOTHER FIENDISH CRIME.'[17]

Lacking any solid clues, the papers filled precious column inches with endless sightings of 'foreign-looking' suspects who they believed matched the description offered by Elizabeth Darrell; men dressed in black, with dark complexions – in other words, most of the Jewish males residing in the East End.

Accounts followed of angry crowds in Whitechapel shouting 'Down with the Jews' and 'It was a Jew who did it'. Meanwhile, *The Star* played on the old legend that the eyes of murder victims retained the images of their killers, suggesting the police should photograph Chapman's eyes.

One of the country's leading experts in criminal insanity, Dr Lyttleton Forbes Winslow, believed the killer was middle-class and claimed to have a plan to catch him. Believing the police were incapable of bringing the murderer to justice using normal means, he deduced that by disguising a dozen policemen as women the killer could be lured into a trap – a plan tried later by journalists.[18]

By 10 September the stumbling investigation appeared to turn a corner. As the press covered the Nichols murder in detail they began to circulate a rumour that the man responsible could be identified by his nickname. An infamous local brute was known to many of the local prostitutes as 'Leather Apron', and that was where the finger pointed. Sergeant Thick was one of many officers who took up the lead presented by the press. After reading the statements of the women who had encountered the would-be killer, he became convinced that he too knew the murderer's identity.

At 8 a.m., two days after the murder of Annie Chapman, Sergeant Thick, accompanied by a fellow officer, knocked on the front door of 22 Mulberry Street in Whitechapel. The man they were there to arrest was a Jewish Cobbler named John Pizer, known personally to Thick as 'Leather Apron'. When the two officers made a search of Pizer's rooms and discovered an assortment of knives, the arrest, at least for a while, looked promising.

After being removed to Leman Street Police Station, Pizer was questioned. He stated that he was unaware that he was known as 'Leather Apron'. He *did* wear an apron for his job, but he also mentioned that his work of late had all but dried up. Though Thick was adamant that Pizer was referred to by the nickname, the suspect's family and friends all refuted such claims.

And, after providing a cast-iron alibi, in which it was proved that on the night of the Nichols murder Pizer was staying in a lodging house on the Holloway Road, he was released.

So the Pizer affair ultimately ended in embarrassment for the police, the suspect cleared and even rewarded with monetary compensation from several newspapers. With Pizer's arrest and subsequent release well publicised, the confidence felt by the real killer could not have failed to grow, safe in the knowledge that the police were without the slightest clue as to his identity.

Although Tracy and KJ had been away from London during 1888, such was the press coverage at the time that when researching the Ripper case five years later, the reporters were able to work from a seemingly endless supply of material: from word on the street and inquest testimonials to detailed accounts of the police enquiries on the ground.

In the case of Annie Chapman, one factor that the reporters were keen to confirm was the amount of time taken by the killer to perform his mutilations. Elizabeth Darrell's sighting at 5.30 a.m., and the subsequent discovery by John Davis at 6 a.m., left a half-hour window in which the murder and 'ripping' must have occurred.

They looked back on the statement made by Dr Phillips, who on 19 September stated his belief that even a skilled surgeon could not have inflicted the wounds found on Annie Chapman's body in anything less than half an hour. That meant that a man of only moderate anatomical knowledge would have taken longer, which left the journalists with one startling conclusion. As John Davis walked along the dark corridor towards the rear door leading to the yard of number 29, Chapman's killer was still in the garden. Now cornered, he would have been left with no alternative. In order to evade capture the killer would need to scale the garden fence and look for a way back to the main thoroughfare.

KJ and Tracy learnt that bloodstains had been discovered by the police at the time of the murder, found on the fences that divided numbers 25, 27 and 29 Hanbury Street. The way in which The Ripper, surprised in his work by Davis, had made good his escape seemed evident. The journalists couldn't fail to see that the method of escape adopted by the killer bore a distinct similarity to the way in which Thomas Cutbush, when evading capture in 1891, leapt over fences and walls before finding an insecure property in which to hide.

A collection of bloody rags found at the rear of number 23 Hanbury Street indicated to the journalists that after leaping from the scene of the murder, the killer had stopped in number 25 to wipe his hands, before throwing the rags into the adjacent garden and disappearing through the unlocked premises, completely unnoticed.[19]

Though hindsight allowed KJ and Tracy to draw such conclusions, to the officers of 1888 such a method of escape was considered only as a possibility and nothing more. To Inspector Joseph Chandler, who pondered on such a theory, one further observation remained perplexing: not one of the flimsy palings on the slim fence running along the left of the yard was broken.[20]

The killer, whoever he may have been, was as light and nimble as a cat.

SIX

Ripper Interrupted

Of all the days of the autumn of 1888 perhaps none were more pleasant than 29 September. With a warm breeze and pools of sunshine cascading onto the streets, many of Whitechapel's residents were encouraged to venture out, exploring the markets of Spitalfields and the shops of Middlesex Street, where on any given day a variety of treasures could be found.

While the rag shops swelled with female trade by late morning the queues of the food stalls began to grow, their yellow sausage meat and battered fish proving popular among the locals. Inside the musty military stores men could be seen to mingle, avoiding the bundles of bayonets that hung like rusted chandeliers from the ceilings, before delving deep into piles of broken pistols and daggers, eager to arm themselves by whatever means.[1]

Beyond the booksellers and butchers the masses could be seen to emerge, the midday rush clogging the streets of Spitalfields with human traffic. Its cobbled ground appeared almost indistinguishable among the costermonger barrows and fruit stalls, all busily serving their hungry customers.

Only as darkness fell did the vibrant atmosphere begin to change, bringing with it a downpour of rain that, unheralded, took London and its people by surprise. As stall keepers attempted to preserve their stock, rooftops began to resonate with a chorus of pelted tiles.

As if bursting their banks, troughs and fountains overflowed – turning streets into rivers and forming dark infested channels of mud and grime to leave the once bustling Whitechapel deserted.[2]

Inside the Bricklayer's Arms on Settles Street, Swedish-born Elizabeth Stride, like many others, sought shelter, choosing to watch the rain from the warmth of a fireside while sipping the last of her ale. Having spent the day cleaning rooms of a Lodging House at 32 Flower and Dean Street, she was enjoying a well-earned rest, sitting on one of two mahogany seats that flanked the fireplace and stole the heat from the remainder of the room.

Hailing from Gothenburg, where she had grown up on a farm with her parents, Elizabeth had been in England since 1866, when she took up residence in Hyde Park before marrying John Stride three years later. An industrious woman, she had once owned a coffee house business and though it, along with her marriage, eventually failed, her desire to work had remained. She earned a wage cleaning for the local Jewish community as well as in a number of lodging houses.

After separating from her husband, Elizabeth moved to Whitechapel, taking up lodgings in Flower and Dean Street in 1882. By then, in an attempt to gain sympathy from those she met, she had concocted a story that her husband and two children had died in a tragic collision between a leisure liner named *Princess Alice* and a collier, an accident recorded as occurring in 1878, near Woolwich on the River Thames. And though 600 passengers lost their lives, Elizabeth's husband had not been one of them; John Stride in fact lived on until 1884, when he died from heart disease.

By 1885 Elizabeth had met waterside labourer Michael Kidney who, at thirty-three, was seven years her junior. The pair had a tempestuous love affair, and Kidney had a reputation for a volatile temper. He often beat Elizabeth and, if he thought that she was venturing to a tavern or beer house, he would secure her in a padlocked room to prevent her from leaving, despite being a drunkard himself.

Having separated from Kidney for the final time in the September of 1888, and being without the support of his wage, Elizabeth worked hard to earn enough to avoid sleeping on the streets. At times when the cleaning work was flourishing, she lived relatively well. When the work dried up she would resort to prostitution. It was something she had done, on and off, since the age of twenty-two.

And though her plight bound her with a great many street women of Whitechapel, to her customers Elizabeth was looked upon as unique. An attractive and slender woman, with an unblemished face surrounded by black curly hair hanging loose upon her shoulders, at forty-five she could have passed for a woman at least ten years younger.

After finishing work at 6.30 p.m. Elizabeth had changed. Dressing in a neat black jacket edged with fur, over a sateen dress and tattered black boots, the darkness of her outfit was broken only by the red rose pinned to her breast.

By 7 p.m. Elizabeth was observed in the Queen's Head on Commercial Street and by 10 p.m. was seen heading towards the Bricklayer's Arms, the light inside spilling beyond its etched windows and acting as a beacon amid the unrelenting rain.[3]

As was customary for a Saturday evening, the mood inside was cheerful. A bawdy scene of excited conversations, of shrieks and hollers and cackled laughter joined by the slurred singing of the confident few, all enjoying the drink and the dry in equal measure.

Surrounded by patrons of every ilk, from seamen and labourers to pimps and their tarts, Elizabeth felt at home – warm, comfortable and safe, sitting beyond a carved divider that separated the crowded bar-room from the quiet seclusion of a fireside. And while some groups of men and women could be seen standing clustered together, almost hidden by smoke, others sat at tables, around open newspapers, where in whispered tones their conversation turned to the more tragic events of recent days.

By the end of September the murders of Mary Nichols and Annie Chapman still remained unsolved and theorising as to the identity of the killer became a common topic for debate.

Though the horrific nature of their murders was bad enough, the press, eager to heighten the fear felt by the majority of London's literate, began to link the killings of the two women with two previous murders that had occurred earlier in the year. That of Emma Smith, a prostitute who fell victim to gang attack,[4] and Martha Tabram, who after taking a soldier client to the darkness of George Yard was found stabbed thirty-nine times, with one of the wounds inflicted with a bayonet.[5]

And though much of the press coverage consisted of repeated accounts of the injuries sustained by the victims, as well as providing names of those men upon whom, without evidence, suspicion was beginning to fall, a common question being asked by the tabloids was whether or not the killer would strike again.

By 1 a.m. the next day the press and the police would have their answer.

As the door of the International Working Men's Club flew open, inside the crowded room of men and women fell silent, their gazes locked upon the club steward, Louis Diemschutz, who was standing in the doorway, trembling with fright and clinging to its frame to keep himself from fainting.

The club, a socialist retreat popular among the local Polish and Russian community and situated in a large yard off Berner Street, had been busier than normal. They had held a debate on the socialism of Jews, and the evening had been well attended. At midnight, though many members had left, at least thirty people remained, relaxing after a night of heated discussion with music and singing.

Beyond the club was a working courtyard used by sack manufacturer W. Hindley, known locally as Dutfield's Yard. A spacious area, that evening it was cast into virtual darkness, the only light coming from the rooms of the Working Men's Club.[6]

The yard could be entered via two large wooden gates that opened inwards and rested against the walls of adjoining cottages as well as that of the club. Beyond the gates lay Berner Street, a short residential thoroughfare branching off from Fairclough Street, on the corner of which stood a boarding school for girls, boys and infants.

Louis Diemschutz knew the area well and that morning, as he drew his pony and trap into Berner Street after a day peddling cheap jewellery at Crystal Palace market, he saw nothing untoward. As he approached Dutfield's Yard, his intention being to unload his unsold stock before stabling his pony elsewhere, he saw that the gates were open.

On entering the yard, with the wheels of his cart jarring against the cobbled road, the darkness inside seemed thicker than normal. With the dull light of the club offering little illumination, had it not been for the reaction of his pony, pulling away to its left, there is every chance he would have failed to see the woman's body lying on the ground to his right.

Leaning over from his cart, Diemschutz peered into the gloom, unable to distinguish much beyond a dark shape huddled upon the floor. Intrigued by his pony's reaction, he dismounted and prodded the object with his whip. Seeing no reaction, he then struck a match and though the flame was almost instantly quashed by a light breeze, saw enough to determine that what he was looking at was a body.

Frightened, Diemschutz made for the club, entered and immediately tried to locate his wife, without a word to the concerned members, who by now were somewhat alarmed by his dramatic entrance.

He explained that he had found the body of a woman, but didn't know whether she was drunk or dead. Diemschutz asked two members to join him: Morris Eagle, a Russian immigrant, and his good friend Isaac Kozebrodsky, whose curiosity, it would seem, was instantly aroused.[7]

Aided by a candle, the three men made their way back into the yard and though the flames flickered and danced in the wind, it held fast long enough to see the body of Elizabeth Stride lying on her left-hand side, alongside the club wall, with a stream of blood running from her neck along a nearby gutter. Diemschutz and Kozebrodsky fled from the yard yelling 'murder' and 'police', making in the direction of Fairclough Street in the hope of finding a patrolling police constable. They continued on to Brunswick and Grove Street but were unable to locate a soul, and it was only on doubling back towards the club, in the direction of Fairclough Street, that they found help in the form of Edward Spooner.

The men explained what they had seen and Spooner proceeded to escort them back to the yard. By the time they reached it, a large crowd had already formed around the body; however, Spooner was the first to touch the corpse. With much trepidation he knelt at Elizabeth's side, delicately lifting her chin and, aided by candlelight, saw for the first time the wound inflicted to her neck.

Within minutes, two police constables arrived in the yard and on seeing the lifeless body, immediately sent for a doctor. While they waited, PC Henry Lamb knelt at Elizabeth's side, taking her wrist in his hand in the vain hope of finding a pulse.[8]

As he soon discovered, she was beyond help.

To *The Sun* reporters, the murder inquiry that followed the discovery of Elizabeth Stride's body provided an array of fascinating witness statements that allowed them to map her movements during the final hours of her life.

They knew that at 11 p.m. she had left the Bricklayer's Arms. That by 11.45 p.m. she had reached Berner Street. They were aware that shortly afterwards she had stopped at Matthew Packer's fruit shop at 44 Berner Street and an hour later she was seen standing outside the gates of Dutfield's Yard. They also knew that on every occasion Elizabeth had been in company with a man whom the reporters believed in all certainly was her killer.

A gentleman who, according to the keen eye of Constable William Smith, was in his twenties approximately 5 ft 7 in., wore dark clothing with a darkcoloured felt hat and was of a respectable appearance. He also saw that the man was carrying a newspaper parcel some eighteen inches in length and six to eight inches in width.[9]

Smith had been on patrol in the neighbouring streets since ten, and on turning into Berner Street at 12.30 a.m. he caught sight of a man and woman standing opposite Dutfield's Yard. He would later confirm the woman's identity as Elizabeth, recognising her from the small flower pinned to her jacket.

The constable would also state that as nothing in their behaviour seemed out of place he had simply continued with his patrol. KJ and Tracy saw that Smith's description tallied with that of Mr Best and John Gardner, who had observed Elizabeth leaving the Bricklayer's Arms at 11 p.m. At that time she was in company with a man described by them as being young and English, who had a black moustache and wore a morning suit and hat. They also added that he bore the appearance of a clerk.[10]

At 11.45 p.m. William Marshall, a resident of number 64 Berner Street, saw the couple heading in the direction of Dutfield's Yard. On passing them, although Elizabeth was quiet, the pair appeared deep in conversation, with the man being heard to comment: 'You would say anything but your prayers.'[11]

By now the couple seemed on good terms and proceeded onwards to a fruit seller on the corner of Berner Street at its junction with Fairclough Street.

Owned by an elderly gentleman named Matthew Packer, among other items the small shop sold fruit and vegetables from its front window, shutting most nights at around midnight.

Packer would later tell two private detectives that on the night of the 29th he had seen a woman matching the description of Elizabeth Stride in company with a gentleman, who had purchased from him half a pound of black grapes. As heavy rain had again started to fall, the couple crossed the road and sheltered in the entrance of the boarding school.

Packer described the man as being young, standing around 5 ft 7 in., wearing dark clothes and having what he perceived as a 'quick commanding way with him'. His story would later be summarised on 4 October by the Assistant Commissioner of the Metropolitan Police, who provided some further details as to what Packer had said, noting that the man was two or three inches taller than Elizabeth and describing him as a young clerk.[12]

Dock labourer James Brown was the next witness to see Elizabeth and her client. On passing along Fairclough Street at 12.45 a.m. he turned and looked down Berner Street. It was then that he saw Stride in company with a man, who at that time appeared to be stopping her from leaving. Brown stated that the man had his arm against the wall of the boarding school, as if blocking Elizabeth, after which he heard her say 'No! not tonight; some other night.' He didn't think anything of it, however, and continued on his way home.[13]

The last of the many eyewitness statements came shortly afterwards. Israel Schwartz, a Hungarian immigrant who lived locally, had turned into Berner Street from Commercial Road. Schwartz was heading home and as he walked in a southerly direction towards Fairclough Street, he started to make out what appeared to be two people standing in the doorway of Dutfield's Yard. As he grew closer, he was able to see that it was a man and a woman standing face-to-face and they appeared to be having a quarrel.

Schwartz then saw the man grab at his female companion and violently throw her to the ground. He would later tell the police that he heard her scream several times but being a small man of quiet demeanour, he kept on walking, more concerned for his own safety than that of the woman.

Schwartz crossed over to the other side of the street, and it was then that he noticed another man standing nearby on the pavement, smoking a pipe. He, like Schwartz, had observed the feuding couple but similarly said nothing and declined from intervening.

On seeing that his actions were being observed, Elizabeth's attacker berated the two spectators, shouting 'Lipski' – an anti-Semitic insult of the time. Now alarmed, Schwartz decided to leave the area as quickly as he could, as did the second man who followed close behind him.

Frightened, Schwartz began to run, and as he thought that the second man (who he had seen smoking a pipe) was pursuing him, he didn't stop until he was clear of Berner Street and under the shelter of a nearby railway arch. When he eventually came to a stop, Schwartz found himself alone, the only sound being that of his rapid breathing echoing in the darkness of the tunnel.[14]

He checked the street beyond its entrance and saw that it was deserted; the second man was nowhere to be seen. By then Elizabeth's screams had ceased; the quarrelling couple had disappeared from sight. And, two streets away, Louis Diemschutz was almost home.

After the discovery of Elizabeth's body, police on the ground worked fast, arriving at the scene in numbers, led by Chief Inspector West and Inspector Charles Pinhorn. In little time the gates of Dutfield's Yard were closed and all the remaining members of the Working Men's Club were ordered to stay.[15] Shining their bull's-eye lanterns across the yard in the hope of finding clues, the constables were greeted by an abundance of bloody footprints, courtesy of the numerous bystanders who had unknowingly stepped in Elizabeth's blood.

By ten past one Dr Frederick Blackwell arrived on the scene. He stated that Elizabeth's body was lying across the entrance to the yard, with her legs drawn up and her feet close to the wall of the club. Though her hands were cold, her neck, chest and legs retained an element of warmth. The doctor also noticed that her right hand had been placed across her chest and was spattered with blood. On turning the body, the doctor saw that her lips were slightly separated, as well as finding that a silk scarf, worn around her neck, had been pulled tight.

Turning his attention to the wound, the doctor noted that her throat had been cut with force, with a deep gash severing the windpipe.[16]

Soon after Dr Phillips arrived, who only three weeks earlier had been summoned to Hanbury Street to examine the corpse of Annie Chapman. In little time both doctors had concluded that, judging by the warmth of the body and the congealment of blood, Elizabeth had been murdered shortly before 1 a.m., around the time that Diemschutz had turned into Berner Street. The assumption was that the killer had heard the rattling of the cart wheels as Diemschutz drove his trap towards the yard and had been interrupted.

Diemschutz could never say whether he had seen any movement in the darkness of the yard as he ran to the club for help, or whether he had heard the steps of the killer scurrying backwards in an attempt to hide. Possibly the singing inside the club was so loud as to have drowned out any sound of the killer skulking in the shadows, though in all likelihood he was there, biding his time before making his escape.

Though forty-five minutes had passed since his discovery, Diemschutz was still in a state of shock. Sitting in the kitchen of the club with his wife by his side, he quietly contemplated what he had seen, pondering on how close he may have been to coming face-to-face with Elizabeth's killer. As he sat back upon a stiff wooden chair and sipped lightly on a glass of gin, offered as a remedy for his ailing nerves, he did so oblivious to the further chaos that was about to ensue, and which would challenge the Metropolitan and the City Police as never before.

As they soon discovered, within an hour of murdering Elizabeth Stride, the Ripper had struck again.

SEVEN

The Worst Yet

As the Ripper fled from Dutfield's Yard, less than a mile away 46-year-old prostitute Catherine Eddowes was awaiting her release from Bishopsgate Police Station. Earlier that night, lying in a drunken heap upon a mudded footway on Aldgate High Street, Catherine had been found by PC Louis Robinson, his attention drawn by a crowd that had gathered around her body.

Although a petite and attractive woman with hazel eyes and a cluster of dark auburn hair, she appeared dishevelled, her clothes in a state of disarray, with her once neat black bonnet hanging loose over her face.[1]

After summoning assistance in the form of PC Simmons, Robinson decided to remove Catherine to his station on Wormwood Street, intending to place her in a cell until morning.

According to gaoler, PC George Hutt, on each of the three occasions that he had checked on Catherine since her arrival at 8.45 p.m. he had found her to be asleep, partially covered by a grey sheet of coarse wool, lying upon a wooden bed that offered as little comfort as the stone floor on which it stood.

So drunk was Catherine that for the four hours of her incarceration she remained oblivious to her surroundings: from the cold of her cell to the vile stench emanating from the brick toilet opposite, the lid of which had been snapped off by the previous occupant.

While most of the cells in Bishopsgate were full, by midnight the station was quiet, leaving Sergeant Byfield and Constable Hutt enjoying a warm mug of tea, listening to the rain as it rattled lightly against the flat roof of the station office.

Ten minutes later the gentle singing coming from Catherine's cell indicated that the prisoner was awake and beginning to sober up. After a further forty-five minutes it was decided that she was fit to leave. PC Hutt ordered the removal of Catherine from her cell so that she could be released.

As Sergeant Byfield opened the thick discharge register, turning to the blank page marked '30 September', he began to hear the sound of movement, with Catherine's shuffling steps indicating that, unlike earlier, she was now able to walk, her skirt of green chintz dragging along the stone floor before coming to a stop at Byfield's desk.

Having already asked for Catherine's name on her arrival, at which time she had replied: 'Nothing', Byfield was insistent that he would only release her if she provided her details. After a moment's hesitation Catherine obliged, giving a name and address before being escorted from the station office by Hutt.

The constable would later remark that as he led Catherine through the swing doors of the station, feeling the chill as he neared the outer exit, she had appeared in good spirits. He reported that before leaving, she had remarked: 'Good night, old cock', after which she turned her back on the constable and slowly began to make her way towards Houndsditch.[2]

As the door shut behind her the constable paused, listening as Catherine's boots, which appeared too large for a woman of her size, lightly scuffed against the cobblestones outside, splattering in the pools of rain as she walked, before disappearing into silence.

Upon the streets and thoroughfares of Spitalfields and Whitechapel, Eddowes was not an unfamiliar figure; they were two areas of London that would later be referred to by Acting Commissioner of the City Police as Catherine's personal 'beat'.[3]

In the seven years that had passed since she had first arrived in the East End, her pleasant manner and kindly nature had won her many friends – as well as securing her a number of regular clients. Catherine's persona, described as 'jolly', may have been a mask for the tragedy of her former life. She had lost both parents at thirteen, and at only nineteen years of age formed a relationship with a man who would go on regularly to beat and abuse her; he was a salesman and former soldier named Thomas Quinn (who outside of his military career used the name Conway).

She met Quinn at the age of nineteen, and they'd had three children together in their home city of Wolverhampton. But the Irishman was at times difficult to live with, and by 1870 had begun to beat Catherine when drunk. Catherine's sister would describe Quinn as an irregular drinker, but when he got his hands on his regular military pension he would generally buy ale. Unable to handle his liquor, Quinn's mood would change dramatically, seeing him turn abusive and leaving Catherine battered and bruised.

For the sake of her children she stayed, though turning to drink herself in the process, and appearing so fearful of Quinn's temper as to stay away from the family home for days at a time. The beatings continued and eventually in 1881, Catherine summoned the courage to leave, taking her daughter Annie with her. She arrived at Cooney's Lodging House on Flower and Dean Street, where soon after she met and fell in love with market labourer John Kelly.[4]

Unlike her previous relationship, in Kelly Catherine had found a friend as well as a lover, forming a strong relationship evident to all who knew them. In order that Catherine should not have to solicit, Kelly worked hard, regularly jobbing at local markets as well as working for a fruit salesman named Lander.[5]

Catherine also tried to make honest money, selling items on street corners as well as cleaning. Together they shared a single bed at Cooney's, costing them eight pence per night, and only when without the funds to pay for a night's sleep would the pair separate, finding their own money and accommodation until they'd earned enough to return to Flower and Dean Street.

While John would often stay in a Casual Ward in Mile End, Catherine would at times be found sleeping in a night refuge on Dorset Street during which time, as a means of buying food and ale, she would resort to prostitution.[6]

By September 1888 the pair had again come together in order to take up their annual excursion to Kent to pick hops on farmland, a popular occupation especially among nineteenth-century city dwellers who could earn close to thirty shillings for a good week's hopping. While working on the farms, accommodation would be provided in the form of tin huts, with workers sharing the food preparation, as well as the washing facilities and a communal toilet. If the blocks were full, then workers would be given shelter of a different kind: sleeping in disused animal sheds and poorly constructed tents.[7]

For Catherine and John 'hopping' was seen as an opportunity to leave the oppressive East End behind and, if only temporarily, enjoy the open countryside, where the air remained clear and untarnished, unlike that of Whitechapel, where the factory smoke blackened even the brightest of skies. John Kelly later recounted that the season of 1888 had not been a particularly good one, and unlike previous years they had only been able to put aside a small sum.

By 27 September both he and Catherine had arrived back in Whitechapel and, having spent what little funds they had on ale, were once again penniless.[8] Lacking the funds for Cooney's Lodging House, they ventured to Mile End in the hope of staying in the Casual Ward at Shoe Lane Workhouse. It was a shelter that, although being of the most deplorable kind with men and women sleeping upon tarpaulin covered benches in infested cellars, was at least free.[9]

The next day, after finding several hours work at the busy Friday markets, Kelly had earned six pence; he gave four pence to Catherine, in the hope that she would use it to pay for a bed at a Lodging House. Catherine declined and insisted that John take the room himself, saying that she was happy to return to the Casual Ward in Mile End.

Early the next morning Catherine made the short journey to Cooney's and by 8 a.m. had arrived and was observed searching for John. By now the need for food took precedence. Again, without funds, John decided to pawn a pair of boots that he had recently acquired, taking them to a pawnbroker in Church Street and with the profits purchasing a feast of eggs and sausages. Predictably, within a matter of hours the two shillings and six pence gained from John's boots were no more.

According to John Kelly, it was 2 p.m. when he and Catherine parted company for the last time. Having made their way to Houndsditch, Catherine had told him that she wished to visit her daughter in Bermondsey in the hope of borrowing some money, promising that she would be back in Whitechapel within a few hours. Oblivious to her true intentions John agreed – not realising it would be last occasion that he would ever see her alive.[10]

Catherine would never reach Bermondsey. She remained in the area of Aldgate, choosing to solicit in order to make enough money for a bed at Cooney's. By 8.30 p.m. she had made her doss money several times over, yet had drunk every penny. By the time PC Louis Robinson found her on Aldgate High Street she was barely conscious.

After leaving Bishopsgate Police Station at 12.55 a.m., not wishing to return home penniless, Catherine decided to search for a client. Walking at a slow pace, she ventured to Mitre Square – a small enclosed court off Aldgate High Street which, being both dark and surrounded by large warehouses, proved a regular venue for the local prostitutes.

Thirty-five minutes later she was observed standing in a covered passage, near to Duke Street, one of three points by which Mitre Square could be entered. By then heavy rain had started to fall once again and, according to witnesses, Catherine appeared to be sheltering, though not alone, observed in quiet conversation with a man standing opposite, her hand resting on his chest.[11]

Three witnesses would later come forward to inform the police that at 1.30 a.m., after enjoying a night at the nearby Imperial Club, they had seen Catherine and her companion as they passed along Duke Street. Although one of the men, a local butcher named Joseph Levy, took little notice of the pair, his friend Joseph Lawende would go on to provide a relatively clear description of Catherine's client. He described him as young, approximately 5 ft 8 in. and of medium build; he had a moustache and wore a salt and pepper loose jacket with a cloth cap.

Harry Harris, the third man in the group, would go on to state that all three men only saw the back of Catherine's companion, with Joseph Levy adding that from his vantage point he could only say that the man was taller than Catherine.[12]

Although the three witnesses had correctly ascertained that Catherine was soliciting, nothing in the couple's behaviour alerted Lawende, Levy or Harris that the man in company with Catherine Eddowes was anything other than a paying client.

Within ten minutes of the sighting Catherine and her companion had left, their place in Church Passage being taken by PC James Harvey, whose usual morning patrols brought him as a matter of course to the area of Mitre Square. He would go on to state that at 1.40 a.m. he had looked in on Mitre Square. Standing in Church Passage he had held aloft his lantern and, while its dull rays did little to separate the darkness, the Square appeared quiet and, as he thought at the time, empty.

Five minutes later the heavy tread of PC Watkins could be heard as he made his way from Mitre Street. Having started his tour of duty at 9.45 p.m., Watkins had already conducted a number of patrols within the Square, the most recent being fifteen minutes earlier at 1.30 a.m., when all had appeared in order. Such was the nature of the Square that every sound made within it reverberated around its high walls.

Watkins could hear his own footfalls echoing as he walked. As he neared the darkest corner, his eyes gauged a dark form lying upon the ground. His steps began to slow. As he looked closer, steadying the lamp attached to his belt in order to shed as much light upon the object as possible, he realised the true nature of his discovery.

When, in 1893, Louis Tracy reviewed the murder of Catherine Eddowes he, like Kennedy Jones, was appalled. Although having worked as a journalist for nine years, never had he seen or read of such brutality as displayed in the murder of the Ripper's fourth victim.

Catherine's body was discovered in the southwest corner of Mitre Square, lying upon her back only yards from a tea warehouse, where a night watchman had been working for most of the evening. Lying on the ground close to a spiked fence that bordered the yard of Heydemann & Co. was Catherine's body, her head resting on its left side, with her arms flat against the sodden ground beneath her.

Catherine's throat had been viciously cut through, creating a gaping wound, below which was another smaller cut. The severity of the attack had separated and divided all the large muscles of the neck, as well as cutting through the larynx; the cuts were so deep as to have reached her backbone.

As PC Watkins discovered, Catherine's clothes had been drawn up in order to expose her abdomen and naked thighs. Her left leg was lying flat, with her right being bent at the knee and, as in the case of Annie Chapman, in an attempt to expose the extent of his work, her killer had ripped away the upper part of her dress.

Catherine's abdomen walls had been laid open from her breastbone, with her intestines drawn out and placed over her right shoulder. In a frenzied assault her killer had violently stabbed and cut at her internal organs, attacking the liver, vagina, and rectum. Before leaving the scene the Ripper turned his attention to Catherine's face.[13]

The mutilation was such as to make the victim almost unrecognisable: the tip of her nose had been removed by what appeared to be a clean cut and another deeper cut was found over the bridge of her nose, extending down through her cheek to the right side of her jaw.

After slashing Catherine's lips, the killer then made several intricate slits to her eyes, along with two inverted 'V' shaped cuts made to her cheeks directly below. It would later be found, after an examination of Catherine's body, that in an effort to mirror his actions in Hanbury Street the killer had again taken a trophy of his kill, removing a kidney and part of the womb.

PC Watkins's initial reaction was to seek help from George Morris – the night watchmen, who was himself a retired police officer. Stepping inside the entrance to Kearley and Tonge's tea warehouse, Watkins soon found Morris, who was by then cleaning the interior steps. Even though the front door had been ajar, Morris would later state that he hadn't heard a sound all night. After being alerted as to the discovery, he quickly collected his own lamp from inside the warehouse and joined the constable in the Square.[14]

News of the second murder soon spread and within minutes City Police Inspector Edward Collard was on the scene, along with three constables. By 2.18 a.m. Dr Gordon Brown had arrived at the square, being joined by Inspector McWilliam, Superintendent Foster and Acting Commissioner of the City Police, Major Henry Smith.[15]

By his own admission, the night of 29 September had proved a difficult one for Smith, who arrived in Mitre Square unshaven and tired. Residing in the private quarters of Cloak Lane Police Station, a building nestled between a busy railway goods depot and a furriers yard, Smith had found it almost impossible to sleep. With a constant clatter of van wheels traversing the nearby causeway and the reek of fur skins pricking at his senses, he had spent the night turning uncomfortably in his bed.

Just before 2 a.m. the Assistant Commissioner was alerted to the murder by a fellow colleague and in minutes had dressed and was standing at the entrance to the station. The hansom cab that arrived shortly after did little to impress Major Smith, who viewed the mode of transport as unsafe and unpleasant.

Accompanied by a burley Superintendent and three detectives who – given the lack of space inside the two man cab – were instructed to cling to the rear, within a matter of minutes the Assistant Commissioner arrived at Mitre Square.

Major Smith would later recall the events of that night in his memoirs, in which he would also draw attention to what he perceived as the failings of his own officers. In light of the Nichols and Chapman murders, Smith had given an order that every man and woman, seen together, be accounted for. In the case of Catherine Eddowes, whom Smith had claimed was well known as being a local prostitute, he could not understand why, after being discharged from Bishopsgate station, she was not followed by officers. A moment of perceived stupidity that ultimately cost her life.[16]

After the discovery of Catherine's body, constables frantically checked the surrounding area in search of the murderer, dipping into the many alleyways and side streets that ran like veins through the heart of Whitechapel. Those secluded places where, being devoid of light, a man could remain unseen among its shadows, watching on from any one of its darkened corners.

Though believing that the killer would have likely distanced himself from the murder scene, officers on the ground diligently checked and double checked the vicinity of Mitre Square, all without success. In order to preserve an image of the crime scene the decision was made to contact Frederick Foster, a city surveyor, so that plans could be drawn of the location as well as sketches made of Catherine's body as she lay in situ.

Foster would go on to draw several images that morning. Alongside those made at the crime scene, he also drew one at 3.45 a.m. depicting Catherine as she had appeared at the mortuary.[17] In 1891 Inspector William Race, when searching Thomas Cutbush's room, found a horrific sketch. It was eerily similar to Foster's illustration, showing how Catherine's body had looked when it had been discovered in Mitre Square.[18]

To Race and the reporters working for *The Sun*, the drawing was almost too close in its detail to be a coincidence, and all three men concluded that in order for Cutbush to have drawn such an image, either he must have seen the drawing made by Foster or – more chillingly – witnessed for himself the injuries inflicted upon Catherine Eddowes.

Although many articles were published in the aftermath of the double murders that concentrated on the gruesome nature of the crimes and the cunning employed by the killer in committing two murders in less than an hour, Louis Tracy would see within the reports another detail of the case that both moved and sickened him.

Within the reports of *The Times* newspaper, Tracy found a true depiction of the horrendous lives being lived by the victims up until the time of their murders, women whose lives seemed to have no purpose beyond mere existence and who, in order to survive, risked everything.

For Louis Tracy no greater example of the plight suffered by Catherine Eddowes was as telling as the description of her appearance at the time of her death. *The Times* reported the many layers worn by the victim, consisting of a jacket, three skirts and petticoats as well as flounces, vests and a white chemise. The paper also detailed the numerous items found among Catherine's clothes, including a match box containing cotton, table knives and clay pipes, as well as a small tin box containing tea and sugar. A check pocket containing pieces of soap was also found tucked inside her coat, along with a pair of spectacles and a large white linen pocket in which she carried a small comb and red mitten.

What Tracy saw in the findings of *The Times* and other contemporary reports was that, without a place to call home or a haven of any kind, Catherine Eddowes had simply walked the streets dressed in every garment in her possession, carrying literally everything she owned.[19]

Tracy would be so moved by the poverty found in the slums of Whitechapel that several years later, after selling his stake in another newspaper and receiving £20,000 in return, he would go on to donate every penny to London's poor. He set up twenty-three soup kitchens that provided 3.5 million meals, something that he would later refer to as his 'greatest achievement'.[20]

Although equally distressed by what he read, Kennedy Jones was keen to keep his emotions in check, focusing on the facts of the murder case as contained within the contemporary reports. What KJ found interesting when reading the newspaper accounts of the double murder, beyond the horrific injuries inflicted upon the victims, were the findings of Dr Gordon Brown in relation to the body of Catherine Eddowes.

Kennedy read that, after Catherine's body had been removed to Golden Lane Mortuary, a thorough examination had been conducted. After instructing that the body be stripped and washed down, Dr Gordon Brown methodically noted each of the injuries inflicted by Catherine's killer. As he turned his attention to her limbs, the doctor noticed something unusual – apparent discoloration upon Catherine's right forearm, which on closer examination appeared to be a tattoo. It consisted of two letters written in blue India ink.

They formed the initials T. C.[21]

EIGHT

'T.C.'

Albert Street, Kennington
December 1893

As the horse began to slow Tracy lifted his gaze from the red notebook resting upon his lap. Sitting inside the cab, dressed in his favoured frock coat of dark wool, the reporter had spent the majority of his journey reading, studying the notes made by Kennedy Jones of an interview held with the relatives of Thomas Cutbush two weeks earlier.[1]

Inside the cab, though the glass windows were secured, the cold of late December could still be felt, offering Tracy little encouragement to remove his black bowler and leather gloves. As opposed to the busy Kennington Park Road, Albert Street seemed ominously still, even for mid-afternoon.

On leaving the cab, feeling the carriage sway as he adjusted his footing so as not to slip, Tracy could hear distant voices coming from the shops and taverns nearby. In Albert Street, save for the rattling of the cab wheels upon the cobbled surface, all was quiet.

Looking above the three-storey houses that flanked each side of the road, the sky appeared heavy, with a veil of grey cloud hanging low upon the chimney tops, broken only by a line of birds flying overhead. As the cab disappeared into Penton Place, with the clatter of hooves ringing in the air, Tracy began to walk.

Straightening his tie, the reporter made his way towards the large door of number 14, located above three steps that rose from a carpet of recently swept leaves lying stiff upon the ground. From KJ's notes, he was aware that a great deal had been ascertained in a previous interview with Cutbush's aunt, as well as the statements of several lodgers who, at one time, had resided in the same house. Not wishing to cover old ground, he hoped to explore an area of their suspect's life that up until now had barely been discussed.

The Sun's chief editor, T. P. O'Connor, was conscious that to present their findings without exploring a motive for Cutbush committing the crimes would prove futile. As such, the directive for Tracy was to elicit information about Cutbush's previous relationships with women, in the hope that he might unearth a clue.

Inspector Race had already informed the reporters that Cutbush had at one time associated with prostitutes and, although aware that to discuss such a topic with his female kin might prove difficult, it was nonetheless an avenue Tracy wished to explore.

Facing the door, he knocked lightly. On receiving no reply he peered in the window to his right, of what he presumed was the drawing room, hoping to see some signs of life. After several seconds, Tracy again rapped the door with his knuckles, harder this time, before hearing what appeared to be distant footsteps moving along a hard floor towards him.

Meanwhile, KJ was sitting among a catalogue of contemporary newspapers in Tudor Street, and came across what he perceived at the time to be a breakthrough in their investigation.

He had already noted the tattoo found on Catherine Eddowes's arm, raising with Tracy the possible coincidence of a victim being marked with the very initials of her would-be attacker.

While Tracy believed that the tattoo was likely to have referred to Catherine's ex-partner Thomas Quinn (who also went by the name of Conway), KJ was of the view that it might, in actual fact, hold an equal significance for Cutbush. In an effort to learn whether any links existed between Catherine and Thomas Cutbush, KJ reviewed the copious articles printed in newspapers of the time covering the murder of Catherine Eddowes and the subsequent inquest.

While many of the accounts related to the manner in which Catherine was murdered, some reported on her movements prior to the morning of 30 September, during which time an alleged revelation had taken place. KJ found that on 28 September, while staying in the Casual Ward, Catherine had taken the superintendent to one side and confessed that she knew the identity of the Ripper.

So confident was Catherine in her claims that, according to the superintendent, she stated that her return to London from Kent had been in order for her to earn the reward being granted at the time for the killer's apprehension.[2]

As KJ knew, around this time several rewards had been offered to anyone who could assist in bringing the killer to justice, the most notable of which was £100 offered by a local MP, considered a small fortune to someone in Catherine's position.[3]

The superintendent warned her to take care that she wouldn't end up a victim herself. To which Catherine replied: 'No fear of that.' As he read of the injuries sustained by Eddowes, it occurred to Kennedy that, while she was undeniably a victim of the same killer as Nichols, Chapman and Stride, there was something in the manner of her murder that set it apart.

Unlike the three previous victims, in the case of Catherine Eddowes, the Ripper had attacked her face. KJ inferred from that detail that there was something far more personal about this crime.

Of course, this could have equally been a sign of the Ripper's increasing madness or confidence, but KJ tended to see a link between Catherine's confession and the fact that on this occasion, unlike before, the Ripper had turned his attention to the very soul of his victim, inflicting wounds to her eyes, nose, lips and cheeks and destroying the one element of her form that made her unique.

Running with his theme, what KJ also saw in the attack on Catherine's face was a correlation to his chief suspect's state of mind at the time. As KJ and Tracy already knew, Thomas Cutbush believed that the lesions on his face were the result of syphilis. Indeed, he was obsessed by the very thought.[4] What if he wished to avenge himself on the class of women he believed had infected him and caused his pains and humiliation at the hands of mocking workmates? To attack a prostitute's face seemed increasingly logical.

And what if Catherine Eddowes had been the very prostitute from whom Cutbush believed he had contracted the disease in the first place? Perhaps, so KJ thought at the time, that very belief might have formed Cutbush's motive.

KJ had also found that, unlike previous victims, Catherine was no stranger to the area in which Cutbush lived. She frequently left east London to visit her daughter who – according to the *Evening News* – had worked as a domestic servant for a respectable family in the neighbourhood of Kennington.[5]

What Tracy had suggested to KJ, prior to his leaving for Albert Street, was for him to attempt to find any sightings of a man in the area of Mitre Square, either before or after Eddowes's murder, that might relate to Cutbush, indicating that he was either with Catherine or at least in the vicinity of the crime scene at the time of her murder.

KJ – although not hopeful – obliged. What he discovered would be more sensational than either man could have hoped.

As the door to number 14 opened Tracy was pleased to embrace a moment's warmth. Greeted by the gentle smile of a female servant dressed entirely in grey, save for a small apron of crisp white, he was invited inside.

Keen to meet Cutbush's aunt, Tracy eagerly followed the servant's steps that fell lightly upon the dark wooden floor of the hallway. Looking around the house, it felt familiar, similar in design to the middle-class homes in which he had been raised in Liverpool and Yorkshire, with the sweet scent of flowers providing a pleasant change from the smoke-filled streets of the city.

Passing a hall table, Tracy noticed a pile of unopened letters stacked neatly next to a folded newspaper of the previous day. As he walked, a sound was heard, the thud of a door closing one floor above followed by that of a key turning in its lock.

On reaching his destination, Tracy noticed that the parlour door was slightly ajar, hearing what sounded like faint footsteps coming from the other side. After placing his hat and coat into the outstretched arms of the servant, who appeared to blush as he thanked her for her assistance, he stepped inside.

As the door opened, initially Tracy didn't see the small figure standing close by the window in the farthest corner, being momentarily distracted by a collection of vivid red ottomans and printed walls. When eventually he saw his host, he noticed that though he had entered the room, with the floor creaking with his every step, the woman's gaze appeared vacant, fixed upon the lengthy garden overlooked by the parlour window.

Eventually, after a long silence as oppressive as the weather outside, Clara Hayne spoke: 'Good morning, Mr Tracy,' she said, her voice carrying a light, yet authoritative tone.

Taking several short steps, Tracy responded: 'Good morning, Miss, thank you for seeing me.'

Gesturing for the reporter to sit, Clara extended her arm, directing Tracy towards an upholstered chair of rich green and only then moving her gaze towards his. After placing his gloves on a nearby table, on top of which he laid his notebook and pencil, Tracy took a seat and only on crossing his legs was he reminded of the spatter of mud upon his trousers, courtesy of a cab driver, who an hour earlier had chosen a puddle as a collection point.

'I'm afraid my sister isn't here,' said Clara, 'though I am sure that should not matter.'

Being an intuitive reporter, Tracy knew when he was being lied to. However, Clara was a vital source, and he chose not to question her statement. 'You recently spoke to my colleague,' said Tracy, 'Mr Kennedy?'

'Yes, and at length I might add,' replied Clara. 'A great many facts I gave him, too.'

'And for that we are grateful, Miss,' replied Tracy, his eyes following his host as she sat opposite him.

'I, however, just have one or two more questions – if that is acceptable?'

Though no words were spoken, with a momentary silence filling the room, Clara offered her compliance. As she moved back from the edge of her seat, resting her hands upon her lap, her fingers fidgeting lightly upon her black dress, she favoured her guest with a delicate smile.

Separated by a cream-topped table on which sat an ornate vase of pink geraniums, the pair began to talk. Throughout the conversation that would follow Clara would reiterate comments made to Inspector Race almost three years earlier. Yes, her nephew had at one time associated with prostitutes, though she expressed the opinion that he had seen the interactions as relationships.

'As I told your colleague, my nephew would often be out late, not returning home until morning. Whether he spent all his time with fallen women, I wouldn't be able to say.'

Realising that, unlike Kennedy Jones, Tracy was refraining from taking notes, Clara changed the topic. 'I suppose you know about the medical books?' she asked, looking at Tracy for a sign of recognition. And without waiting for confirmation, she continued: 'He studied a good deal, Mr Tracy – sitting up until late, reading. I understand from your colleague that this is important to your ... investigation?'

'It is,' replied Tracy, nodding, 'and my colleague has told me all that you have said, however I am keen to know – did Thomas ever return home with any of the women with whom he associated?' After a moment's pause, Clara replied: 'No, Mr Tracy!' somewhat vexed by the implication. 'He only ever returned home alone.'

Standing, Clara moved towards the window overlooking the garden: a large bay edged with gold drapes that defined the slightness of her form even more than before. 'He used to come from the garden,' she continued, 'I mean, the mews that borders our garden, passing the outhouse before coming inside.'

Keen to return to the topic of women, Tracy again attempted to push the matter, trying to delve deeper into Cutbush's private life. Clara, however, had other ideas: 'Tea – Mr Tracy?' she said, the sentence appearing more an announcement than a question. Before receiving a reply, she had traversed the sizeable room and was already opening the parlour door.

By the time he accepted, she was already halfway down the hall. Although somewhat frustrated, while his hostess made her way to the pantry, Tracy used the unplanned pause as an opportunity to take in his surroundings, including a collection of high-quality paintings and prints hanging from the walls. Looking around, he saw portraits of aged relatives set within fine gold frames: of stern, unsmiling men dressed in black, with sunken eyes surrounded by a mass of grey hair, as well as several women, attired in neat evening dress, one of whom resembled Tracy's hostess – though younger.

Although displeased by the untimely break, as the tea kettle whistled in the far-off pantry, Tracy suddenly found himself overcome by thirst. Led by her servant, whose small hands appeared hidden under a large tray of china, on which sat a pot of tea and two cups,

Clara emerged.

Eager to revisit his previous line of questioning, Tracy drank fast, burning his tongue in the process, while attempting to return to the topic of Cutbush's behaviour. After watching as his hostess took a final sip and placed her cup upon its saucer, he pressed on, asking whether or not Thomas had ever demonstrated violence towards any of the women in his company.

Unable to look directly at her guest, choosing instead to cast her gaze towards the parlour window, Clara replied: 'There was one woman. He saw her often, so we were led to believe. Our nephew wasn't inclined to keep such matters from us, Mr Tracy, though most men would, I'm sure. The relationship, if you can call it that, stopped quite suddenly.'

'And this happened – when?' asked Tracy.

'The exact date escapes me, though it was prior to 1888, of that I am sure,' replied Clara.

Though seemingly hesitant to explain fully the reason behind the relationship ending, Clara eventually admitted all she knew, stating that while in a fit of rage her nephew had viciously attacked and raped the woman whom he had been seeing.

As Tracy placed the small notebook upon his knee, attempting to scrawl an accurate account of the revelation, Clara, in an effort to appease the guilt surely felt by herself and her sister, wished to state that they had originally believed the assault had occurred under the influence of passion, giving this as her reason for not communicating with the authorities.[6]

Later, as she escorted Tracy to the parlour door, while calling for her servant to bring his hat and coat, she returned to the subject. 'I now see,' she continued, 'that our interpretation of the events was not correct, Mr Tracy. That it was something else creating the madness inside him – something far more sinister.'

After assuring Clara that, as previously promised by KJ, this would be the last visit, Tracy bade her farewell, and though the meeting had ended earlier than expected, as he walked towards Kennington Park Road in order to find a cab, he did so more enlightened than he could ever have hoped for.

Travelling back to Tudor Street, he contemplated what might have led Cutbush to assault the prostitute. Sitting inside the cab as it traversed the irregular cobblestones leading towards London Bridge, his mind wandered to a man he had once known during his time working in India, a soldier of quiet temperament and gentle nature, who went on to commit a most horrendous crime.

Tracy recalled the surprise he had felt when, after serving twenty years, the soldier returned to his homeland and on arrival in England, without warning or hesitation, murdered a prostitute in cold blood. From what he knew of him, the soldier had contracted syphilis from the same prostitute two decades earlier and though many years had passed, on returning home he was overtaken with the desire for revenge.[7]

It threw up the possibility that Cutbush had come to believe that the prostitute whom he attacked had given him syphilis, the disease for which he had sought treatment when contacting Dr Brooks in July of 1888.

Although Brooks had stated that Cutbush was not infected, as Tracy was aware, in some cases the idea of having syphilis can produce the

71

same form of mania as observed in an actual sufferer. It was something he himself had witnessed and would later write of in an article for *The Sun* of 13 February 1894.

On arriving in Tudor Street, Tracy reflected on the final statement made by Clara Hayne that, like the soldier prior to his arrest, Cutbush's behaviour had dramatically changed, his mind becoming quite unhinged. She had concluded by saying that his persona was 'strange'.[8]

Walking inside *The Sun*'s offices, welcomed by a cacophony of noise emanating from the print room, Tracy was met by Wolff, the assistant manager, who hastily informed him that T. P. O'Connor had called an urgent meeting. Eager to enlighten his chief editor as to his findings, Tracy was keen to attend.

Inside O'Connor's office, cast in the sepia glow of a single gas-light, he found KJ sitting awkwardly upon a wooden chair. Next to him was O'Connor, whose large frame appeared to dominate what Tracy considered to be one of the more untidy offices in Tudor Street.

Eager to keep abreast of the investigation, O'Connor wished to receive a full update from his editors, including the results of Tracy's recent enquiries. For two hours every aspect of their findings to date were discussed, along with the testimony of Clara Hayne. And, even though experienced in the field of journalism, all three men couldn't fail to be excited. The wealth of evidence being accumulated against Cutbush, from the findings of Inspector Race to family confessions, appeared overwhelming and, while being open to any contradictory evidence that might surface to prove their suspect's innocence, as far as they could see, none appeared to exist.

During the meeting T. P. O'Connor drew parallels between Cutbush and another serial killer with whose crimes he was acquainted, a man referred to by him as 'Neill', referring to Thomas Neill Cream, who like Cutbush had associated with the very class of women who would later become his victims.

It was believed that Cream had contracted syphilis from a prostitute he had met in 1876. Fifteen years later, he would poison four prostitutes in the area of Lambeth, seemingly for no other reason than to satisfy his own sadistic whim.[9]

It was only at the conclusion of the meeting that KJ spoke of his findings, reminding Tracy of his instruction prior to visiting Kennington and informing him that he had discovered something quite unexpected.

Although all three men had been aware of the sighting made by Joseph Lawende on the morning of Catherine Eddowes's murder, of the man seen in company with her in Church Passage, what they hadn't known was the existence of two further sightings.

Some had judged Lawende's observations unreliable, with his friend Harry Harris stating that they only saw the man's back and Lawende himself admitting to not being able to recognise the man again. However, the newly uncovered sightings came directly from the police.

As KJ explained, the first observation was of a man seen in the vicinity of Mitre Square only ten minutes after Catherine's release from Bishopsgate Police Station. A night duty constable had observed a young man, whom he described as tall, with a dark complexion and a black moustache, who appeared to be wearing a cap, hurrying towards the area of Mitre Square.

While not seeing anything peculiar in the man's behaviour, the constable did observe that he appeared to walk at a sprightly pace.[10] The account was evidently compatible with the appearance of Thomas Cutbush.

KJ also discovered something of which, up until December of 1893, both he and his colleagues had been unaware. On 2 October 1888, the City Police had offered an official description of the murderer.

Though usually vocal, both T. P. O'Connor and Tracy fell silent as KJ described the man whom the police believed was responsible for the Mitre Square killing: 'He was aged twenty-eight years old,' announced KJ – his voice growing louder as he talked, 'he appeared to be of slight build, with his height given at 5 ft 8 in., and had a dark complexion. He was described as having no whiskers, wearing a hard felt hat and a black diagonal coat with collar and tie, appearing altogether respectable. He was also seen to be carrying a newspaper parcel.'[11]

From a bound ledger KJ produced a sheet of white paper folded in two. Palming it open, he slid the note along the surface of the table, only stopping as he reached the cupped hands of O'Connor lying outstretched upon the table top. On it, written in Kennedy's neat hand, was the official description of Thomas Cutbush as he had appeared in 1891 on his admittance to Broadmoor:

Age – Twenty-five years old
Build – Slight
Height – 5ft 9½ in.
Complexion – Dark
Very short whiskers
Previous occupation – Merchants Clerk [12]

Removing a pair of spectacles from his waistcoat that clung tight to his girth, T. P. O'Connor read on. Impressed, he nodded as he read, flitting a glance of recognition towards KJ before passing the note to Tracy. KJ also informed his colleagues of the testimony of Matthew Packer, who on the night of the double murders had sold grapes to the companion of Elizabeth Stride and subsequently claimed that her client had spoken like an educated man, having what he perceived to be 'a loud, sharp sort of voice and a quick commanding way with him'. It was identical to the manner in which Cutbush was said to have spoken.[13]

What was becoming clear to all three men, as they sat around a small table in the heart of Fleet Street, was that in Thomas Cutbush they had found a man with all the credentials to be the Ripper, someone who not only fitted the description of the killer but who was also capable of great violence.

By the end of the day a new-found confidence had emerged. New evidence had been brought to light and as the three men left for home they were bound by the same astonishing conviction: that Thomas Cutbush was looking more and more like the man who would be Jack.

NINE

The Ripper Speaks

On 27 September 1888, a correspondence was received by the Central News Agency in the City of London: a letter, hand-delivered to the chief editor by two of his journalists and addressed to 'The Boss'.

25 Sept. 1888.

Dear Boss,
I keep on hearing the police have caught me but they won't fix me just yet. I have laughed when they look so clever and talk about being on the right track. That joke about Leather Apron gave me real fits. I am down on whores and I shant quit ripping them till I do get buckled. Grand work the last job was. I gave the lady no time to squeal. How can they catch me now.

I love my work and want to start again. You will soon hear of me with my funny little games. I saved some of the proper red stuff in a ginger beer bottle over the last job to write with but it went thick like glue and I can't use it. Red ink is fit enough I hope ha.ha. The next job I do I shall clip the ladys ear off and send to the police officers just for jolly wouldn't you. Keep this letter back till I do a bit more work, then give it out straight.

My knife's so nice and sharp I want to get to work right
away if I get a chance. Good luck.
   Yours Truly
   Jack the Ripper
   Don't mind me giving the trade name.

This was followed by a second postscript, which read:

Wasn't good enough to post this before I got all of the red ink off
my hands curse it. No luck yet. They say I'm a doctor now ha ha.

Although the Central News Agency believed the letter to be a practical joke, two days later the editor decided to pass the correspondence on to Scotland Yard. One detail seized on at the time was the fact that the letter referred to the murders as being a 'job', perceived by some as indicating that the murderer worked within the medical profession. And then there was the statement that more murders were to come: a prediction that would come to fruition.

On 1 October, two days after the murders of Elizabeth Stride and Catherine Eddowes, the *Daily News* was given permission to publish the letter in full. Facsimiles were produced and put up as posters; anyone who recognised the handwriting was asked to come forward.

Later that day another communication was received by the Central News Agency, in the same hand as the previous letter. The writer wished to inform the editor that his last communication had not been a joke. It read:

I wasn't codding dear old boss when I gave you the tip. You'll
hear about saucy Jackys work tomorrow double event this time
number one squealed abit couldn't finish straight off. Had not
time to get ears for police thanks for keeping last letter back till I
got to work again.
   Jack the Ripper

Due to the postcard containing an identical signature to that of the previous letter, the correspondence was passed to the Metropolitan Police, who by now were taking both communications seriously. The fact that the writer of the postcard made reference to the two murders in a single night (the 'double event) this was seen by the police as an important clue.

Yet as *The Sun* reporters discovered, news of the murders had in fact been in the public domain within hours of the killing of Catherine Eddowes. Several of the Sunday newspapers covered the story, meaning that as well as the killer, many of London's literate would have also had knowledge of the murders, which of course allowed a hoaxer to pen the correspondence and include a certain amount of detail. This fact, though important, made little difference to how the letters were perceived by the public.

To the people of London it appeared that the killer had suddenly found his voice. And so on 27 September 1888, the Ripper and his legacy were born, with the press no longer referring to the killer as the 'Whitechapel Monster' or 'Leather Apron', it was now 'Jack the Ripper' who was responsible for the crimes.

The decision to publicise the letters would prove particularly unwise, for instead of obtaining any leads in the way of identifying the writer, it opened the floodgates for hundreds of imitators. With an immediately identifiable name and a wealth of gory details to pore over London quickly found itself in the grip of hysteria.

Soon a mass of correspondence was received from those wishing to imitate the previous letters, scribing their own threatening messages from London and beyond – and in turn causing the police to waste valuable time chasing false leads.

While some newspapers chose to identify a local as the culprit, others turned to the new and increasingly popular phenomena of spiritualism for help. The police also had to contend with numerous individuals who appeared overwhelmed with the desire to state their guilt.

Alfred Napier Blanchard was one such man who early in October, while in a public house in Aston, was overheard confessing to being the killer. Blanchard was then arrested, though he later claimed to have made the confession while drunk, only being released after it was discovered that he was in Manchester on the nights of the murders.[2]

By mid-October the police were inundated with suggestions as to the identity of the killer, mainly perpetuated by the press of the day, who by then had decided that a foreigner was responsible.

As far as the London *Echo* was concerned, the Ripper was an Austrian seaman who had sailed away on a Faversham vessel and whose hand-writing resembled that of the 'Dear Boss' letter.

According to another press source 'Jack' was a German thief who killed in order to embrace an ancient practice of 'Diebslichler' or 'thieves candles', in which the light of candles made from the uteri of women was believed to induce a deep sleep in anyone upon whom it fell, becoming an invaluable tool for those involved in robbery and theft.[4]

In an attempt to pursue every avenue of the investigation requests were made for more constables to be drafted in from Greater London. In addition the police also entertained the notion of using bloodhounds to bring the killer to ground. Yet, despite the efforts of the authorities no positive lead would emerge.

It wasn't until mid October that another letter of true significance was received, adding a disturbing twist to the Ripper case. Rather than the Central News Agency the unfortunate recipient on this occasion was George Lusk, the president of the Whitechapel Vigilance Committee.

A little over a month earlier Lusk and fifteen other local tradesmen had met in the Crown Public House in Mile End Road. Their inten-tion was to form a committee that would not only offer assistance to the police but would also aid the rejuvenation of trade in the East End that since the start of the murders had dwindled.[5]

One of the first objectives of the committee was to seek a reward for the apprehension of the killer and as such they wrote directly to the Home Office hoping to persuade them of this new course of action. Their opinion held little sway with the Home Secretary, Henry Mathews, who immediately refused their suggestion on the basis of a government ban on monetary rewards.[6]

Although the committee were without government backing they decided it was necessary to find their own funds and in addition sought to provide an increased presence on the streets of Whitechapel, organising a band of men, most of whom were unemployed, to walk the alleys and courts of the East End in search of the killer.

The efforts of the Whitechapel Vigilance Committee were well documented in the press and though having in their number a music hall star in the form of Charles Reeves, it was Lusk who would take center stage and quickly became a local celebrity.

While Lusk himself was happy to court the spotlight all too soon it appeared that his work was attracting the attention of a more unsettling audience and quite possibly the Ripper himself.

At 5.00 p.m. on 16 October Lusk received a small cardboard box in the post. It was wrapped in brown paper and accompanied by a short letter that opened with a chilling salutation. It read:

From Hell

Mr Lusk
Sor
  I send you half the kidne [sic] I took from one women prasarved [sic] it for you tother piece I fried and ate it was very nise I may send you the bloody knif that took it out if you only wate a whil longer
  signed
  Catch me when
  you can
  Mishter Lusk.

Inside the cardboard box was half a human kidney preserved in spirits. Although initially greeted with amusement by Lusk, who believed the letter to be a hoax and the kidney to be that of a dog, he was eventually persuaded by his committee members to have it examined at The London Hospital.

To Lusk's surprise the examination produced a chilling verdict. Dr

Openshaw, the pathological curator at the hospital, would go onto state his belief that the kidney was most definitely that of a human, and had been preserved in wine.[7]

Within a day of Dr Openshaw's examination the letter was published. Immediately a frenzy ensued with the press and the public alike deciding that the letter was an authentic communication from the killer.

Though the style of handwriting differed greatly to that of the 'Dear Boss' letters, the inclusion of the kidney had led many to speculate that to find the writer of the Lusk letter was to discover the true perpetrator of the Whitechapel murders.

Dr Sedgewick Saunders, the City Pathologist, had differing views. He concluded that it was impossible to ascertain the sex and age of the person from whom the kidney had been taken. Although he held that it had been preserved in spirits he concluded that it was more likely to have come from a hospital than an individual. Saunders advanced an alternative thesis: that a medical student, in an act of high jinks, had thought it would make a good practical joke.[8]

An analysis of the accompanying letter threw up an interesting debate. The words 'Sor', 'Knif' and 'Mishter' gave rise to two schools of thought. Either the writer was deliberately masking his identity by these usages, or he was in fact an Irishman.

This second angle was supported by the statement of a young woman named Emily Marsh. Miss Marsh claimed that on 15 October she had come into contact with a man she believed to be the writer. At around 1.00 p.m. while working in her father's shop on the Mile End Road Marsh recalled that an Irishman had entered the store. On stepping inside he remarked on a poster in the shop window that referred to Lusk's Vigilance Committee and the reward being offered for the killer. Before leaving the shop, the man asked whether or not Miss Marsh knew the address of Mr Lusk.[9]

Although the shop girl was able to provide the authorities with the man's description, the police were unable to discover the true identity of the person responsible for the Lusk letter.

Should the motive for writing the communication have been to fuel the hysteria being felt within the capital, it proved most effective. In a matter of days following the double murder of Elizabeth Stride and Catherine Eddowes, a new form of panic and terror gripped the entire populace of London.

With endless newspaper columns now dedicated to the letters and the futile search for their writers, by late October hoax communications began pouring in from virtually every corner of the British Isles. From Manchester, where the writer claimed he was in hiding, to Glasgow, where, in a correspondence comprising of newspaper cuttings, the author informed the Metropolitan Police that he intended to take sixteen further victims. It appeared the Ripper's reach had extended further than anyone had imagined.

In this maelstrom, as Kennedy Jones was to note in 1893, incidents of real significance appeared to have been simply overlooked.

With no murders occurring in October a belief was beginning to spread among the populace of London that with the murder of Catherine Eddowes, the Ripper's spree had ended. The Whitechapel Vigilance Committee shared the belief and by 20 October a number of members had stood down. Without the support of his men and exhausted through worry and concern for his own safety Lusk resigned.[10]

By the following month George Lusk and the rest of the world would discover that the Ripper was still as active and as dangerous as he had ever been.

It was at this point in the unfolding events of 1888 that KJ found a single reference to an incident that should have placed the investigating police forces on the right track – but didn't. Appearing in a daily paper shortly before the murders of Stride and Eddowes under the heading 'ANOTHER JACK THE RIPPER SCARE', was the story of a disturbance in Mile End.

During the September of 1888, a man entered a public house located on the eastern edge of Whitechapel – a young man of slight build and sallow features who, once inside, promptly sat at the bar next to one of several prostitutes for whom the pub was a local haunt.

Within a matter of minutes, the once-bustling tavern fell silent as the female with whom the man was talking began to scream. Immediately the young man made for the exit, barging through the double doors into the street, and, once outside, began to run. Though many patrons attempted to pursue him, by the time they reached the pub's exit the man had disappeared from sight. Inside, as the woman's screams faded into little more than a whimper, she exclaimed that the man with whom she had been talking was Jack the Ripper.

After conducting an interview with the woman, the press issued a description of the man: young (aged twenty-seven or twenty-eight), of slight build, with his face appearing sallow and thin.[11] On being arrested, as Kennedy Jones was all too aware, Cutbush had admitted to Inspector Race that he had been responsible for the Mile End incident and stated that he had 'just missed her'.

TEN

HE STOLE HER HEART

Up until the morning of 9 November, Thomas Bowyer had led a particularly average life. Known locally as 'Indian Harry', due to him having served with the Indian Army, Bowyer scraped a living working for a local businessman named John McCarthy.[1]

Working in Dorset Street, Bowyer acted as an assistant in McCarthy's chandler's shop, where bowed wooden shelves held a plethora of items much-needed by the locals, from groceries and soap to cheap candles of every size. As well as assisting in the shop, Bowyer would also help with other jobs, such as collecting rent from tenants who occupied several buildings owned by McCarthy.

It had rained heavily throughout the previous night and the morning was yet to recover, the sky overcast with dark clouds. The shop in which Bowyer served was located at number 27 Dorset Street, home to a number of common lodging houses and named as being one of the most violent streets in all the capital; a place where only the bravest of constables dared to venture.[2]

Though some looked upon Dorset Street with fear, for John McCarthy it was simply a workplace, where to his credit he successfully operated two businesses. As well as the chandlers, McCarthy also owned several local properties for which he was the landlord, situated in the nearby Miller's Court; it was known locally as 'McCarthy's Rents'.[3]

Although most of McCarthy's tenants paid their rent promptly when due, one particular occupant of room number thirteen – a young woman named Mary Jane Kelly – was less than diligent when it came to such monetary matters, accumulating arrears totalling twenty-nine shillings.

Though a hard businessman, McCarthy had allowed the tenant a period of grace. By 9 November, his leniency had reached its limit, and at 10.45 a.m. he requested that Bowyer visit Miller's Court to collect what he was owed.

Positioned to the right of McCarthy's shop, 26 Dorset Street was a sizeable building used in the main as a shed. In order to maximise its capacity the back rooms had been partitioned off, jutting out into Miller's Court, where six two-roomed properties could be found, each whitewashed to the height of their first floor windows. Lit by a single street lamp, the courtyard appeared cramped and gloomy, and housed only two outside amenities: a small bin and an external water tap that ran cold and was used by only the bravest tenants as a place to wash.[4]

Entry to the court was by way of a small covered archway leading from Dorset Street, where just inside on the right was the door of number thirteen. Having been asked to collect the rent Bowyer hurriedly made his way to the room, trying to avoid the rain that had started moments earlier. Walking through the archway, he noticed a partially torn poster clinging to the damp bricks on the side of the wall – one of several in the area offering a reward for the discovery of the Whitechapel murderer.[5]

Eager to return to the warmth of the shop, Bowyer hurried towards the door, realising as he did so that it had in fact been two days since he had last seen the tenant, when he had observed her standing in the court with a male companion.

On reaching the door Bowyer knocked twice, his thuds resounding inside the 12 ft room beyond. Receiving no answer, he decided to venture around the corner in order to look through one of two windows that offered the room its only natural light.

The farthest pane of the first window had been broken some days earlier and, in order to keep out the draught, a makeshift curtain of rags had been draped behind it. So as not to prick his skin on the glass Bowyer moved his hand slowly through the hole, feeling as he did so the warmth from within. Taking a light grip of the rag with the tips of his fingers, he pulled it to one side. Beyond the makeshift curtain, at first all he could see was darkness mixed with the faint smell of sweat and smoke.

Though the room housed a small fireplace no flames were visible, with only daylight aiding his vision. As his eyes adjusted to the dimness of the room, initially his gaze fell on a small wooden table that stood next to Mary's bed, on which two darker objects could be made out. After a moment he realised what was lying on the table – two lumps of human flesh.[6]

Turning away from the sight – later recalled by those who saw it as being 'the work of the Devil' – Bowyer did his best not to vomit.[7] In a state of shock he looked again, and this time made out the sight of a body lying on the blood-soaked sheets of a wooden bed. Now traumatised, Bowyer rushed back through the archway of Miller's Court, barely able to stay upright, before slamming through the door of his master's shop and almost collapsing upon the stone floor. Facing John McCarthy, somehow he managed to find the words to describe what he had seen. Somewhat disbelieving of his servant, McCarthy wished to see inside the room himself before taking any further action.

After returning to Miller's Court, McCarthy took a look inside the room. With the makeshift curtain having been pulled away by Bowyer moments earlier, the room was now well illuminated. After seeing the corpse for himself, McCarthy instantly jolted back from the window, his revulsion almost sweeping his legs from under him and leaving him fighting the urge to collapse.

Leaning backwards against the brick wall, bent double, he blurted out an indistinguishable garble – a jumble of words that made no sense to the equally bewildered Bowyer. Unable to remove his gaze from the cobbles beneath him, McCarthy spoke again. Though his words were fast, they were more composed; he ordered Bowyer not to tell anyone of their discovery and to find a police constable immediately.

While McCarthy attempted to calm himself, Bowyer ran – arriving in the nearby Commercial Street Police Station at 10.50 a.m. On seeing two officers near to the entrance he hurried towards them, attempting in vain to make himself understood. Fortunately for Inspector Beck and Detective Constable Dew, John McCarthy soon followed and was able to provide an account of what the two men had seen.

Inspector Beck, accompanied by Dew, followed both Bowyer and McCarthy back to Miller's Court, wanting to see for themselves exactly what the two men believed they had witnessed.

Constable Dew was the first to emerge from the covered archway inside Miller's Court. After initially attempting to open the door and finding it locked, he made his way round to the broken window in order to peer inside. Before being allowed to go any further, Inspector Beck intervened, placing an arm across Dew's chest and easing him backwards, before stepping in front.[8]

Even with seventeen years of experience behind him, nothing could have prepared Walter Beck for what he was about to see. The corpse of the once vivacious Mary Jane Kelly was almost unrecognisable as a human form. Lying upon her bloodied bed sheets, Mary's body had been virtually skinned.

What remained of her legs had been spread wide apart, with her left hand resting on her exposed rib cage and her head turned to its left; directly facing the window from which she was now being observed. As well as her body, Mary's face had suffered a horrendous attack, leaving only the faintest traces of her once pretty features intact.

On seeing the carnage inside the tiny room the Inspector, almost unable to control his emotions, stumbled backwards away from the window – his face turning ashen with horror and immediately advising his colleague not to look.

Dew, however, ignored the Inspector's words of advice and saw for himself what was left of Jack the Ripper's fifth victim.

When news of the Miller's Court murder hit the newspapers Catherine Pickell, a young flower girl and friend of Mary Kelly, couldn't believe how close she herself had come to being embroiled in the Ripper saga. Had Catherine looked through the window of Mary's room at

7.30 a.m., when – with the intention of borrowing a shawl – she had knocked on the door, then it would have been she and not Thomas Bowyer to discover the remains of her friend; the thought would haunt her for the rest of her days.[9]

After Inspector Beck and Constable Dew had looked inside the room the decision was made to seal off Miller's Court, placing officers at the entrance to prevent access and preserve the crime scene.

The Divisional Surgeon was sent for at the request of Inspector Beck and arrived within fifteen minutes. On seeing Mary's remains from the window Dr Phillips reached two rather obvious conclusions: the body was beyond all help and there was no other person inside the room who needed assistance.

Inspector Frederick Abberline followed soon after, and on arrival was briefed by Inspector Beck as to the circumstances of the discovery as well as the actions taken up until that point.

Following new guidelines, Beck informed Abberline that two bloodhounds had been sent for. It was a new approach believed at the time to be a practical method of tracking the killer. For two hours entry was delayed.

While the officers on the ground battled with a growing crowd of spectators, Abberline waited patiently for the arrival of the hounds. Only with the arrival of Superintendent Thomas Arnold at 1.30 p.m. was Abberline informed that his wait had been in vain as the order for the use of dogs had been countermanded.[10]

Superintendent Arnold wasted no time in taking control of the scene and immediately spurred the investigation back into action, ordering that the door be forced open. John McCarthy obliged and with the aid of a pickaxe broke down the wooden door, allowing the long awaited entry to be made.

Only when Dr Phillips entered the room did he see the true extent of the Ripper's work. As the door swung open – hitting against a small table that had been positioned next to the bed – the doctor stepped inside. To his right lay the corpse of 25-year-old Mary Kelly.

What greeted the experienced eyes of Dr Phillips was a once beautiful woman completely obliterated. What the Ripper had achieved during his time in Miller's Court, while safely locked inside the tiny room with his victim, was to explore every twisted fantasy that his mind could conjure up.

Dr Bond, who like Dr Phillips examined Mary's body, was to report that the remains were discovered in the middle of the bed, with Mary's shoulders flat against the mattress and her left forearm lying across her abdomen. Her right arm was resting at her side with her fingers clenched. Having virtually gutted his defenceless victim; the doctors found that the killer had removed the surface of Mary's abdomen and thighs, and emptied the abdominal cavity of its viscera.

With his fifth victim the Ripper had methodically taken his knife to every part of her body, severing Mary's breasts and placing one under her head and the other by her right foot. Between her feet he had placed her liver and either side of her body had positioned the spleen and intestines.

Mary's neck had been brutally severed down to the bone and her face gashed in all manner of directions, partly removing her nose, cheeks, eyebrows and ears. Before a full examination was complete a shocking discovery would be made that would indicate the Ripper had once again taken trophies of his kill. As the doctors searched among the mutilated remains they were shocked to discover that Mary's heart was missing.[11]

For ten months, Mary Kelly had lived in the 12 ft room just inside Miller's Court, surviving on the favours of others as well as turning to prostitution when money was tight. Only twenty-five, she attracted a great deal of attention from the men in the area and at 5 ft 7 inches was considerably taller than the average woman.

Born in Limerick in 1863, she hailed from a large Irish family but spent much of her youth living in Wales with her father. At the tender age of sixteen Mary married, becoming the wife of a man named 'Davies' – a collier, who died three years later during a pit explosion. It was only with Mary's subsequent departure from Carmarthenshire to Cardiff that she fell in with bad company and thus started her career in prostitution, with her age and Irish beauty winning her many admirers and no doubt acquiring a higher price for her services. In 1884 she left Cardiff and moved to the West End of London, finding work in a high-class brothel, where by her own admission she began to associate with a number of affluent customers; one of whom grew so fond of Mary that he took her to Paris for several weeks.

According to Joseph Barnett, Mary had taken a dislike to France and was happy when she returned home to London, staying for a while at Pennington Street in Tower Hamlets. Questioned later, Barnett said that after meeting in 1887, he and Mary soon started living together, first in George Street and then Paternoster Court. Due, however, to the couple's habitual drinking and lack of funds they were promptly evicted and subsequently lodged in Brick Lane, until finding their way to 'McCarthy's Rents' in Miller's Court.

Until July 1888 the pair had lived in relative comfort, with Barnett's earnings as a porter at Billingsgate Fish Market enough to keep a roof over their heads and put food on the table. When Barnett was fired, Mary once again turned to the streets as a means of earning an income.[12]

On 30 October the couple had quarrelled – Barnett had discovered that Mary had brought a female prostitute back to their room. After the quarrel he moved out, taking lodgings elsewhere, though returning most days to give Mary what money he had managed to scrape together.[13]

On the night of 8 November, at 7.30 p.m., Barnett visited Mary and was observed drinking with her in The Horn of Plenty public house in Crispin Street. Now back on good terms, he had decided to put aside his differences with Mary's friends and took drinks with the very prostitute who had caused the argument in the first place.

Two and a half hours after officers first stepped into room number 13, Mary's body was removed from Miller's Court and taken to Shoreditch Mortuary. In placing two officers at the entrance to the court the Metropolitan Police were sending a clear message that no one other than officials was permitted near the murder scene; the police believed that there were possible clues yet to be garnered from the room and its vicinity.

Inside, Inspector Abberline made a thorough inventory of its contents, paying special attention to the fireplace opposite the front door. He determined that a large fire had blazed for some time during the previous evening, burning so fiercely as to melt the spout of a kettle hanging nearby.

On bended knee Abberline inspected the ashes, feeling a dull warmth emanating from the grate. In it he found traces of clothing, presumably used to feed the fire and provide light within the room. Judging from the heat still present, it appeared that the fire had only recently been extinguished.

Abbeline's discovery meant that in all likelihood the Ripper had stayed with his victim all night – that there was every chance he had left just before the arrival of Bowyer and was still somewhere close by, on his way to work – or home.[14]

ELEVEN

The Kennington Connection

Unbeknownst to Inspector Abberline, thirty-five minutes before Thomas Bowyer's gruesome discovery in Miller's Court, a man had been seen hurrying away from the area covered in blood.

The witness, a local businessman, had been on his way to work and, aware that the main thoroughfares were likely to be congested with the Friday markets, had decided to take a shortcut through Mitre Square.

Although the location had already become synonymous with the brutal killing of Catherine Eddowes, in daylight it gave little hint as to the depravity that had taken place a month earlier; seeming unusually peaceful to the businessman, who had used the route on many an occasion when running late for work.

Keen to avoid the shower that had been threatening since dawn, the man walked through the deserted square at a sprightly pace and only on reaching its centre, in the shadow of Kearley and Tonge's tea warehouse, did he notice another man walking towards him from the opposite direction.

With his swift steps becoming almost a sprint, the man appeared to be in a hurry and was in a state of obvious excitement. He was tall, well dressed and appeared to be carrying something like a parcel under his arm. According to the witness he seemed anxious and was disoriented, running straight into the surprised businessman, who only then noticed that the man's face, shirt and collar were splashed with blood.[1]

With the body of Mary Kelly yet to be discovered, the businessman, though somewhat perplexed, simply continued on to his place of work and only after reading of the atrocity in the nearby Miller's Court and realising the direction from which the man had been hurrying, did he think to contact the authorities.

At 11.45 a.m. the man was seen again, three miles from Mitre Square. This time a more detailed description was obtained. As well as being described as thin and clean shaven, save for a brown moustache, he was also said to have a sallow complexion. It was also noted that his smart attire consisted of a dark suit, along with a black coat and hat, with the parcel under his arm being described as a small leather bag. As had been observed in Mitre Square the man was bespattered with blood and was seen to bend down and wash his hands in a rain puddle.[2]

This second sighting had taken place not in Whitechapel or Spitalfields, but in the small thoroughfare of Clayton Street in Kennington, only a short distance from the home of Thomas Cutbush.

The *Evening News* was in no doubt that the sightings related to the Ripper; in their edition of 12 November they ran with the sub-heading: 'supposed killer seen at kennington'.

Thomas Bowyer had seen a similar-looking man with Mary Kelly on 7 November, two days before her murder. Shortly after serving Mary in his shop and selling her a half-penny candle, Bowyer had walked into Miller's Court. Once there he noticed Mary talking with a young man.

Something about the man's appearance seemed to strike Bowyer as odd; he described his peculiar eyes, a detail to add to the general impression of a man in his twenties, of smart appearance and with a dark moustache. As it was then evening, Bowyer took the man to be merely another of Mary's clients and thought no more of the matter until after her murder.[3]

Mary was seen again with the same male only hours prior to her killing at 11 p.m. on the evening of 8 November. They were drinking together in the Britannia Public House on the corner of Commercial Street. At that time, according to the witness, Mary seemed drunk.[4]

The last time Mary was seen alive was at 2 a.m. George Hutchinson, a young labourer returning to Whitechapel from Romford, was approached by her in the street. Hutchinson claimed that, prior to reaching Flower and Dean Street, Mary had stopped him and asked if he could lend her sixpence. Short of money himself, Hutchinson was unable to help and watched as Mary walked on, before stopping and talking to another man standing nearby.

Hutchinson went on to state his belief that the pair appeared to be on good terms, with the man seen to place an arm around Mary's shoulder as they walked back up the street towards him. Standing close to the Queen's Head Public House, he watched as Mary and her client walked back to Dorset Street and into Miller's Court.

Hutchinson furnished the police with a detailed description of the man, stating that he seemed of a Jewish appearance, was in his thirties and had a dark complexion with equally dark eyes. According to Hutchinson, the man wore a moustache and was respectably dressed; he also informed the police that his attention had been drawn to the fact that the man 'walked very sharp,' implying that he moved briskly.[5]

As *The Sun* reporters were aware from reading the official records relating to the appearance of Thomas Cutbush, he had what were described as striking and protruding blue eyes. They were able to establish that his complexion was often described as sallow or dark and that by his own admission he was sometimes mistaken for being Jewish. As they were aware, Cutbush was tall and slim and due to the nature of his work generally bore a smart and respectable appearance. On occasion he sported a moustache.[6]

KJ and Tracy soon realised that, time and again throughout the entire Ripper murder investigation, a young, respectably dressed man who had the mien of a clerk was seen with the victims or near the murder scenes, both before and after the crimes.

Respectably dressed men were few and far between on the streets of Whitechapel after dark, let alone after midnight. Matthew Packer, who claimed to have seen the Ripper on the night of the double murder, believed that he was most definitely not a working man or anything like the people living in Whitechapel.[7] To *The Sun* reporters this description made sense. Contrary to the already growing local legend, it just didn't seem logical for the Ripper to have looked like a monster.

The officers who entered Mary Kelly's room discovered that her clothing had been neatly folded on a small wooden chair, with her boots left warming by the fireplace, indicating that she had willingly invited her killer inside, believing him to be a client and before being killed had undressed for sex.[8]

Whoever the Ripper was he had been able to convince Mary that he was just another client, who was gentlemanly enough to let her fold her clothes. With the previous murders, the threat of discovery had been constant. But once inside Mary's room it was no longer a concern. On entering, she had readily locked the front door so as not to be disturbed by any unwanted guests; her killer was safe in the knowledge that he now had the luxury of both time and privacy.

On Monday 19 November the remains of Mary Kelly were carried by open hearse from the Shoreditch Mortuary to St Patrick's Cemetery in Leytonstone. Ten days earlier, amid a scene of confused excitement, the body of the Ripper's fifth victim had been removed from Miller's Court and conveyed to the mortuary amid a sea of onlookers.

Due to the press coverage, a wave of sympathy had engulfed not just London but the entire country. A Mr Henry Wilton, the sexton attached to St Leonard's Church in Shoreditch, volunteered to pay for Mary's funeral. Well publicised, the event attracted a mass of spectators, who on the morning of 19 November congregated outside the church gates, all eagerly anticipating the departure of the funeral car.

At 12.30 p.m. the coffin was placed upon an open hearse, drawing an emotional response from the crowds outside; while many lowered their heads and removed their caps, others – women who at one time or another had shared the streets with Mary – began to sob. As the hearse, drawn by two large horses, slowly passed through the crowds the coffin became visible; of fine oak and pine, it was adorned with two crowns of artificial flowers and a cross of heartsease. Such was the size of the crowds outside that even with the aid of many constables the hearse struggled to pass, moving at a slow pace through the streets blocked with onlookers and abandoned carts.

By 2 p.m. Mary's body had reached St Patrick's Church in Leytonstone, where a small group of mourners had gathered in a huddle at her graveside. Though no family were present, Joseph Barnett was in attendance, attempting desperately to fight the tears welling up within his closed eyes as he listened to the coffin being lowered into the earth.

As flashes of sunlight emerged from the brooding sky above, with its rays dancing through the bare branches of the trees that surrounded the small churchyard, Mary Kelly's body was laid to rest.[9]

TWELVE

Profiling the Ripper

Although many men were arrested following the murder of Mary Kelly, all would eventually be released without charge. While stopping short of reporting names, many newspapers were keen to expand on the cases of men upon whom suspicion had fallen.

The *Evening News* of 10 November 1888 told the story of one such man, described as an 'unfortunate foreigner', who was arrested by officers of the Commercial Street Police Station. Only on reaching the desk sergeant did it become apparent that it was in fact the third occasion that the man had been arrested, his 'odd face' proving enough to warrant his detention.[1]

As weeks passed the police continued to make arrests based on little or no evidence and by 8 December their desperation had reached a new level. It was on that day that a local vagrant, by the name of Edwin Burrows, was arrested solely on the basis that his peaked cap resembled that allegedly worn by the killer.[2]

The general impression at the time was that the police were without the slightest clue as to the identity of the murderer, leaving Londoners horrified that the Ripper was still at liberty. Queen Victoria was equally concerned and keen to make her feelings known she wrote to the Prime Minister, Lord Salisbury, stating the absolute need for action.

The Royal correspondence instructed the Prime Minister that all of the courts in Whitechapel were to be lit, as well as improvements made in the detectives working on the case. As a result of the Queen's intervention a proclamation was made in Parliament, that anyone who led the police to the Ripper would be given an official pardon.[3]

Such bold strokes would yield little in the way of positive leads and instead the police were left to continue their hunt unaided by clues of any true significance.

The public, who by now were avidly following every aspect of the case, were well aware of the difficulties facing the rank and file of London's constabulary. Thus, in an effort to have their voices heard the men and women of England began to bombard the pressrooms of Fleet Street with curious notions as to how the killer might be captured.

One suggestion was that every man living in the district should report to the nearest police station before going to bed,[4] whereas *The Daily Telegraph* asked that every London constable be given the power to stop and search any man in case they carried a knife of the type used by the killer.[5]

In an attempt to offer the women of Whitechapel greater protection another proposal suggested that every prostitute be armed with a pistol.[6] Personal safety was always a concern to the working women of the East End and within a month of the murder of Mary Nichols many prostitutes in the district took to carrying knives in case they should encounter the killer.

Mr. E.H. Pickersgill, M.P. believed that a change in footwear was the answer, stating that the police were at a disadvantage in their hunt for the killer due to the design of their boots. According to Mr Pickersgill the heavy military tread of the policeman could be heard of an evening for up to a quarter of a mile. In an effort to remedy this issue and allow silent patrols Pickersgill suggested that constables be supplied with the costly yet effective rubber soled boots.[7]

The perception that the police required assistance was not without foundation and as if to epitomise their need for a new approach, in November 1888 Assistant Commissioner Robert Anderson decided to adopt an innovative tactic.

Anderson would turn to police surgeon and forensic specialist Dr

Thomas Bond in an attempt to seek a clearer understanding as to the nature of the killings. To allow Bond a full overview of the case Anderson sent copies of the inquest evidence from the previous murders and asked the doctor for his expert opinion.

In his report, delivered on 10 November, Bond would not only outline his thoughts on the case, but would make history in providing one of the first ever criminal profiles of a killer.

Bond stated that in his view the murders of Nichols, Chapman, Stride, Eddowes and Kelly were all committed by the same hand. He believed that the killer attacked with speed to allow the victims no time to scream or to call for help. In opposition to the popular belief at the time Bond wrote that while mutilation was the object of the murders the injuries showed no indication that the killer had anatomical knowledge. In his opinion the Ripper did not even demonstrate the expertise of a butcher. Bond also estimated that the weapon used in the attacks was a strong blade, six inches in length.[8]

In profiling the type of man responsible for the killings Bond observed that he must be a man possessed of great strength and daring. That he worked alone and suffered bouts of homicidal mania, developed from what he termed a 'brooding condition of the mind'.

Bond believed that externally the killer would appear quiet and harmless and estimated that he would be of middle age. He would dress respectably yet would be without steady employment, being a man of solitary habits, living among 'respectable persons'. Although the killer was undoubtedly cunning Bond surmised that those closest to him would have some knowledge of his character that would ultimately lead to their suspicion.

The profile indicated Dr Bond's incredible insight into the inner workings of the killer, accomplished through detailed analysis of the crimes as well as his vast experience in the field. It went beyond the popular characterisation of the killer as a simple maniac and showed an understanding of the type of person who can commit multiple murders and get away with it.

While Bond was the first to create such a profile he was not alone in his appreciation of such scientific techniques. Within a month of Dr Bond's report, the American lawyer and author Mr Austin Abbott made his own contribution to the Ripper story.

On 13 December, at New York's Academy of Medicine, the Society of Medical Jurisprudence met for the fifty-eighth time. The topic of discussion that night was a paper read by Mr Abbott entitled 'Whitechapel Murders and Criminal Lunacy'.

Like Dr Bond, Abbott looked beyond the horror of the crimes and instead took an analytical approach as to the type of man responsible for the killings.

'He may not be a surgeon or a butcher', Abbott said, 'but evidently he is accustomed to swift manipulation. It was probable he was not a resident of that quarter. So many successful acts proved that he was a man of great resources. He had all the qualities, moreover, of a low, ignorant, brutal nature. If he should be captured the question of his mental condition would at once become of interest all over the civilized world.'[9]

Mr Abbott also wished to delve into the killer's motives for selecting Whitechapel as his killing ground, noting 'first, his victims there are less apt to find friends to succor and avenge them. Second, the district is less dangerous for the assassin. Third, the prevalence of disease among the women of Whitechapel.'[10]

At his conclusion Abbot surmised as to whether such mutilation of the body and genitalia inferred sexual gratification and stated that, in his opinion, 'the barbarous pleasure of inflicting mutilation could not co-exist in the sane mind at the same time with the sexual passion: that the activity of the one is inconsistent with the simultaneous activity of the other, and that their co-existence is evidence of a deranged mind.'

Bond and Abbott would never know how close they came to painting a true image of the killer. Just like the rest of the world the two professionals could only watch on as the Ripper story ran its course, hoping that their efforts might in some small way assist in the killer's apprehension.

As the December of 1888 rolled into January of the following year the police continued the hunt and although the Ripper remained at large, to their relief, there had at least been no more murders. For the authorities the cessation in activity meant only more puzzling questions.

Where had the killer gone? Was he in jail, abroad or simply lying low?

In 1893, looking back, *The Sun* journalists believed they knew the answer– Jack the Ripper was taking some sea air.

THIRTEEN

Some Bracing Sea Air

As is common with serial killers the frequency and period over which their murders occur will often vary. While for some the killing spree is relatively short, for others, the murderous campaigns will at times span years. History tells us that some murderers, who may kill in rapid succession over a period of months and years, will stop for no apparent reason, with lulls in activity lasting, in some cases, decades.

As for the Ripper, many were baffled as to why the killings should suddenly cease, causing the press and the public to speculate as to where he might be. *The Sun* journalists, however, thought they had found the answer.

From a previous interview conducted with Clara Hayne, Kennedy Jones had learnt that whenever her nephew's behaviour became too much to handle, his mother would look to send him away. When Cutbush stepped over the mark, which was often, Kate would look to remove him from London, sending him to the Isle of Thanet, where he would stay intermittently in several of the coastal towns.

His latest crime had been to attack a servant girl, who had tried to enter his attic room without permission.[1] After the attack Cutbush had rampaged through the family home, smashing furniture, including an expensive chandelier, while hurling vile obscenities at anyone in his path. He finally disappeared into the rear garden.[2]

Concerned for their own safety, Kate and her sister believed that once again a break was required. With its beaches and open skies, Kate hoped Ramsgate might offer her son the space he needed, serving as a remedy to his increasing anxiety and within a matter of days had arranged for his carriage to Thanet. It followed a regular pattern established in late 1888, and which carried on until the autumn of 1890.[3]

The Sun journalists discovered that during this period Cutbush had befriended Mr T. J. Crotty and his wife, who lived in one of the town's larger properties. Cutbush managed to convince Crotty that rather than being a clerk he was in fact an 'ex-medical man from London', who had led 'a very fast life'. Talking extensively and expertly about medicine and anatomy, Cutbush managed to persuade the family that he was a doctor. Eager for free medical advice, Crotty allowed him to treat four members of his own family for a variety of ailments, though any resulting cures or side effects were never established.

From this encounter, it was clear that despite his strange and aggressive behaviour, Cutbush was able to put together a convincing argument when he wanted to. Crotty recalled that when in Ramsgate Cutbush would pay for two cabmen to drive him about the town, almost exclusively after dark, and that whether being driven or walking, he would be out every night.

During a conversation on the subject of family, Cutbush had lied and informed Crotty and his wife that he was the son of a clergyman, after which he changed the subject and instead chose to discuss his ill treatment at the hands of Dr Brooks.

On another occasion, while finding himself alone with Mrs Crotty, Cutbush let slip that he had done 'something' to a woman and 'she would not live'. As the days passed, the Crottys started to distance themselves from the eccentric 'doctor', whose odd behaviour appeared to grow steadily more erratic.

Then one day – unexpectedly – Cutbush vanished.[4]

For Sarah Smith, manager of the Whitechapel Baths and Washhouses on Goulston Street in east London, the morning of 17 July 1889 was the same as any other. Sitting upon her bed in the dim light of a candle's flame, she once again struggled to sleep.

While her husband had fallen into an easy slumber as soon as the pair ventured to bed, Sarah had not been so lucky and chose instead to read in the hope of tiring her eyes. Though the snoring of her husband filled the silence of the room, outside appeared quiet save for the light pattering of rain falling upon the window.

As she turned the page of her book, pulling the warm bed sheets towards her chest while leaning back upon the wooden bedstead, Sarah was unaware of what was taking place just beneath her window. Down below, in a short passageway known as Castle Alley, an aged prostitute was fighting for her life.[5]

Earlier that night, forty-year-old cleaner and prostitute Alice McKenzie had left her lodgings on Gun Street and, in company with a young blind boy named George Dixon, had ventured to a pub close to the Cambridge Music Hall on Commercial Road. Feeling the cold pinching at her skin, Alice walked fast, leading her young friend by the hand and attempting to avoid any obstacles.[6]

Unlike other younger prostitutes in her acquaintance Alice bore the appearance of a much older woman. Standing only 5 ft 4 in. and being small in stature, her clothes were a patchwork of rags, consisting of a red stuff bodice, a brown skirt and a petticoat, along with mismatched stockings. Though her complexion was fair, with freckles dappling her nose and cheeks, her skin appeared tired and marked by several large scars obtained in youth.[7]

With a mouth of ruined teeth, Alice would often refrain from smiling and, with her worn clothes reflecting the dismal living conditions in which she existed, her general appearance was less than attractive.

Passing through the pub's entrance, she and her companion couldn't fail to hear the noise from the music hall next door, excited conversation and laughter forming a distant drone under the singing of a stage performer.

The public house was equally busy, though to the knowing eye of McKenzie not all the punters crowded under its high ceiling were there for pleasure; spotting several local pickpockets who saw the crowded barroom as an opportunity to prosper.

Eventually Alice made her way to the bar, leading George Dixon by the wrist. Once there she was heard to speak to a man, asking him to buy her a drink, to which he agreed.[8] In little over an hour Alice left in order to escort George back to his lodgings, walking unsteadily across the cobbled streets with the weariness of drink suddenly upon her. On reaching Gun Street, after entering the lodging house, she bade her young companion goodnight.

At 11.30 p.m. Alice was seen for the last time by friends on Flower and Dean Street, appearing to be in a rush as she passed. She was heard to say that she was unable to stop, seeming as if she were in a hurry to meet someone.[9]

PC Walter Andrews, a constable with the Metropolitan Police since 1880, had been treading his regular beat on the evening of the 16 July, conducting a foot patrol of an area which included Goulston Street, Wentworth Street and Old Castle Street, and also encompassed the smaller passage of Castle Alley.[10]

He had last been there at 12.20 a.m., wending his way past the numerous wagons and vans of the local costermongers that were regularly stored there throughout the night. Checking that no unwanted guests had bedded down in the carts, PC Andrews ascertained that the alley was empty, with only the noise of the nearby Three Crowns public house to hold his attention, and by 12.30 a.m. that was beginning to close.[11]

Another constable by the name of Joseph Allen was also out on patrol, covering the same beat as Andrews and pausing momentarily in the seclusion of Castle Alley in order to eat his supper.[12] After spending eighteen minutes checking on the neighbouring streets and making sure all was in order, Constable Andrews returned, entering Castle Alley from its northern junction with Old Castle Street, before continuing onwards towards Whitechapel.

As he walked down the western side of the alley, diligently checking the rear doors of several properties to make sure that they were secure,

Andrews suddenly noticed what appeared to be the body of a woman lying hidden between two parked wagons.

Discovered slumped in a pool of blood was the body of Alice McKenzie. With her face partially lit by the dim rays of a nearby lamp, Andrews could see that her throat had been punctured by two stab wounds, as well as noticing that her clothes were in a state of disarray.

Instinctively, he crouched on the ground, twisting his body to get as close to Alice as possible. Touching her cheek in order to gauge warmth, he saw that she was beyond all help; with a stream of blood gushing from her neck indicating the severity of the cut.[13]

Moments earlier, according to the account of Sergeant Stephen White, who had been patrolling near Whitechapel High Street, a man had been seen hurrying out of Castle Alley, before disappearing into the darkness of a neighbouring street.

Within minutes, like Andrews, Sergeant White was standing over the body of Alice McKenzie, observing her raised skirts that exposed a brutal attack to her genital area and a long jagged cut that ran from below her left breast to her belly button, a rip indicative of only one man.[14]

As London was about to discover – Jack was back.

FOURTEEN

Near Miss

By the time Dr Phillips arrived in Castle Alley dressed in his black overcoat and top hat, with his grey whiskers resting untidily upon his shirt collar, the rain was already falling hard, rattling the tops of the carts parked nearby like a drum roll.

On reaching the murder scene, Phillips noticed the victim's eyes were open, staring upwards towards the light of a street lamp, her pupils fully dilated, while from her neck a stream of blood had formed a red outline around her body.

As Dr Phillips knew all too well, although the light was poor and the weather conditions impossible, an examination of the body was required. Aided by the belt lamp of a nearby constable, Phillips saw a space where he could position himself and leaning against a wagon knelt uncomfortably upon the ground, feeling the wet of the cobblestones upon his left knee as he leant closer towards the body.[1]

Initial observations concluded that the blood had flowed from a jagged cut to the victim's neck and that on the doctor's arrival at 1.10 a.m. it had already begun to clot. Phillips saw that the clothes had been turned up, exposing the genitals and abdomen, both of which had sustained an attack, as well as noting that while the exposed skin was cold, the areas of the body that had remained covered were still warm.

On the removal of the body to the mortuary shed, in the nearby Pavilion Yard, the remains of the victim were placed upon a large table.

Although the mortuary attendant was keen to keep what little warmth remained inside the yard, no sooner had he closed the door than it was again forced opened, with Superintendent Arnold and Chief Inspector West entering at an eager pace, followed moments later by Dr Phillips.

Inside the mortuary Phillips noticed that the neck wound was much deeper than he had originally thought and he would later confirm that death had been caused by the severance of the vessels of the neck. Finding bruising upon the victim's chest and collar bone, the doctor concluded that the killer had used force to hold Alice to the ground and once under his control had inflicted the fatal wound.[2]

After waking to a chorus of shouts and police whistles in the street below, Sarah Smith had become curious. Looking on from the shelter of a doorway Smith watched as a throng of constables and doctors surrounded an object partially hidden by a wagon.

Only on spotting the mismatched stockings of Alice McKenzie protruding beyond the cart did she realise the nature of the disturbance. Later that day Sarah would be called to identify the body, confirming that Alice had been a customer at the washhouses for which she was deputy. She told the police that Alice would attend regularly in order to wash her clothes, though she only knew her by the name of 'Kelly'.[3]

James Monro, the new Commissioner of the Metropolitan Police, received word of the murder at 3 a.m. and immediately made his way to Castle Alley, wasting little time in announcing his belief that the man responsible was the Ripper. Some hours later Monro would admit that while all precautions had been taken to prevent a recurrence of the murders of the previous year, the killer had managed to enter Whitechapel and commit his heinous crime without leaving the 'slightest clue'.[4]

In the days that followed, in an act of desperation, huge numbers of police reinforcements were drafted into Whitechapel. Once there and under the direction of Chief Inspector Donald Swanson constables and sergeants were asked to exchange their uniforms for plain clothes, before being posted day and night in every quarter of the East End.

After the discovery of Alice McKenzie, the thoroughfares of

Whitechapel and Mile End became crowded with residents, all anxiously discussing the tragic events as well as the growing belief that the Ripper had returned.

Such was the effect of the murder that as darkness began to fall the commercial roads of Whitechapel, that would usually be teeming with prostitutes well after the closure of the public houses, were near deserted.[5]

Unlike the previous murders, after the killing of McKenzie the police were inundated with potential leads. According to Inspector Henry Moore, on the day of the murder two suspects were brought into Commercial Street Police Station, where they were questioned about their involvement with the crime. One of them would later be named as John Larkin Mills, who was interviewed during the afternoon of 17 July for two hours, only to have his identity and good character confirmed. It was soon established that he had no connection to this or any of the previous murders.[6]

As for the identity of the second suspect, that would remain a mystery, with only the newspapers of the day offering the briefest of details. According to the reports a suspicious male had been seen fleeing the area of Castle Alley in the early hours of the morning of the murder, much like the male observed by Sergeant Stephen White, who was seen walking out of Castle Alley moments before the discovery of the body. The press stated that his movements were observed by a nearby police officer who, after detaining him, brought him to the station for questioning. While the police were reluctant to divulge details, it seemed that they had attached some significance to his identity although he would later be released without charge.[7]

The two arrests were followed by the confession of William Wallace Brodie, who on 18 July walked into Leman Street Police Station and while under the influence of alcohol admitted to being the Whitechapel murderer and having committed all the atrocities attributed to Jack the Ripper. After thoroughly investigating his background it was discovered that Brodie, who was homeless, had been travelling on a vessel in the area of South Africa for almost the entire period of the Ripper murders.[8]

Such evidence proved categorically that Brodie was in no way connected to the killing. Somewhat disheartened by the results of their initial enquiries, the police were anxious to follow up on another potential lead and began to make a concerted effort to trace the whereabouts of George Dixon, believing the youth to be a potential key witness.

The task of locating McKenzie's teenage acquaintance fell to Sergeant John McCarthy, who less than two years later would assist in the arrest of Thomas Cutbush. After much effort, trawling the nearby taverns and public houses, McCarthy eventually found George Dixon at 29 Star Street in Commercial Road.

Sitting in the small bricked kitchen the sergeant took a detailed account of Dixon's night spent with the victim, charting their movements after leaving the lodging house on Gun Street and in particular the details of the man heard in conversation with Alice later that evening. Although only hearing the man speak briefly Dixon confirmed that his voice contained such strange tones as to make it distinctive. He told Sergeant McCarthy that he would be able to recognise it again, should he have the opportunity.[9]

Although they were yet to hear it for themselves, *The Sun* journalists had already encountered several people who had mentioned Cutbush's unusual voice. One such person was the owner of a Kennington tobacco shop, Mr H. D. Thatcher.

In a letter sent to *The Sun* Thatcher wrote that he had known Cutbush for some time and about five years earlier had been a regular customer of his, often visiting the shop late at night to purchase tobacco.

According to the shopkeeper Cutbush would never talk to other customers and only ever spoke to him, his speech at times being fast and excitable while on other occasions appearing dazed, as if he had just woken. Thatcher confirmed that Cutbush's conversation would almost always centre on the fact that his face was twisted and causing him pain and on more than one occasion told the dramatic tale of the doctor who was trying to poison him.

Thatcher also mentioned occasions when Cutbush alleged that he had communicated with eminent politicians, including Henry Labouchere, in order to bring in a Bill to prevent doctors dispensing new prescriptions.

So wrote Thatcher, Cutbush would regularly place envelopes upon the shop counter, addressed to individuals of rank, presumably officials within the police, and without encouragement would talk endlessly about anatomy and chemistry. One other point observed by Thatcher was that Cutbush's hands and coins were almost always stained with the same black chemical.

On one night, well remembered by the shopkeeper, the conversation took a darker turn when Cutbush brightly started to discuss how easy it was to get away with murder. When Thatcher jokingly called him 'Jack' he left instantly and never returned to the shop.[10]

Thatcher's letter proved particularly enlightening and provided further evidence of Cutbush's passion for chemistry and medicine as well as his desire to impress whomever he met with his knowledge of the subject. The shopkeeper's testimony also added weight to a hypothesis as to the reason why Cutbush should have chosen to adopt an alias.

Cutbush's interest in chemistry and medicine was well known to his family and acquaintances and so it is likely that his mother, a woman born in Philadelphia, would have mentioned the famous doctor of chemistry who had made his reputation in her home city. A man whose name just happened to be Dr James Cutbush.

Should Thomas have needed a reason for using the alias of 'James' or 'Jim' then this appears as logical as any other. Time and again Cutbush described himself as a medical man and in James Cutbush, he had found someone with whom he shared many similarities. Both being young, with James Cutbush dying at only thirty-five and both being avid writers with a shared thirst for knowledge.[11]

Although only a theory, it seems a logical one.

The journalists also found interesting, from the shopkeeper's testimony, a confirmation of the depth and persistence of Cutbush's anger at Dr Brooks and his perceived poisoning. By then, in November 1890, such was Cutbush's conviction that his life was at risk that he had made up his mind to kill Dr Brooks, having approached an old work colleague in the hope of obtaining a pistol.

As Tracy had discovered, the former colleague – referred to as 'SY' by *The Sun*– refused to assist Cutbush with his plan, choosing instead to warn the doctor of Cutbush's intentions. In a letter sent to Dr Brooks on 15 November 1890, 'SY' communicated his concerns.

Having known Cutbush for some time and having already observed his peculiar behaviour, Dr Brooks became fearful and that evening visited Lambeth Police Station, where on his arrival he presented the desk sergeant with the letter.

Dr Brooks was asked to wait in the station office while the correspondence was passed to the Inspector, who, according to the doctor, was less than impressed with his claims, suggesting that he contact the local workhouse in Newington. The Inspector stated that, should they deem it necessary, the workhouse could take action and institutionalise Cutbush. The next day, in order to ascertain Cutbush's state of mind, the workhouse sent a Medical Officer along with a Justice of the Peace to 14 Albert Street.[12]

On hearing the muffled conversation from his bedroom, Cutbush sprinted down the stairs and seeing the men at the door leapt the last of the steps. Landing on the wooden floor of the hallway he began to sprint to the rear of the house, knocking over the hall table in the process.

Before the two officials could react, Cutbush was already in the garden. By the time they reached the parlour window, he was scaling the garden wall and though pausing only to see if he was being pursued, in less than a second, he was out of sight.

On his return home later that day, creeping silently through the house, Cutbush was surprised to find both his mother and aunt still awake, sitting inside the parlour, awaiting his return. After hearing movement, Kate shouted for her son to join them, her voice quivering as she spoke.

As Cutbush stepped inside Kate informed him that in light of the day's events they were left with no choice other than to return him to Ramsgate. Cutbush would offer no reply and turned to leave without a single retort to his mother's comment or concern for her obvious state of upset.

In response Kate rose to her feet. 'Thomas,' she said, her voice louder than before, 'I have no choice in this, you must understand that. I will be watching you closely from now on.'

After momentarily pausing, his frame barely distinguishable in the darkness of the hallway, Cutbush spoke. Tilting her head towards the doorway in an attempt to hear his words, Kate was unable to understand her son. By the time she asked him to repeat what he had said, Cutbush was gone.

FIFTEEN

He Went for Her Throat

Swallow Gardens, just beyond the boundaries of Whitechapel, was a short, narrow and poorly lit alleyway that ran under a decaying railway arch from Chamber Street to Royal Mint Street. It provided darkness and isolation: a perfect place for prostitutes to work.[1]

Frances Coles, or 'Carroty Nell' as she was known locally, was a regular visitor: a petite woman, twenty-six years old and gifted with the complexion and looks of youth, with large brown eyes and an oval face flanked by a mass of dark hair.[2]

At 1.45 a.m. on 13 February 1891, having taken breakfast at Shuttleworth's Eating House on Wentworth Street, Frances went looking for trade, walking through the murky backstreets of Whitechapel, passing the partly occupied buildings and warehouses nearby, before taking her place in the arch.

For eight years, she had done her best to keep the truth of her troubles from her family, with her elderly father and sister unaware of her chosen profession, believing instead that Frances had found steady employment in the Minories, a lengthy street within the boundaries of the City of London.

Her sister Mary Ann Coles, who unlike Frances lived in respectable circumstances in Shoreditch, would later recall that during the Christmas of 1890, on a visit from her sister, she had noticed that Frances appeared dirty and smelt of liquor. Although concerned by her sister's appearance,

Frances reassured Mary Ann that she had found regular lodgings with an elderly lady on Commercial Road. Mary Ann would later discover, however, that this was yet another lie.

Up until the February of 1891, Frances had known little in the way of stability, moving around between the many doss houses of Whitechapel and Shoreditch, and when lacking the funds for a bed, sleeping rough on the streets. Although Frances had at one time found work as a labeller for a chemist in the Minories, the manual nature of the work eventually proved too painful and she chose instead to use her looks as an easier means of income.[3]

Mrs Hague, the landlady of Thrawl Street lodging house, had Frances as a resident for some time up until the January of 1891, at which point she disappeared while still owing rent. On 12 February Frances unexpectedly returned, promising to pay her landlady what she was owed. She'd acquired the funds from one of her regular clients who had recently returned from sea.

James Thomas Sadler, a ship's fireman, was older than Frances. He was a stout, muscular man of fiftythree, with a grey beard that hung ragged on his weathered face and whose worn cap did little to hide the scars of many a previous fight.[4]

As Frances knew all too well, Sadler was not averse to confrontation and was well known in the bars and taverns of Whitechapel for being something of a loose cannon. A man who, though pleasant when sober, would become quarrelsome and ill-tempered when drunk.[5]

After the S.S. *Fez* had docked in London, following some time at sea, Sadler was keen to step ashore and indulge in all that Whitechapel had to offer. In possession of several months unspent wages, he was discharged, leaving the St Katharine Docks at 7 p.m. before making his way to the nearest alehouse.

As one of Frances's regulars, Sadler was aware of her haunts and in no time had found the girl he was looking for standing at the bar of the Princess Alice. After several drinks together they moved on to The White Swan, and were later seen wearily making their way to White's Row, where they lodged for the night, sleeping in a double bed paid for by Sadler.

Waking with a hangover, by noon the next day the couple were up and back out on the streets – and once again in search of liquor. For the next five hours they visited a number of pubs, spending as much of Sadler's wages as possible, as well as using some of his money to treat Frances to a new black hat and a pair of earrings from a shop on Brick Lane.[6]

By 5 p.m. Sadler and Coles were taking food at Shuttleworth's Eating House on Wentworth Street and forty-five minutes later had moved onto the Marlborough Head in Brick Lane. Inside, amid the smoke-filled bar, Sadler's deep voice roared, cheerfully raising a glass of gin while offering to buy drinks for a number of his fellow patrons. While palming a handful of coins upon the bar, he was oblivious to the three bystanders, who on seeing the fireman's generosity were taking a keen interest in his apparent wealth, noticing several notes protruding from his waistcoat pocket.

By the time Sadler and Coles left the pub and ventured onto Thrawl Street, the bystanders had made up their minds. Though Coles was standing by Sadler's side, the three strangers were undeterred and jumped upon Sadler as soon as he left the pub's entrance.

Sadler was violently struck over the head. Having been taken unawares, he was unable to fight back, falling to the ground and instinctively grabbing for his head in an attempt to shield his face from another attack. After being jumped upon, with his attackers kicking and striking him in the stomach and legs, eventually the assault came to an end.[7]

Staggering to his feet, bewildered and bruised, Sadler watched as the men who had attacked him walked off, counting their spoils, having stolen the remainder of his wages. Only on patting at his pockets did he realise that along with his money, they had also stolen his only timepiece.

Leaning back against a shop front, wiping the blood from his nose, Sadler berated Frances, who for the duration of the attack had been standing close by. Realising that his shouts were attracting a crowd, Sadler fell silent, before turning his back upon his young companion and heading off to the St Katharine Dock, hoping that he would be granted permission to sleep aboard ship.[8]

Deciding not to follow, Frances made her way to Montague Street. There she entered one of its many taverns and was seen by her former landlady in the company of a man, being treated to drinks. Having taken little notice of the pair, Mrs Hague could only provide scant details of Frances's companion, describing him as having a fair complexion and a moustache.[9]

Meanwhile, Sadler had arrived back at the dock, his heavy steps resounding upon the wooden platform. He approached the two police officers guarding the S.S. *Fez*. After being told that he was not permitted to board the ship due to his drunken state, an argument ensued, with Sadler cursing the officers, though barely able to stand upright. After receiving little in the way of retort, he turned his anger on a passing dock labourer, berating the worker with a series of slurred obscenities.

Unlike the police officers, the dock labourer responded, leaving Sadler flat out on the dock, having taken a punch to the ribs and several kicks. Though he hit the ground hard, Sadler tried to get up and fight back and only then did he notice the blood running down his cheek, from a gash above his right eye caused when he collided with the edge of a gate as he fell.

While the police officers watched on, Sadler managed to get back to his feet, staggering as far as Nightingale Walk before falling to the ground from the pain of his injuries. He attempted in vain to gain sanctuary in a lodging house in East Smithfield but owing to his appearance was immediately refused admittance.[10]

After wandering the streets a little longer, using the house walls and shop fronts as a means of support, Sadler eventually arrived back at the entrance to White's Row lodging house, where he had stayed the previous night with Frances. Standing under the yellow rays of the large lamp outside, he began to check his appearance, seeing the blood on his brown jacket and the ragged flesh of his knuckles from when he had fallen to the ground.

In the kitchen Sadler discovered Frances slumped on the table, head in arms, sleeping off the effects of the day's drinking.[11] Now without funds, Sadler was merely allowed to stay long enough to clean himself up before being evicted by the deputy. With little fuss, he left and was seen staggering slowly along the Whitechapel Road, eventually arriving at The London Hospital, assisted by a young constable who had taken pity on him.

On waking, Frances left the lodgings in White's Row and took the short journey to Wentworth Street, where she used the last of her money to purchase breakfast. Joseph Haswell, an employee of Shuttleworth's, would recall seeing Frances Coles that morning, remembering that she had asked for a piece of mutton and a slice of bread and that, after she had finished, she appeared eager to stay indoors. Needing to close the shop, Haswell thanked Frances for her custom before asking her to leave. Frances's reply was not so polite – telling Haswell to mind his own business.[12]

Tired and offended, Haswell wasted little time escorting Frances from the premises, grabbing her by the arm and moving her into the street, at which point she turned right, walking towards Brick Lane. Haswell would later state that by the time Frances left it was 1.45 a.m.

By 2.15 a.m. PC Ernest Thompson was turning into Swallow Gardens, noting the time on the large clock tower of the Co-operative Store in Lehman Street. As he entered, surrounded by the silence of early morning, Thompson heard footsteps hurrying out of the other end of the alley towards Mansell Street. Having been an officer for only six weeks this was Thompson's first night patrolling alone and unbeknownst to him he was about to stumble across his first murder case. In fact, had he arrived just seconds earlier, Thompson may have saved Frances's life.[13]

As the constable slowed his pace a dark shape came into view, lying motionless upon the ground in the dim light of the archway. Steadying his lamp in order to get a better look, Thompson suddenly became aware that the object was a woman lying on her back. Initially he saw the blood pouring from her throat and then, as he leant closer, noticed Frances open one eye and then slowly shut it. Realising that the woman was still alive, he blew hard upon his whistle; his lips drying as shock began to take hold.

Fortunately, Thompson didn't have to wait long for help to arrive in the form of fellow constable George Elliott, an undercover officer who was outside a factory in Royal Mint Street, and Constable Hyde, who had been patrolling close by.

On their arrival and on seeing the body lying upon the ground Hyde was immediately dispatched to locate the local doctor, Dr Oxley, who resided ten minutes away in Dock Street. Not long after his arrival in Swallow Gardens, Oxley was joined by Dr Phillips, who had also been summoned. By the time both men arrived Frances was dead.

Within an hour the area around the small archway was flooded with police officers, with Inspector Moore and Assistant Commissioner Anderson, as well as the Chief Constable Sir Melville Macnaghten, all standing in the gloom of Swallow Gardens, panicked by the thought that the unfortunate woman was probably another victim of Jack the Ripper.[14]

Initial checks of the area did little to assist the police on the ground, with officers ordered specifically to inspect the walls of the archway and its nearby hoardings, looking for any further messages left by the killer.

An examination of Frances's body revealed that she had been thrown to the ground with great force, causing an injury to the back of her head. Her attacker had then gripped her by the chin and cut her throat twice.

To the officers working on the murder case, this part at least was a sign of the Ripper's handiwork.[15] Although some believed that, due to the absence of any mutilation, Frances Coles was not a Ripper victim, others thought differently. Their theory was that PC Thompson had disturbed the Ripper and that the footsteps he had heard running out of Swallow Gardens had belonged to the killer, making good his escape before having the time to leave his gruesome trademark.

Initially, unlike the previous six murders, it appeared the police knew exactly who was responsible, finding a prime suspect in James Sadler. He was located on 14 February in the Phoenix public house and taken to Leman Street Police Station for questioning, and was subsequently arrested, appearing at Thames Magistrates Court, where he was charged with murder.

The detectives believed they had caught Frances's killer and the notion began to circulate that perhaps the Metropolitan Police had finally apprehended Jack the Ripper.[16]

James Sadler, however, was no killer. After his arrest, numerous witnesses came forward to substantiate his claims that he had not in fact been in company with Frances in the hours before her murder, while finding corroborating evidence to confirm that he had been assaulted three times in one night.

Sadler was also provided with an alibi in the form of Sergeant Edwards, who at 2 a.m. had observed the fireman outside the Royal Mint, at that time described as being so drunk as to be almost unable to stand. As a result, by 2 March all charges against Sadler were dropped.[17] Such was the press coverage surrounding the arrest that on Sadler's release from Thames Magistrates Court he was met by a cheering crowd of men and women who had gathered outside to hear the verdict.

On being released, Sadler became enraged by the accusations made by the press and sought compensation from the various newspapers that had labelled him (incorrectly) a killer. And, as the hysteria of the case began to dwindle with other headlines taking precedence over the once sensational story, one question remained unanswered: if it wasn't James Sadler who had killed Frances Coles, then who was it?

The lodger living at 14 Albert Street had grown accustomed to Thomas Cutbush's strange behaviour, so he wasn't altogether surprised when one night in 1891 he heard Cutbush breaking the parlour window and climbing into the house. The only thing of which he couldn't be certain, when Kennedy Jones questioned him two years later, was exactly which day it was.[18]

By 1891 Cutbush had become a virtual recluse, sleeping all day and venturing from his room only after dark. His mother Kate would later confirm that, by then, her son's studying had reached an excessive level, with Cutbush's conversation only ever relating to the topic of medicine.

As she began to realise that his mental state was in decline, Kate debated contacting the local authorities, aware that the trips to Ramsgate were no longer the solution. One night Cutbush chose to discuss the Whitechapel murders, recounting in graphic detail the manner in which the prostitutes had been killed. Kate came to the conclusion that the time had come to take action.

As February rolled into March, she believed she had found the answer: that for her son's benefit and the safety of her family, he needed to be removed from the house and placed in an asylum.

As she attempted to broach the subject on the evening of 4 March 1891, Cutbush drew his Bowie knife and leapt for her throat.

Artist's impression of Thomas Cutbush
courtesy of Steven Bullock

MR. W. N. RACE,
EX-INSPECTOR, L DIV., METROPOLITAN FORCE.

Image of Inspector William Race kindly
provided by Stewart Evans

LOUIS TRACY.

Image of Louis Tracy courtesy of John D. Squires

Blackjack truncheon once owned by Charles Henry Cutbush
- courtesy of Claire Chevin

Photograph of the area in Nunhead Cemetery where the grave of
Thomas Cutbush was located - taken by the author.

No. 25.

Warrant of removal of a Criminal
Lunatic, ordered to be detained
during Her Majesty's pleasure,
from Prison to Broadmoor.

CRIMINAL LUNATIC ASYLUMS ACT, 1860.

23 & 24 V., c. 75, s. 2.

(a) Registered No. of Criminal Lunatic	(a)	X32007
(b) Name	(b)	Thomas Cutbush
*(c) Offence charged	(c)	Maliciously wounding
†(d) Date when on arraignment prisoner was found to be then insane, &c.		
(e) Court	(e)	14 April 1891
	(e)	South London Sessions, Newington
(f) Order of Court	(f)	To be detained during Her Majesty's pleasure.
(g) Prison in which confined at date of this Warrant	(g)	Holloway

*Warrant of Removal of a Criminal Lunatic, ordered to be detained
during Her Majesty's pleasure, from Prison to Broadmoor.*

I hereby authorise and require you, the Governor of the above-named Prison, to cause the Criminal Lunatic above described to be removed from the said Prison to Broadmoor Lunatic Asylum, and to transmit with the same a Certificate in the form annexed, duly filled up and authenticated; and you, the Superintendent of Broadmoor Lunatic Asylum, to receive and there to detain the said Criminal Lunatic until further order.

Henry Matthews

One of Her Majesty's Principal Secretaries of State.

Whitehall,

15th. day of April 1891.

To the Governor of H.M. Prison at Holloway.

AND

To the Superintendent of
Broadmoor Lunatic Asylum.

---

* (c) Insert Offence charged, or Offence of which convicted, as circumstances may require.
† (d) Insert, as the circumstances may require:—
Date of conviction, the Jury returning a special verdict in pursuance of the Trial of Lunatics Act, 1883.
Date when, on arraignment, Prisoner was found to be then insane by a Jury specially empanelled for the purpose; or
Date of trial when Prisoner appeared to the Jury charged with indictment to be then insane; or
Date when Prisoner was brought up before Court to be discharged for want of prosecution, and found to be then insane by Jury empanelled for the purpose.

S. & S. (35,570a) 300 7—89

3/H19/22/2/4/1523/1

Warrant for the removal of Thomas Cutbush from Holloway
Prison to Broadmoor Lunatic Asylum - reproduced by permission of
the Berkshire Record Office

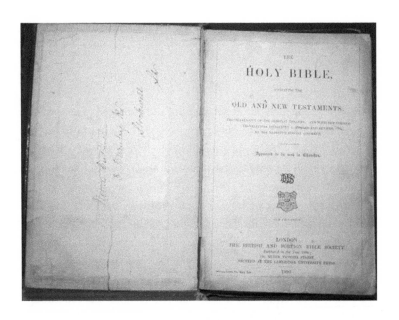

The Holy Bible once owned by Helen 'Nellie' Cutbush
- courtesy of Claire Chevin

SIXTEEN

On the Run

Fortunately, Kate saw the attack coming and managed to escape from the parlour into the hallway. Fumbling with the door key in an attempt to secure her son inside, she pressed her weight against the door and only after finally hearing the bolt snap into the frame did she begin to scream for help.[1]

Hearing her sister's cries, Clara ran from her room to find Kate huddled on the floor of the hallway. After listening intently to her sister's explanation, she held her in her arms, with both women realising that the moment they had feared for so long was now upon them.

After sitting in silence for almost ten minutes the sisters dared re-enter the room, discovering once inside that Cutbush had escaped through a window which had been left ajar.

For Kate, the attack represented the final straw: seeing her son for the first time as the violent young man he truly was. Although he had taken his knife to a servant only months earlier, never did she anticipate that he would turn his anger on her.

Deciding that swift action was needed in order to protect herself and her family, Kate communicated with the parish authorities, informing them of her concerns, of her son's increasingly strange behaviour and her fears for her own safety.[2]

The church clock had barely struck eleven when Cutbush returned home, his light footsteps splitting the stillness of the house as he scaled the stairs towards his attic room. Throughout the dark hours that followed, Kate remained awake, lying in bed unable to sleep for fear of what her son might do, should his anger resurface.

It was 7 a.m. when the heavy tread beyond her window indicated the arrival of the four warders outside. As a result of her distress and her admissions, Lambeth Infirmary had decided that, for public safety, it was time for Cutbush to be admitted.

Although barricading herself and her sister within the rear pantry, Kate could still hear her son's screams as the guards entered his room, the commotion as the fight broke out, with the sound of bodies hitting the floor of the attic, of kicks and punches followed by a sudden – almost eerie – quiet, as Thomas fell onto the floorboards of the landing, having been struck in the face.

Had the guards taken a moment longer in placing Cutbush in the waiting cab, then in all certainty they would have seen Kate emerge from the pantry in an attempt to plead for her son's release, her guilt being so great as to numb the fear that had consumed her the previous night.[3] As was the case, by the time she reached the open front door and called her son's name, the cab was already out of sight.

By 1 p.m. news of Cutbush's escape from Lambeth Infirmary had reached Albert Street, with a local constable breaking the news to the now distraught sisters, along with a clear directive that should Cutbush return home then they were to contact the police immediately.

For almost eight hours he was lost from sight. While every police station in London was being wired the particulars surrounding his escape and urging a speedy apprehension, Cutbush was lying low, walking along the banks of the Thames while quietly contemplating his next move.

By the time he crossed Westminster Bridge, in an attempt to hide within the more populated City of London, the skies were already beginning to darken. Burrowing his chin deep into the collar of his newly acquired coat, he skulked along the edge of the bridge, passing a procession of omnibuses that creaked with the weight of their passengers. Adorned with the adverts of the day, the large carriages offered the perfect cover, allowing him to cross onto the Embankment, unnoticed and unobserved.

Although much of his time at large would remain a blur, Cutbush recalled that from Westminster he had ventured to Hyde Park Corner. There, having covered his face with mud, he hid, lurking within shop fronts and yards. Hours seemed to pass before the first police activity became noticeable. Cutbush observed two constables checking the area of the nearby Grosvenor Crescent. A lantern's beam was the first indication of their arrival, stretching out through the still night air, scanning the walls, with the red brick appearing bright, almost luminous, against the thick darkness that surrounded it.

When Cutbush saw another officer walking close by, he made a break for it. Fighting the urge to run, he kept his pace steady and fast. He didn't know whether they were there for him, whether he had been spotted or even if the whistle that sounded somewhere behind him was theirs. Only on reaching Belgrave Street did he begin to sprint, his panic too great to remain under control. Exhausted, Cutbush desperately crossed to the western edge of the city in the hope of escaping those he would later refer to as 'the runners'.

Only on reaching Holborn did he pause for the first time, pushing gently on an open gate and ducking inside an empty grocer's yard. Kneeling behind a cart, surrounded by the stench of rotten fruit, Cutbush gagged, though having eaten nothing for a day he was unable to be sick.

As usual, Holborn was busy. Filled with a hundred footfalls the street seemed alive, with distant conversations and the clatter of cabs seeping into the yard. Only as Cutbush stood, heaving himself to his feet while leaning on the barrow wheel, did he contemplate his next move. Peering through the gap in the gate, he could see the City Temple, its grand pillared entrance standing majestic on the opposite side of the road.

Cutbush had visited the Temple many times before to listen to the sermons of Dr Joseph Parker, London's most popular preacher. Believing the Temple might offer him the sanctuary he so craved, he emerged from his hiding place and, after pulling his cap low over his brow, again began to walk.[4]

Mr Clark, the sexton of the City Temple, had been working in the vestry, tidying Dr Parker's books, when the rattle of the entrance doors indicated the arrival of an unexpected visitor. Peering through the peep hole, fitted in the door at the request of Dr Parker in order to peruse his audience, Clark caught a glimpse of the visitor slowly making his way towards the stage.

Cutbush had never seen the Temple empty and had only ever arrived amid a throng of crowds, all eager to listen to the preacher. Although the Temple usually appeared bright, with its ornate ceilings gleaming in the light of a row of hanging lamps, now it wore a different aspect. The pews and the stage on which Parker had talked so passionately about the plight of society and the truth of religion were picked out solely by the dull light from the vestry door.

For a while Cutbush was given sanctuary inside the Temple, the sexton's wife offering him a seat and a glass of water. After thanking the sexton and his wife for their generosity, Cutbush left, heading into Fleet Street before backtracking to the Embankment. For a while he simply stood, leaning upon the steep wall of the Thames, seeing the empty steam boats below, weightless upon the water's edge and the distant lights of smaller crafts amid the darkness of the water, pools of moonlight caressing the waves as they lapped at the banks of the river.

As Big Ben struck eight, Cutbush had already crossed the bridge and within half an hour had reached Kennington Park Road. It was there that he spotted his next victim.

Florence Grace Johnson was younger and prettier than any of the Ripper's previous victims. Her pale face lifted by the brightness of her youthful eyes, with a mass of thick dark hair pulled neatly into a bun.

Having spent the evening with a friend, by 8.30 p.m. Florence was on her way home to Fentiman Street. Walking a route that she had taken many times before, in company with a female companion, Florence felt safe. As she passed the tobacco shop on Newington Butts she didn't notice the tall man standing under the hoarding. Had she looked closer, then possibly she would have seen the glimmer of the blade held in Cutbush's right hand, a large Bowie knife acquired during his time at large. Had she seen it then perhaps she would have had time to flee.

As Florence and her young companion neared the end of Kennington Park Road, only then did she sense something was wrong, hearing footsteps moving at a fast pace close behind. Only as she felt warm breath upon the back of her neck did she begin to run. In two paces Cutbush had caught up, pulling on Florence's dress with one hand while plunging his knife into her lower back with the other. As her companion began to scream, attracting assistance from a nearby butcher's shop, Cutbush fled, looking back only once before disappearing from sight.

After being carried to Kennington Lane Police Station by her father, Florence soon relayed the details of the attack, describing the assailant's appearance and stating emphatically that she would be able to identify him again, should she get the chance. As she explained, although she had fallen to the ground after feeling the knife penetrate her back, she had turned and had seen her attacker.

Screwing up her eyes, Florence trembled as Dr Farr lifted her once neat dress, its pale blue now turned a deep red as the blood streamed from her wound. Farr would later tell reporters that Florence had sustained a clean, deep incision to her lower back, and though not being life-threatening, it was still serious.[5]

As word of the incident spread, every constable in Lambeth was placed on high alert. With the Metropolitan Police now aware that Cutbush was again in hiding somewhere within the district, officers were ordered to comb the area in an attempt to locate him. Yet again, Cutbush had simply vanished.

By midnight he was back in Albert Street, clambering over the back wall before slowly making his way to the rear of the house. For almost four hours Clara and her sister tended to Cutbush, placing bandages on his blistered feet and running him a bath. Perhaps born from fear more than compassion, neither sister contacted the police as asked and instead assisted Cutbush in changing his clothes.

Only as her son was about to leave did Kate speak openly about what had occurred and her reasons for contacting the infirmary. Having had a change of heart, she offered Cutbush a way out. She gave him ten shillings and suggested that he flee to Thanet, instructing him to travel by train to Margate and on arrival send word via letter. In order for Cutbush to stay away for a length of time, Kate told him that she would send more funds and possibly join him there herself in due course.

Cutbush, however, had other ideas and would never reach his coastline retreat. Hearing the heavy thread of constables outside the front of the house he scattered towards the rear garden and in no time had distanced himself from the threat of capture.

He waited until Saturday morning to reappear. Under the cover of darkness Cutbush made his way to the Minories, to Mrs Dickinson's gunsmiths shop near the Tower of London, where he remained, skulking in the shadows until the doors were unbolted and the shop opened for business.

Once inside Cutbush wasted little time in spending the money given to him by his mother, purchasing a new Bowie knife and sheath. For the remainder of the day he kept clear of Kennington, aware that the police presence would be too great to risk returning home.

Only as day turned to night did Cutbush begin his journey back to Albert Street and by 10.15 p.m. had reached the Kennington Road. Although Cutbush would later testify that the knife purchased from the Gunsmiths shop was to defend himself against foreign sailors, as Isabelle Fraser Anderson was about to discover the weapon had been acquired for one reason, and one reason only.[6]

According to Robert Smith, a clerk who was also walking home along the Kennington Road, he had first been alerted to the altercation by a woman's screams. On looking behind him, Smith saw a young woman approaching, who appeared noticeably distraught.

Eighteen-year-old Isabelle Anderson explained that moments earlier she had felt a tug from behind as she walked along the road, then heard the sound of her own dress being ripped as a knife tore through her garments.

While listening to Isabelle's panicked words, Smith saw Cutbush running in the opposite direction. Almost unable to speak, Isabelle cried out that the fleeing man was her assailant;

Smith immediately gave chase.

Racing ahead, Cutbush somehow managed to convince John Barton, a milkman working in Princes Road, that he had been 'larking' with a girl and was being chased by her relatives, who intended to 'pitch' into him. Incredibly, Barton agreed to hide him in his cellar. Cutbush would later recall seeing Smith's boots as the cellar door closed, hearing his panting breaths as Cutbush himself attempted to contain his own, standing motionless on the stairway below. Fifteen minutes later, the street silent, Cutbush lifted the trap door and slowly made his way from the confines of the dairy.[7]

It was 12.15 a.m. on 8 March when Cutbush finally returned home. He was found skulking in the back garden by his aunt, his eyes large and wild, resembling that of a hunted animal, and with hands trembling in the cold air. Fearing capture Cutbush would stay only four hours before taking to the streets once more.

Later that day Cutbush returned home to eat and stayed for six hours, during which time he retired to his room. While her nephew slept, Clara noticed a knife jutting from his coat pocket and fearing for her own safety, tentatively removed it, leaving only the sheath in its place before hiding the blade behind a piano.

By 7 p.m. Cutbush had woken and had again taken to the streets, only this time, as he loitered among the shadows cast by the Georgian properties of Kennington, he did so oblivious to the fact that the police were now closing in.

Whilst he roamed the streets, Inspector Race arrived at Albert Street and during his time inside discovered vital information on Cutbush. As well as taking possession of the knife used to stab Isabelle Fraser Anderson, Race had seen Cutbush's room. He had observed the drawings of the mutilated women and the books on surgery, along with blood-stained clothing stuffed up the chimney breast, covered in turpentine.

Aunt Clara assured Race that her nephew was likely to return at some point in the coming hours, so the Inspector seized the opportunity and by midnight had returned with Sergeant McCarthy and Chief Inspector Chisholm. They positioned themselves at the rear of 14 Albert Street, waiting patiently for Cutbush to return.

At 7 a.m. their patience was rewarded. Inspector Race was the first to see Cutbush's distinctive figure walking slowly towards them, clinging to the wall of the mews in an attempt to stay out of sight. Oblivious to the officers waiting for him, Cutbush made ready to scale the garden wall. As he did so, Race laid a hand on his shoulder.

Finally, Thomas Cutbush was under arrest.[8]

SEVENTEEN

A Strange Trial

Only as the tall-sided police wagon pulled out of Albert Street and turned into Penton Place did the prisoner utter his first words. Until then, he had appeared quiet, as if in a trance, his gaze fixed upon the scarred wooden floor beneath his feet, ignorant to the sights and sounds beyond the small barred window in the rear door.

It was during his journey to Kennington Lane Police Station that Cutbush would make his confession, asking whether his capture was for what he called the 'Mile End job'. Race would ignore the suspect's rant and would only truly discover the significance of his claims in 1893, after the diligent Kennedy Jones discovered an account of Cutbush's attempt to accost a prostitute in Mile End.[1]

As Race didn't know about a 'Mile End job', he said not a word until arriving at Kennington Lane Police Station. Only then did he speak, ordering Cutbush to stand, before walking him backwards down the slim steps of the wagon.

Though having been talkative while en route, once inside the near-empty station the prisoner fell silent once again, appearing more sullen as Race and McCarthy searched his pockets in the presence of the desk sergeant.

As expected, the sheath found in the waistband of Cutbush's trousers was empty. After removing a bag of damp tobacco from the prisoner's coat pocket, Sergeant McCarthy then discovered several torn pieces of paper, which when pasted together made for a shocking image, much like those found by Race in Cutbush's room; it consisted of another sketch depicting the mutilated torso of a woman, her abdomen ripped wide open with its walls resting on either side of the body to expose the bloody intestines.[2]

The interview that followed would do little to elicit the truth behind Cutbush's actions. He stated (incorrectly) that he had no knowledge of Whitechapel. He offered no explanation as to why he should carry a knife sheath and fabricated stories in an attempt to explain his need for making such drawings, while at all times appearing calm, almost confident, as if under the misguided belief that he would soon be set free.[3]

Within a matter of hours Cutbush was transferred from his police holding cell to Peckham House Lunatic Asylum, a large mansion set in acres of expansive grounds that, although once home to the Spitta family, reputed for their lavish lifestyle, was now a brutal establishment for the insane.[4]

Within the lightless cell Cutbush remained for several weeks, his time in the asylum broken only by the sporadic visits of the police. During that time he spoke very little, in the main conveying his displeasure with the quality of food, which brought little response from his chief warder, a short yet fierce-looking man, whose temperament was as cold as the corridors in which he patrolled.

During his stay Cutbush would be positively identified by his two victims. The first to enter the confines of Peckham House Asylum was Florence Johnson. Nursing her wounds, she walked at a slow pace accompanied by Inspector Race and was followed shortly afterwards by Isabelle Anderson, who sheltered desperately under the arm of her father.

Cutbush also discovered, during an early visit from his aunt and mother, that prior to his arrest his knife had been handed over to Race. He had previously been ignorant of this particular detail and the revelation provoked his only recorded outburst.

On 21 March 1891, before Judge Hopkins of Lambeth Police Court, Cutbush was charged on remand with feloniously cutting and wounding

Florence Grace Johnson with intent to do grievous bodily harm. He was also charged with attempting to wound Isabelle Fraser Anderson.[5]

Commissioner Sir Edward Bradford sent Chief Inspector Chisholm to attend the court on his behalf. Upon his arrival, the Chief Inspector ordered, very unusually, that only sworn information relating to Cutbush be read, making it clear that it was the Commissioner who had made this request and indicating that under no circumstances could Cutbush's possible connections to the Ripper case be discussed.[6]

Prosecutor Angus Lewis opened with a brief outline of the case, calling Miss Anderson as his first witness. After reiterating an account of the attack, Isabelle explained that the man who assaulted her was in appearance like the prisoner, as well as stating, in almost a whisper, that she had noticed the knife as the attacker made off. 'It was held in his right hand,' she said.

Next to take the stand was Clara Hayne. Shuffling towards the dock in a bemused state, she acknowledged that she had lived with her nephew for some time. Keeping her gaze low, she explained the circumstances surrounding his removal to Lambeth Infirmary, stating that as a consequence of his condition, application had been made to the parish authorities that had led to his removal to the infirmary.

On the subject of her nephew's escape and subsequent arrest, Clara spoke openly and explained that during one of the occasions when he returned home, she had found a knife in his coat pocket. Clara continued that for two years her nephew had been unable to work, with the condition of his mind brought about through what she deemed as 'excessive study'.

Dressed smartly in his pressed uniform, Inspector Race took his place in the dock by midday. After confirming his name and rank, Race stated that he had been present with Chief Inspector Chisholm when the prisoner was arrested, as well as presenting the knife used by Cutbush in his attack on Isabelle Fraser Anderson.

After Florence Johnson offered her account of the stabbing, Mr Hopkins had heard enough, informing the court that Cutbush would be committed to trial at the next Sessions.[7] For three weeks Cutbush remained in Holloway Prison. Confined in his cell, often appearing dazed and incoherent, his mental health was in a steady state of decline. Although wishing to appear confident, in the face of overwhelming evidence he continued his claim that he was innocent and anticipated his release.

On 14 April 1891, Cutbush returned to court.

At the London County Sessions in Newington, reporters working for *The Standard* and *The Times* jostled for position as they entered the courtroom. Aware that the 'Kennington Stabbings' had caused something of a minor sensation, the journalists were keen to get prime seats in order to capture every detail of the trial.

Before the experienced Sir Peter Edlin, Q.C., the first of the day's cases was heard: that of Phillip Phillips, an elderly criminal suffering with nerves in the face of an unexpected audience, who shifted awkwardly into the dock. After a moment Phillips spoke, his words appearing soft, while his lips remained almost indistinguishable amid a beard of unkempt grey. Only once did his gaze lift from the wooden floor beneath him, in order to plead guilty to theft, having stolen 8lb of meat from a local butcher's.[8]

After a lengthy pause, Cutbush entered the courtroom. Dressed in a linen shirt buttoned to his neck, along with a black jacket and grey trousers, the defendant was ushered to his seat. Keeping his head low, his chin almost resting on his chest, Cutbush took his place at his solicitor's side.

During the previous case, he had sat in the defendant's room, reiterating to his solicitor, George Kirk, that he was not to blame for the stabbings and that another man was the culprit.[9]

Sitting quietly in his seat, Cutbush eyed his solicitor as he prepared his papers while the Prosecutor for the Crown, Mr De Michele, began to speak. Michele asked directly whether the defendant was in a fit state to plead. As Cutbush looked towards his solicitor, gripping the table's edge in front of him, Dr Gilbert of Holloway Prison stood to present his opinion. The prison doctor confirmed that since 14 March Cutbush had been under close observation and during that time he had come to the conclusion that he was practically insane, or at any rate sufficiently so as not to understand the nature of the charge against him. The jury agreed with the findings of Dr Gilbert and instantly found Cutbush insane. As he was deemed 'incompetent', Cutbush was told that he would be held in a lunatic asylum for the remainder of his life.[10]

As a wave of dismay spread throughout the courtroom Cutbush was removed from sight, casting only a glance towards his mother sat amid a sea of spectators, consoled by her sister as she held her head in her hands, unable to look at her son for even a moment.

Reviewing the abortive trial in 1893, KJ and Tracy were amazed by the sudden conclusion of the proceedings, especially in light of the fact that in Prosecutor Mr De Michele's brief and in the instructions of the solicitor who defended Cutbush, they had found the same startling statement: the defendant was suspected of being Jack the Ripper.[11]

However, because the Crown had raised the issue of insanity, any mention of their suspicions would be precluded, only made public three years later by *The Sun*. The treatment of Cutbush, when compared to other criminals charged with similar offences, struck both reporters as odd. John Donkin, a qualified doctor from Northumberland, would serve only three months imprisonment in Newcastle for assaulting a number of women during 1881.

Like Cutbush, Donkin was a man who took pleasure in instilling fear in others and would often boast of his crimes to complete strangers.[12]

Equally, in German-born Charles Ludwig, who in September 1888 was charged at the Thames Police Court for threatening to stab Alexander Finlay in Whitechapel, *The Sun* journalists saw a similarity to Cutbush.

In the early hours of 18 September, Ludwig – who by trade was a baker – had been refused service at a coffee stall on the Whitechapel Road owing to his drunken state. He became highly agitated and attempted to stab Mr Finlay, who was merely standing close by. Ludwig proceeded to chase Finlay around the stall, thrusting at him several times with a 'long bladed knife' until he was arrested by a local constable.

Like Cutbush, Ludwig had a history of accosting women and that morning, while walking through the Minories, had pulled a knife on a prostitute in a secluded courtyard. According to the papers Ludwig was a man of dirty habits who enjoyed frightening people. To the amazement of KJ and Tracy, although Ludwig was clearly a dangerous man who, similarly to Cutbush, owned a knife and had attempted to feloniously wound at least two individuals, for his actions he was remanded in custody for just one week.[13]

The disproportionate treatment of Cutbush staggered both reporters, finding the Crown's wish to send him to Broadmoor an indication that the authorities knew more than they were letting on.

To KJ and Tracy the trial had presented an opportunity for the truth of Cutbush's criminal past to be made public. Aware that both the defence and prosecution had suspicions as to Cutbush's involvement in the Ripper crimes, the journalists were deeply alarmed by the court's decision to remove the suspect to Broadmoor and thus dismiss the opportunity for the true facts to be made clear.

Unlike Charles Ludwig and John Donkin, Cutbush would be detained for the remainder of his life in the most secure asylum in the land, unable to speak out or allow the truth of his previous crimes to be made public. The day after Cutbush's trial, Home Secretary Henry Matthews sent a warrant to the Governor of Holloway Prison, requesting Cutbush's removal to the remote and highly secure Broadmoor, where he was admitted eight days later.

Although the trial had ended, with Cutbush's fate now being determined, the story would continue to intrigue reporters and received much coverage in the press. Interestingly, in many of the newspapers that had covered the trial, such as the *Northampton Mercury* and *The Times*, Cutbush was referred to not as Thomas but by his alias of 'James'. Other journalists would conduct their own interviews with Cutbush's relatives, as well as publishing a statement made by his solicitor in relation to the sudden cessation of the trial.

The *Lloyd's Weekly News* decided to pursue the matter. On 19 April 1891, they demanded a full investigation be undertaken into Cutbush so that justice could be done and the doubts of the public laid to rest. They stated that in 'certain police circles' there was a growing feeling that the case may prove to be connected with the 'darker and more tragic mysteries of the East End'.

The investigation never came. To *The Sun* journalists looking back on this case in January 1894, there was one very obvious course left open to them: they must visit Broadmoor and confront Thomas Cutbush.

EIGHTEEN

Face to Face with 'Jack'

The two reporters travelled the last stage of their journey by cab over rough and muddy roads. Staring into the dense Crowthorne woods as the four-wheeled dogcart ascended a frosted hill, both men sat in silence, quietly contemplating what the coming hours might bring.[1]

Broadmoor, home to the country's most dangerous lunatics, was a handsome, imposing building that sat on the crest of a wooded hill. With its light stone, its trees, its evergreens and flowerbeds, to the approaching journalists the building looked almost pleasant. Almost.

Behind the great iron-studded door and the barred windows of the porter's lodge were 600 men and women, of whom more than 100 had taken the lives of others, often under the most ghastly circumstances.

Dr David Nicholson, Broadmoor's genial Medical Superintendent, greeted the visitors at his house, a charming little villa under the lee of the asylum. For an hour KJ and Tracy took tea overlooking the valley while the doctor filled them in on the highlights of his seventeen years of service among 'the worst ruffians in Great Britain'. Dr Nicholson bore the scars of several assaults and had survived two murder attempts but still spoke kindly of his charges.[2]

The three men then walked to Nicholson's office, where a warder was waiting to tell him that a male patient had developed 'dangerous symptoms' overnight and now required the constant supervision of three attendants as he had threatened to 'do for' a number of individuals, including himself.[3]

From the female ward came the report that 'Tottie Fay' had turned 'maniacal' and had been removed to a padded cell, where there was no furniture to break nor glass to smash.[4]

There were many infamous patients behind Broadmoor's thick walls, including the Reverend Henry John Dodwell, who claimed he'd been unfairly sacked from the chaplaincy. Unfortunately, he tried to bring attention to his case by firing a pistol at a judge and was duly incarcerated.

The case became famous when doctors disagreed over his sanity, leading to debates in the

House of Commons. Not long after the Royal Psychological Society published a pamphlet asking for his release, Dodwell attacked Dr Orange, Broadmoor's Medical Superintendent, by hitting him over the head with a stone concealed in a handkerchief.[5]

Also present in the asylum was William Chester Minor, a schizophrenic American army surgeon who fatally shot George Merrett, whom Minor believed had broken into his room, on 17 February 1872. At the time Merrett had been on his way to work to support his family of six children.

Thanks to his army pension, Minor was able to live a comfortable existence in Broadmoor and would go on to become one of the largest contributors of quotations to the *Oxford English Dictionary*. This happy and productive period would be short-lived as Minor's condition quickly deteriorated.

In 1902 Minor would cut off his own penis and in 1918 he would be diagnosed with 'dementia praecox, of the paranoid form' He would die in 1920 having been deported to America.[6]

Security at Broadmoor had been tightened after the 1888 escape of wife-murderer James Kelly, who made duplicate sets of keys and vanished. Kelly reappeared in 1927 when he presented himself at Broadmoor's main gate, asking to be readmitted. Old and profoundly deaf, Kelly knew he'd be looked after and sure enough they let him in.[7]

KJ and Tracy explained to Dr Nicholson why they were there and what they needed from him. Nicholson's initial surprise was tempered when, after consideration, he came to think that perhaps their claim was not so fantastic after all.

He fetched a large brown envelope which contained all of the documents relative to the patient of interest. After allowing the reporters the chance to peruse the documents, Dr Nicholson then took his guests on a journey through Broadmoor, starting with the kitchen in the women's wing, which contained 200 patients.

Tracy would later remark that it seemed 'impossible to associate with these women the frightful deeds to which they owed a lifelong detention'. This was with good reason. The vast majority weren't criminals in the normal sense at all. As the reporters would learn many of Broadmoor's female patients had killed their own children as result of post-natal depression

Susannah Bradley was one such patient, who on leaving her home one day walked to a nearby canal and on reaching the bank leapt into the cold waters with her baby in her arms. A boatman rushed to their aid and though Susannah was still alive, for her infant son it was too late.

It was later discovered that Susannah had written a suicide note to her husband in which she claimed that she was an unfit mother. On a judges ruling she was sent to Broadmoor and would remain there for several years until being released into the care of her husband.[9]

As KJ and Tracy passed the kitchen, they noted that dinner consisted of 'Roast pork, pease pudding, potatoes, vegetables and tapioca pudding' and that each of 'the poor creatures was allowed half a pint of mild beer with the meal if she desired it, though the attendants endeavour to encourage them towards total abstinence'. Their spirits lifted at the sight of the female kitchen and wards, which were 'pleasant and cheery' and well lit by the sun through generous windows.

'The plan of the buildings,' wrote Tracy on 16 February 1891, 'consisting, simply speaking, in each block, of a wide longitudinal corridor, with bedrooms or general apartments running out of it, gave ample facilities for the diffusion of light and heat, and the otherwise unfortunate inmates were certainly made quite as comfortable as circumstances permitted.' The journalists were also surprised to observe that the women were allowed to walk the corridors and pass unescorted between floors on their way to the recreation room or library, or to their private apartments.

The female wing of Broadmoor did much to confound the stereotypes associated with Victorian lunatic asylums. Dr Nicholson only restricted the freedom of those individuals who had proven more than once that they were driven uncontrollably to commit violence.

As Nicholson guided them through, KJ and Tracy tried to hide their nervousness as some of the patients shrieked as they passed, while others answered Nicholson quietly when he enquired after their health. There were other patients who displayed typical symptoms of the mentally ill, gazing unresponsively as if staring at a fixed point in space, invisible to anyone but them.

The larger male wing of Broadmoor was quite different. 'It was at once clear that the tidiness and generally homelike air of the place had disappeared,' wrote Tracy. Although the wards were spotlessly clean, the comfort and warmth of the female section was no longer present. The warders took on a more severe appearance, some carrying batons, while the patients were dressed in drab uniforms.

Dr Nicholson seemed on the best of terms with most of them. Many shared a pleasant word with him as they passed, and one man laughed heartily as he showed Nicholson a local newspaper, which had written an article about the asylum but had got many of its facts wrong.

KJ commented that the inmates seemed quite harmless, and many of them behaved as though they were perfectly sane. 'Once the trait of homicidal insanity has exhibited itself it is impossible to know the moment when it may recur in violent and unexpected form,' Dr Nicholson replied. 'The most dangerous lunatics are those who believe that some person or persons – vaguely alluded to as "they" – are seeking to do them harm.' Such was the case with the man they were about to visit.

As they progressed deeper into the asylum, the journalists passed through strong iron gates and were joined by an extra force of warders. Soon they stood at the iron door to Block One, home to the fifty most dangerous men in Britain, to be brought face-to-face with the man whom they had travelled for six hours to interview.

Tracy wrote:

'Perhaps we were depressed by the morbid surroundings, added to a hypersensitive appreciation of the strange, wild, devilish personality of the man we were about to see. Whatever the feeling, there can be no doubt that some of the brightness had gone from the sunlight, some of the purity from the air, as we looked out through a grated window into a spacious courtyard of asphalt; bounded on two sides by a high wall, and on the others by the tall buildings which shut out the now declining rays of the January sun.'

The male patients were taking exercise in a cold and dreary enclosed space; most were simply loitering, but on peering through the grated window, one particular patient caught their eye. 'There he is!' the chief warder said, pointing to a stooped figure who was as far removed from the others as it was possible to be, his cap pulled over his brow. 'Bring him here,' Dr Nicholson said to one of the warders.

Tracy later recalled the madman's face as 'animal', 'unconscious of life, care, or hope'. As his startling blue eyes caught the January sun, Tracy saw no soul behind those windows, writing that 'in such a man all actions were possible, that it was as simple to put a knife upon a human throat as upon a piece of tobacco'. These were, the two men now fully believed, the eyes that had witnessed the dying throes of at least seven women in Whitechapel.

As Cutbush approached with his guard beside him, Dr Nicholson broke the spell. Putting on a cheery tone, he asked: 'Well, my man, how are you?' Cutbush said nothing. Instead, he yanked his shirt open and bared his chest, as if he were about to undergo a medical examination.

'Yes, yes, that's all right,' Dr Nicholson said. 'You are comfortable here?'

Silence.

'Would you tell these gentlemen how you are getting on?'

It was useless. They would never hear the distinctive voice once heard by George Dixon.

147

'As we gazed at him we wondered whether awful visions of the past did not at times flit across his brain and twinge with horror that impassive face – visions of squalid, ill-lighted streets and alleys, with draggle-haired women, of whispered consultations, of sudden stabbing and hacking at palpitating bodies, of hair breadth escapes from capture, and mad races for life through the darkness and gloom of London.'

Cutbush fastened his shirt and made to go. As he did so, a warder reached towards him to escort him back. His hand flew up, blocking his arm, before doing 'a strange thing. He grasped his throat with his left hand, threw back his head, and placed his right hand at the base of the skull.'

The meaning behind Cutbush's actions was unknown to Dr Nicholson or to the warders present. Rather than reacting to the demonstration Nicholson simply informed the journalists that Cutbush was no longer verbally communicative and was in the 'final and most troublesome stage of lunacy'.

Within a matter of seconds Cutbush was led back outside into the open air where he immediately took up his position by the deserted wall.

The journalists, profoundly disturbed by their visit, hurried back to London, determined after many months of investigation to lay their case before the world. Upon their return to London, however, KJ and Tracy soon discovered that their scoop, one they believed would save the ailing newspaper and in turn their livelihoods, was about to be ripped from their grasp.[10]

NINETEEN

Stealing the Scoop

12 February 1894
Tudor Street, City of London

Avoiding the sudden downpour, KJ and Tracy tumbled into the cab
parked at the corner of Tudor Street, having sprinted from *The Sun*'s
offices. Paying the driver enough to enable a speedy journey, by 7 p.m.
the two reporters arrived at Westminster. Although they knew that T.
P. O'Connor (now an MP) was attending a parliamentary meeting at
the House of Commons and that to disturb him would be less than
well received, the journalists were aware that their editor needed to
hear the news.

While the information pertaining to Thomas Cutbush had been in
the possession of *The Sun* for many months, on the afternoon of 12
February, KJ had learnt that within *The Sun*'s offices there was a mole.

As the reporters discovered, both *The Morning* and another rival
newspaper had been offered a portion of their story from a member of
staff, no doubt with the promise of hefty financial gain. On hearing
the news KJ and Tracy were devastated. Although they had worked
diligently for months collating information, conducting interviews and
undergoing painstaking research in order to present the identity of the
Ripper to the world, as both men knew, their findings would mean
nothing if they were not the first to present them to the public.

While *The Morning* stated that they would respect *The Sun's* exclusive, the second newspaper (unnamed by *The Sun*) wished to take their find to print. With no plans to publish their story for two weeks, KJ and Tracy were now faced with the challenge of their careers. If they were going to beat their rival and be the first to publish their findings, then they would need to go to print sooner than anyone had anticipated.

Unflinching in the face of such a mammoth task, T. P. O'Connor accepted the news with his trademark calm. Explaining to his two journalists that if they were to retain the scoop of the century and save their newspaper, they would need to pull every resource they had and, for one day only, change their method of working. As O'Connor would later explain, 'There was consequently nothing for it but to stop up all night and bring out *The Sun* as a morning paper at five o'clock instead of an evening paper at the usual hour.'

In the great tradition of newspaper editors who ask much of their employees, O'Connor at once hailed a cab and returned to Tudor Street and on arrival, gathered his men. In the space of an hour an editorial team was assembled, with word being spread to all staff members that they would be working through the night.

'Our staff – editorial, compositors, machine men and cart men – were summoned,' recalled

T. P. O'Connor. 'We all stayed through the watches of the night in consultation and in preparing the matter for publication; and day had already broken before any of us were able to start for our homes.'

Next morning the story of Thomas Cutbush finally hit the newsstands.

From the outset KJ and Tracy wanted to make clear in their articles that in Cutbush they had found a man who fitted the profile of the Ripper in every conceivable way. Keen to address a question that, for three years, had dogged the Ripper investigation, KJ explained why the murders had suddenly ceased in the February of 1891.

While some theorists believed that the logical reason for the cessation of the murders was the killer's death, KJ wished to explore another possibility, writing that to his mind the murderer only stopped killing because of an inability, physically, to kill. If the Ripper no longer roamed the backstreets of Whitechapel stalking his victims, then it followed that there would be no more murders.

'A homicidal lunatic may sometimes try his hand at murder without success,' wrote KJ on 13 February, 'inflicting, perhaps, only a wound – sometimes only causing a fright, and, caught in these comparatively minor offences and being unmistakably a lunatic, may thus be locked away, without noise, without attracting attention, without even a paragraph in the newspapers.' To *The Sun* reporters, Cutbush was seen in a similar vein to another of history's killers: Charles Peace, a criminal who, although being arrested on a charge of burglary, was in fact a murderer. Like Cutbush, the killings obviously ceased after his confinement.

Over the course of a week *The Sun* explored Cutbush's character, showing that he exhibited the cunning and simplicity attributed only to true madness, describing him as a 'poor simple creature who while under the watchful gaze of his jailers would deny his charges, though at the same time plotting his escape'.

On 17 February, Tracy would write that 'clues, elusive and slight' had been followed up. That 'witness after witness had been examined, with every line of evidence having been sifted, weighed and collated'. From the outset, *The Sun* wished to explore their evidence and use their incredible witness testimonies as a way to show the world the true psyche of a killer.

One of their first interviews had been with a former lodger of Albert Street, a man named by *The Sun* only by the initials 'H. L.' and who had known Cutbush for some time. The report on 17 February 1894 carried his story. 'H. L.' confirmed that Cutbush was an idle, dissolute young man. He had actually been present in the house when Cutbush attempted to slit his mother's throat, and believed categorically that the police thought Cutbush was in fact the Ripper.

Others who had stayed in Albert Street had similar recollections, stating that Cutbush was a curious fellow who led an eccentric life, and they recalled his strange habit of walking the streets, as well as his love of anatomy.

Another lodger, named as 'S. K.', thought Cutbush to be dirty in his habits and mind and, on being questioned by Kennedy Jones, stated how repulsed he was by Cutbush's desire to associate with prostitutes. 'His appearance suggested filthy habits,' said 'S. K.', before reiterating the testimonies of others: that the police had great suspicions that the young man living in the attic room was the Ripper.

Neighbours had also been interviewed throughout 1893 and added to the picture of a man of weak mind. His slender figure was observed by them on numerous occasions, scaling the back wall of 14 Albert Street in the early hours of the morning, skulking through the rear garden before disappearing into the house, often appearing dazed.

As Tracy explained in the second of *The Sun*'s articles, in appearance Cutbush was distinctive: tall and of slight stature, he walked with a stoop, as if troubled by a weak chest. His face was narrow, with a high forehead, and as Tracy recalled, he had 'large dark eyes'.

On detailing his visit to Broadmoor, Tracy wrote of the expression on Cutbush's face as he sat opposite, having the look of a hunted beast, 'his nose prominent, his lips full and his jaw signifying much power'. From Cutbush's career working in the tea trade in the East End to his eventual dismissal for the assault on an elderly colleague, the reporters provided an in-depth exploration of their suspect, as well as illustrating the lengthy feud with Dr Brooks.

In order to show Cutbush's state of mind, on 13 February, *The Sun* published a transcript of a letter found in his room. It showed a growing paranoia that the doctor had poisoned him, after a recent visit to his surgery:

'He told me that I need not trouble, as there was nothing the matter with me,' wrote Cutbush in a peculiar sloping backhand, 'and he gave me a bottle of mixture. I thought no more of the matter until a day or so afterwards, when I came on very ill. All the nerves and bones in my head seemed dropping to pieces.'

The paper laid out the story of Cutbush's terrible anxiety and fear as red irritant patches came upon his face, accompanied by burning pains down his left side. Soon after, such was his belief that Dr Brooks was poisoning him that's his thought turned to the doctor's murder.

Then came the findings of Inspector Race in which he explained that the discovery of the drawings in Cutbush's pockets, as well as those that had adorned his bedroom floor: pictures of mutilated women lying on their backs with their abdomens ripped open, reminiscent of the Ripper's victims, along with the medical books that filled the wooden desk of his sparsely furnished room.

Race provided the journalists with a facsimile of the knife, described as of a Bowie design, six inches in length, with the blade tapering at the point. It bore the name of the firm based in the Minories. Intrigued by the fact that Cutbush had stuffed blood-stained clothes up his chimney, Race was keen to relay his findings to the reporters, believing that only one reason could exist for such actions.

Over the course of the week, *The Sun* illustrated that in Cutbush was a man possessed of so many traits of the Ripper: that he was able to make off at great speed and, like the Whitechapel killer, was so fleet of foot as to evade detection. Taking great pains to show the care with which they had gone about their investigations, KJ wrote of the great scrutiny to which the facts had been subjected, and the months of work dedicated to the enquiry.

Although Florence Johnson hadn't wished to talk to Tracy, her father had agreed to offer a brief testimony based on his daughter's account. He said that after the attack he had written to the police, expressing his concerns and his belief that the knife found on Cutbush matched that used by the Ripper. He also saw another similarity to the Whitechapel killer, stressing in his communication that, like the Ripper, Cutbush attacked from behind and was 'catlike in approach', stalking his victims unheard and unobserved.

The Sun covered Cutbush's murderous attack on his mother, his midnight walks, his knowledge of Whitechapel and importantly, his knives, painting a clear image of their suspect as a strange and violent individual.

When it came to recounting Clara Hayne's testimony, Louis Tracy evidently felt a debt to his source and the piece was most respectful.

Writing on 14 February that Clara, along with her sister, had tended to Cutbush, nursed him, watched for him, borne with him with a patience that never tired, with a love that never waned. While he has been out through the watches of the night on his fiendish work, one of them has sat up, waiting anxiously for his return – frightened at every noise – apprehensive of every possible form of mishap; in imagination picturing this tiger who marched from crime to crime as some innocent, harmless, and helpless child in need of protection. As she had done two years earlier, in 1893 Clara Hayne provided a wealth of information on her nephew. While relaying accounts of his strange behaviour, she spoke openly of Cutbush's violent nature, stating that he had attacked a servant with a knife as well as viciously assaulting a prostitute sometime prior to the commencement of the Ripper murders.

Clara also provided what KJ and Tracy saw as an answer to one of the biggest mysteries of the Ripper investigation. As the police were aware, from almost every one of his victims the Ripper had taken trophies. What baffled the officers on the ground, as well as senior officials working on the case, was where the killer would have kept them.

In 1893, Clara offered up a clue. During an interview with KJ, she informed the reporter that in the rear garden of 14 Albert Street stood a brick outhouse, a place used solely by Cutbush. Kate had entered it once and though never enlightening her sister as to what she had discovered inside, on the day of her son's arrest she arranged for it to be pulled down and destroyed, with the rubble removed immediately, leaving no trace of what once stood in its place.

As for Cutbush's motive, KJ and Tracy were clear that their suspect had committed the murders while suffering from a form of 'mania' brought on either from the deterioration of his mind or a consequence of syphilis. Tracy would write that, for some, the belief of having contracted the disease is sometimes enough to turn men to murder and, in Cutbush's case, spur them on to take revenge on the very class of women accused of spreading the disease. Above all, the reporters looked upon Cutbush as a lunatic, a criminal who exhibited little fear or moral guilt for his actions.

The reporters were convinced that Cutbush was the Ripper. In their minds he *must* have been the elusive killer, who had evaded the police for three years: 'In bed most of the day,' Tracy wrote, 'out most of the night, engaged exclusively in the study of anatomy and the drawing of mutilated women – is not that exactly the picture one would form of the type of lunatic who would commit the Whitechapel murders? When it is added that, altogether outside the Whitechapel horrors, the creature who so lives has committed other homicidal offences, the case becomes irresistible.'

By mid-February the series of articles had run its course. The reaction, when it came, was extraordinary.[1]

TWENTY

The Floodgates Open

T.P. O'Connor expressed surprise at the reaction the articles provoked. Whether through faux naivety or an underestimation of the power of the revelation, *The Sun* was inundated with sacks of letters from readers, some wishing to congratulate them on their find, as well as others from those who knew or had encountered Thomas Cutbush prior to 1891.

One of the first letters received at *The Sun*'s office was from a gentleman who had been accosted by Cutbush in Camden at 10.30 p.m. on the night of his escape from Lambeth. The man explained that for his own safety he wished not to be identified by the papers.

The Sun respected his wishes and on 15 March published his remarkable tale. The man and his young fiancée had just disembarked from a train at Camden Road and were hurrying homewards close to Camden Street when a figure came at them from the darkness of a ruined building.

He was tall, thin and slightly stooped. He looked cold, the young man thought, and as he drew closer, he saw that the stranger's collar was turned up, while his hat was pulled low over his face. He noted the extraordinary blue eyes, which shone in the lamplight.

Speaking hurriedly, Cutbush pleaded with the couple to hide him as 'the runners were after him', before claiming that he was a medical man and innocent of all charges laid against him. Continuing, he claimed that there was a £500 reward for his capture. As the writer recalled, Cutbush had said that 'they' had forcibly put him in a room but he'd escaped. If returned, he said, the doctors would certify him as mad and send him to an asylum, where he would be murdered. He admitted to being wanted on a 'grave and serious charge' and, on seeing a coming cab clattering along the road, Cutbush suddenly stepped back into the shadows and cried: 'Here they come!' After the carriage passed, he continued: 'You must know that they say I am Jack the Ripper – but I am not, though all their insides are open and their bowels are all out.'

He was clearly delusional, the young man thought, but because of his polite manner and clothing, took him to be a gentleman. 'I am a medical man, you know,' Cutbush continued, 'but not Jack the Ripper – you must not think I am. But they do … I have only been cutting up girls and laying them out.'

Cutbush gave the address of his mother and aunt and implored the man to write to them on his behalf and explain everything. After the couple said they were unable to help, he grew agitated. 'Then show me the way to the fields – where I shall be safe!' he said. The gentleman immediately directed Cutbush to Hampstead, after which he vanished from sight.

A man of his word, the gentleman wrote to Clara and Kate informing them of their nephew's whereabouts and that in his opinion Cutbush was suffering from delusions.[1]

Others who had come across Cutbush in the years prior to *The Sun*'s publication were equally keen to come forward. Such as Mr Crotty, the shopkeeper who eagerly recalled his strange conversations with Cutbush; that he would talk of the ease with which murder can be achieved and recalling that he often appeared excitable and talked endlessly of medicine and chemistry.

Then came the story of Mr T. J., who for a time had shared his home in Ramsgate with the unstable Cutbush. In *The Sun* article of 19 February, Crotty spoke openly that Cutbush had convinced both him and his wife that he was a doctor, that he often roamed the streets at night and had informed his wife that he 'had done something to a woman' and she would not live.[2]

On seeing the sensation caused by *The Sun*'s claims, other newspapers were keen to get involved in the story. The *Morning Leader* was one of the first and by the afternoon of 13 February (the day of the first *Sun* article), they had successfully secured an interview with

Inspector Race, keen to learn more about his involvement in the Cutbush affair.[3]

While working on the Whitechapel case, Race became fascinated by the identity of the killer. He acquired dates, clues and theories against Cutbush, as well as getting hold of his knife, which he submitted to Scotland Yard for inspection. Race also illuminated the reporter working for the *Morning Leader* that for his efforts he was awarded a bonus from his superiors.

As he commented, however, he didn't 'rest satisfied' with the offer of money. What he wished for was a full investigation in order to prove Cutbush was the killer and for the Ripper finally to be brought to justice for his crimes. The *Morning Leader* also reported that, although Cutbush was in Broadmoor and his mind lost to madness, his conversation and confessions related solely to the Ripper murders. After informing the reporter that very little had been done with his findings, when asked how he hoped to secure the conviction of Thomas Cutbush with respect to the Ripper's crimes,

Race's answer was immediate: 'Only with the aid of the press can I hope to succeed.'[4]

He was in luck; with the publication of *The Sun* and the *Morning Leader* came a whirlwind of media hysteria, with almost every major newspaper covering the story, some providing verbatim accounts of Race's sensational interview, while others chose to use *The Sun* as their primary source.

In the days that followed the publication of *The Sun*'s first article on 13 February 1894, it appeared the world suddenly woke up to the idea that the Ripper had been identified. Everyone, it appeared, had an opinion when it came to unmasking the true identity of Jack the Ripper. One particular man, whom KJ and Tracy were keen to interview, was the MP Henry Labouchere. A man not only connected to the Cutbush case, in that Thomas had previously written to him, but who had also expressed a great interest in the Ripper investigation.

Labouchere had previously provided his opinion on the case in an interview with the *Dundee Courier* in the summer of 1889, shortly after receiving the correspondence from Cutbush. What KJ and Tracy found fascinating, and ultimately furnished their reason for wishing to interview Labouchere themselves, was that when the MP came to explain the type of man most likely to be Jack the Ripper, he described, almost perfectly,

Thomas Cutbush.

In the article published on 19 July 1889, Labouchere suggests that the Ripper was a man who lived at a distance to Whitechapel and that he must have 'some hiding place in which to conceal his clothes'. Garments like those found hidden in the chimney breast of Cutbush's room in 1891 that could 'hardly escape bloodstains'. On the subject of madness Labouchere deduced, with his inimitable smile, that the killer was 'conspicuously sane'. After referring to the police investigation as 'bungled', he wished to state his belief that the killer's taste for murder developed as a result of the killing of Mary Nichols, after which time, as the MP stated, he simply 'went on'.[5]

To their surprise, on the seventh day of publication, KJ and Tracy scored a coup when Labouchere agreed to be interviewed. In his interview, reported in *The Sun* on 19 February, Labouchere was quoted as saying that 'the Broadmoor lunatic may have been Jack', with the MP concluding that in his opinion the Ripper would have been the same sort of man as Cutbush.

Much to the satisfaction of *The Sun* reporters, Labouchere had been greatly interested by their articles and though emphatically unwilling to support their theory, commented that they had made out a fair case for public investigation. This is something that in *The Sun*'s final instalment KJ and Tracy had been keen to reiterate, concluding with their wish that the Cutbush story be subjected to a thorough police investigation.

Before finishing his brief yet enlightening interview, Labouchere made one final comment. While puffing on his cigarette, the MP leant towards the reporters and with a determined tone, gave a last piece of advice: 'If I were Mr Asquith, I should elect a clever officer to look into the matter.'[6]

But Home Secretary Herbert Asquith did not, and the police remained silent.

TWENTY-ONE

A Misleading Memo

While the paper was inundated with calls for an investigation from the public and secured the backing of an influential coterie of MPs, the Yard responded with silence, a tradition long maintained in their dealings with the press.

Questioned by journalists working for the *Western Mail*, three days after his interview with the *Morning Leader*, Race appeared guarded, stating that: 'I must be careful in expressing an opinion,'[1] aware that by speaking out he would, or possibly already had, displeased his superiors.

The Inspector had no idea how much. William Race was a first-class officer with scores of arrests to his name. His investigations had proved popular with the press and often featured in the newspapers, yet after the Cutbush affair his career nosedived.

Frustrations with the job led to ill health and depression. The promotion he had expected never came and instead Race would be invalided out of the force on a small pension on 1 April 1898 at the age of forty-three, after eighteen years of service.[2]

The police investigation into Cutbush for which Race had fought for up until leaving the force in 1898 never came. In response to *The Sun*'s investigation, Chief Constable Sir Melville Macnaghten produced a memo for Chief Commissioner Sir Edward Bradford (no doubt in case *The Sun*'s story generated inquiries from the Home Office), stating that Cutbush was not a viable suspect. He listed the names of three other men whom he considered were more likely to have been the Ripper.

And there the Cutbush story would have ended– save for one amazing development some sixty years later.

In 1959, while researching the Ripper case, TV journalist Daniel Farson was interviewing Lady Christabel Aberconway, the daughter of former Chief Constable Sir Melville Macnaghten. During the course of the interview she mentioned that she had transcripts of her father's notes relating to the Whitechapel murders, papers that had never previously been made public.[3]

These notes turned out to be one of the most important Ripper-related documents ever discovered. In his report, Macnaghten had named three men as more likely suspects than Thomas Cutbush. The first name presented was that of Mr M. J. Druitt, whom Macnaghten referred to, incorrectly, as a doctor. Druitt was said to have disappeared after the murder of Mary Kelly in November 1888 and a month later was discovered floating in the Thames by a waterman.

At the time of writing his memorandum, Macnaghten believed Druitt to have been 'sexually insane' and (allegedly) believed to have been the killer by his own family. In reality, Mr Druitt was a tragic young man, real name Montague, who taught at a boys' boarding school in Blackheath and who studied law.

Believing that he was suffering from the hereditary mental disorder that had affected his mother (who in the July of 1888 was admitted into an asylum), Druitt decided to take his own life. After his body was found, a suicide note was also discovered within his chambers; it confirmed that the young teacher had believed he was going mad like his mother, and that the best thing was for him to die.

Druitt never demonstrated any signs of violence towards anyone. He was never known to associate with prostitutes or indeed to show hatred towards women in any way. In 1888 his life began to spiral out of control, initially with his mother's admittance into an asylum and then with his dismissal from his teaching position in the November, due to him having been in what the papers referred to as 'serious trouble'.

Such an expression possibly indicates that Druitt had become involved, sexually, with one of his pupils, a suggestion which is supported by Macnaghten's claim that he was 'sexually insane', a naive term used in the Victorian era when referring to homosexuality. Druitt believed he was going mad and, with his career now in tatters due to the nature of his dismissal, he simply gave up on life.

No evidence exists that links Druitt to the Ripper crimes, yet Macnaghten seems somewhat impelled to convince his readers that he was a more likely suspect than Cutbush. The Chief Constable went on to state, without any supporting evidence, that the Ripper's mind gave way after the 'glut' in Miller's Court, after which he immediately committed suicide.[4]

The second individual mentioned in Macnaghten's memorandum was a man named Kosminski, referred to as a Polish Jew living in the area of Whitechapel. He, according to Macnaghten, became insane through years of indulgence in solitary vices, meaning masturbation. Kosminski allegedly had a hatred of women, specifically prostitutes. He was removed to an asylum and according to Macnaghten was a 'strong suspect'.

The full name of this second suspect was Aaron Kosminski, a man who ended his days confined within Leavesden Asylum after being transferred there from Colney Hatch in 1891. Kosminski was a vagrant, driven to the streets of London by the voices in his head. Refusing to work, he would often be found eating from the gutters and chose never to wash.

Unlike the Ripper, Kosminski was a feeble man of unsound mind, who exhibited only mild violent tendencies: on one occasion he threatened his sister with a knife and on another, an incident which occurred during his confinement, he threatened an attendant with a chair. These, however, were his only known outbursts and he was generally described as harmless by those who knew him.

Without any clear evidence in his possession, Macnaghten reiterates the point: a second named suspect, a weak, malnourished man who by the time of the murders had lost his grip on reality and who in 1894 was safely under lock and key in Leavesden Asylum, was more likely than Cutbush to have been the Ripper.[5]

Many of the officers involved in the Ripper investigation held different beliefs as to the killer's identity, though the idea that the murderer was a foreigner appeared to find favour with several of the key players in the investigation. Attaching blame to an Englishman seems to have been something that, from the start of the investigation, the police and indeed the press were less than willing to countenance.

When the Ripper first struck it was the Swiss and Polish Jews who were initially blamed by the press and,[6] as the months and years passed, the focus shifted onto Italians,[7] Americans[8] and even Norwegians.[9]

Kosminski appears to have been a strange individual who was known to the police and to some fit the mould of what a serial killer was. What is certain, however, is that the police were attaching blame without having acquired conclusive evidence to indicate why.

Chief Inspector Swanson, another of Macnaghten's colleagues, also held suspicions in relation to Kosminski, though the extent of his knowledge appears limited. Swanson claimed with some certainty that Kosminski was the Ripper and that he was sent to Colney Hatch Asylum, where he died shortly after being admitted. In actual fact, Aaron Kosminski was sent from Colney Hatch to Leavesden Asylum in 1894 and lived on a for total of twenty-five years.[10]

In naming Kosminski in his memorandum, Macnaghten appears to have chosen the preferred suspect of his colleague Chief Inspector Swanson. Picking a man who, for some, appeared to fit the bill. Macnaghten provided only the barest of facts in relation to Kosminski and proved unconvincing in his attempts to suggest that the weak-minded Pole was more likely than Cutbush to have been the killer.

A study of the report reveals Macnaghten's desire to cast blame onto men for whom being labelled a killer would then cause little stir or unwanted attention. Druitt was dead and Kosminski safely confined in an asylum. In choosing his third suspect, it appears that Macnaghten was simply plucking a name from the air, that of a man who, though at times demonstrated violence, could not rationally be considered capable of anything on the scale of the Ripper's crimes.

Michael Ostrog, like Kosminski, was a foreigner. He hailed from Russia and in 1888 was fifty-five years old. He claimed that he had worked as a surgeon in the Russian Navy and on occasion used an assortment of aliases. Ostrog was in essence nothing more than a con artist and a thief, who spent much time travelling around Britain stealing from colleges in Oxford and Eton.

Ostrog's one act of violence came in 1873 when he pulled a pistol on a police officer; aside from that, it is wholly unclear as to why Macnaghten should mention him at all.[11] Astonishingly, there is every indication that Michael Ostrog was incarcerated in France at the time of the Ripper murders, for what was described as a petty crime, and is therefore completely exonerated from involvement in the Whitechapel murders case.[12]

Looking back, it seems clear that historians owe a debt of gratitude to William Race for going to *The Sun*. Without him, there would have been no Macnaghten report, and without the report there would have been no Kosminski, Druitt or Ostrog– whose names, though carrying little weight as suspects, reawakened the interest of researchers across the world, an interest that has continued to the present day.

For an inspector to go the press was extraordinary. Race was normally a sober and dedicated officer and taking such a step was an outright betrayal of the profession. In order to have risked his career, one he loved dearly, he must have been utterly convinced that the man he arrested on the morning of 9 March 1891 was the Ripper.

Race's concerns and risks were ill served by the flawed Macnaghten report, finding the Chief Constable steadfast in his defence of Cutbush. One of Macnaghten's final observations in his report was that Thomas Cutbush was actually the nephew of Executive Superintendent Charles Henry Cutbush,[13] an officer responsible for the policing of Whitechapel's lodging houses and in 1888 actively involved in the hunt for the Ripper. He was even based in the same building as Inspector Abberline.

What Melville Macnaghten hadn't known at the time of the memo was the fact that Charles Cutbush was suffering from intense depression and paranoid delusions, similar to those exhibited by Thomas.

To the shock of all who knew him, two years after the memorandum was written, Charles Cutbush committed suicide, shooting himself in the head in the presence of his young daughter at his home in Stockwell.

TWENTY-TWO

Twists of Fate

In the August of 1891, only four months after Thomas Cutbush was admitted as a patient to Broadmoor Asylum, the impressive career of Charles Cutbush came to an unexpected and abrupt end.

For Charles, becoming a police officer was a lifetime's ambition which, at the age of twenty-three, he eventually realised. During the winter of 1867 Cutbush joined the Metropolitan Police Force and was posted to A Division's King Street Station, where he patrolled the area of Whitehall.[1]

Within a matter of months, Charles was successfully appointed to the position of Assistant Clerk to Chief Superintendent Walker and by 1871 assumed full charge of the divisional office. It was there that he carved out a reputation for being a superior officer and a 'very excellent detective'.[2]

Considered a natural leader, Charles was soon offered a swift promotion to sergeant and in no time was presented with the opportunity of further progression. Impressively only six years after first lacing up his police boots Charles Cutbush achieved the rank of inspector.[3]

During a year of change that saw the Metropolitan Police acquire nine new police stations within their jurisdiction,[4] as well as introducing lighting into many of their cells,[5] Charles decided to broaden his horizons. By the December of 1873 he bade farewell to Whitehall and transferred to St James's Division, taking up a spacious office in Little Vine Street.[6]

Under the direction of Superintendent J. H. Dunlop, in his new role of inspector, Charles actively looked to suppress the 'notorious' activities occurring in the lodging houses of nearby Panton Street, which at that time were being used as brothels.

In an attempt to improve the reputation of the lodging houses the establishments became police regulated, with every room being inspected for cleanliness and space before being allocated a set number of beds for which they were then licensed. In an effort to tackle disease an order was passed that fresh linen was to be used on a weekly basis, as well as establishing improved ventilation.

To avoid the lodging houses being used for immoral purposes a high proportion were categorised as single sex, with only a small number allowing unmarried men and women to sleep under the same roof. For those couples who were married a number of tiny rooms were provided, partitioned off from the remainder of the house.[7]

In the role of inspector Charles proved popular among his colleagues and would later be referred to by *The Morning Post* as 'one of the best known heads of police'. While garnering the respect of all who knew him, in no time his talents caught the eye of the then Secretary of State, who would go on to commend him for what was vaguely described as 'services rendered'.

Although the move to Vine Street found Charles taking on a more administrative role, throughout his first years there his abilities as a detective would often be called upon. In February of 1875 his name appeared in numerous articles in connection with the death of 63-year-old widow Mary Young, who was discovered lying on the floor of her apartment in Leicester Square surrounded by a pool of blood, her neck having been slashed with a large table knife.

In an excellent piece of quick detection, Charles Cutbush determined that, far from being the gruesome murder it appeared at first blush, Mrs Young's death was in fact suicide. On the evening of 9 February, a verdict was given that she had 'destroyed her own life while in a state of temporary insanity'.[8]

When in 1876 Colonel Labalmondière, the then Assistant

Commissioner, offered Charles a move to Scotland Yard he eagerly accepted and immediately arranged for the contents of his office to be moved. As principal assistant to Superintendent Harris, Charles worked within the Executive Department, controlling police personnel engaged in duty as well as the continued regulation of lodging houses.

Other administrative duties included the dissemination of ambulances to divisional police stations, replacing the ancient wooden stretchers with the more practical wheeled carriage, invented by Herr Neuss, that offered a more viable solution to the conveyance of bodies.[9]

Three years after his move to Scotland Yard, Charles was promoted once again, filling the vacancy left by Harris in 1879.[10] While his career flourished, beyond the offices of Scotland Yard, his personal life was equally successful. After marrying the loving Ann, the pair had six children and eventually settled at 3 Burnley Road in Stockwell, a large family home that was big enough to accommodate his children and servants, as well as his elderly mother, Amelia.[11]

Like many of the men in the Cutbush family Charles cut a dashing figure, being tall and of a slender frame and always smartly attired, both in and out of the station. Only once during his career did Charles ever contemplate leaving the Metropolitan Police, when he applied for the post of Chief Constable for Birmingham.

Such was his reputation that from ninety applicants he successfully made the final five and although ultimately losing out to Joseph Farndale, the former Chief Constable of Leicester Constabulary, Charles remained happy in his work.[12]

As Charles discovered, the role of superintendent offered far more variety than any previous position. For example, in 1882 he was asked to organise a summer fête in benefit of the Twickenham Police Orphanage. Charles had approached the matter with his trademark enthusiasm. As reported by *Reynolds Newspaper* the event, held at Alexandra Palace, was enjoyed by many thousands and considered a great success despite poor weather.[13]

Six years later, Charles found that working at Scotland Yard provided more than its fair share of new challenges. Like so many of his colleagues, during the autumn of 1888, Charles too became embroiled in the hunt for Jack the Ripper. Among the surviving police files are several reports which bear the name 'C. H. Cutbush, Supt.', addressed to H Division and relating to the identification of those victims thought to have been murdered by the elusive killer.[14]

Working in the same offices as Inspector Abberline, who had direct control over the Ripper investigation, Charles acquired a sound knowledge of the police efforts at the time of the murders, as well as sharing the anxiety felt by all at Scotland Yard as the Ripper continued to evade capture.

Beyond work and family, the most important aspect of life for Charles was religion. Although a driven worker he would always make sure there was time for the church and kept a bible close at hand alongside his service revolver in the top drawer of his desk.[15]

By the time the Ripper investigation came to an end in 1891, Charles had changed dramatically. Unbeknownst to his colleagues, he had become a regular patient at Dr Waite's surgery on Lambeth Road, where he complained of depression as well as increasingly disturbing delusions. As his hallucinations worsened and a growing insomnia started to affect his ability to work, Charles grew deeply concerned about his future at Scotland Yard. After Dr Waite concluded that his patient had an infection of the brain there was no other option but to retire.[16]

By the August of 1891, much to his regret, Charles Cutbush stepped through the doors of Scotland Yard for the last time and said farewell to the profession he had loved so dearly.

As the winter of 1892 approached, his paranoia worsened. He informed his doctor that he was being stalked and that day and night he felt the presence of 'Roman Catholics' following his every move and looking to bring about his ruin.[17]

For Charles, the dawn of 1893 brought an increasing anxiety that ultimately led him to fear for his own life. As a result, Charles chose to arm himself with a leather-bound blackjack, secreted in the pocket of his trousers.

By the time *The Sun* published its findings in 1894, and perhaps as a consequence, Charles's mental health began to decline at an alarming rate. Although Melville Macnaghten would be the first to officially name Charles as Thomas's uncle, Louis Tracy also became aware of the connection and, being conscious of the possible reaction from the public, wrote a short, yet powerful statement in his article of 14 February 1894: 'Jack the Ripper has relatives,' wrote Tracy, 'some of them in positions which would make them a target for the natural curiosity.'

Whether other journalists eventually discovered the links and sought to question Charles is not known. What is certain is that within two years of the publication of *The Sun*'s claims Charles Cutbush had committed suicide.

Such was the tragedy of Charles's end that the family were left devastated. Although to the outside world it appeared that he had taken his life due to a failing mental health, those closest to him believed that there was another, more disturbing, motivation behind his death.

Claire Chevin had been aware of her great grandfather's death ever since her youth. As a young girl, raised in the same house that Charles had called home until his demise, she had learnt a great deal about the circumstances surrounding his suicide.

Whenever she would question relatives as to why Charles should have taken his own life, the same story would be told. That Charles had been the uncle of Thomas Cutbush and that on hearing that suspicion was falling upon his nephew, connecting him to the Jack the Ripper murders, he had fallen into a dark depression. Finding it impossible to cope with the family connection to one of history's most notorious serial killers, on 5 March 1896, Charles took drastic action.

That morning Charles's health had worsened. The family doctor was called and on his arrival at Burnley Road Charles spoke at length about his condition. By mid-afternoon his mood had shown little improvement; he was speaking hardly a word and appeared 'very strange'.

Charles's 25-year-old daughter Helen was present in the house at the time and at 2 p.m. left her father sitting on the sofa in the drawing room. Only as she stepped into the hallway did she hear the gun shot: a single, thunderous blast that would leave her and her family reeling.[18]

By the time Helen reached her father it was too late; finding him lying upon the wooden floor of the drawing room with blood flowing from a bullet wound to his temple, his eyes lifeless as they stared through his distraught daughter, whose screams could be heard two houses away.

Five days later the *Morning Post* carried the results of Coroner George Wyatt's inquiry into Charles's death, that prior to the tragic events of 5 March, the 52-year-old had suffered greatly from depression. On many occasions he had threatened suicide, carrying a revolver in his pocket at all times. The last testimony reported in the article would come from Dr Waite, who confirmed that Charles had appeared excited on the morning of his death.[19]

For Helen Cutbush (known to her relatives as 'Nellie') the shot that had killed her father would ricochet throughout the remainder of her life with damaging consequences.

Deciding to remain in the family home, Helen lived as a spinster in Burnley Road for many years to come. As she grew older her mental health began to deteriorate, finding her becoming increasingly disturbed. For solace Helen would turn to religion but what began as belief soon transformed into an obsession. The bible, engraved with her name, would rarely leave Helen's side and eventually would become a weapon used for self-abuse.[20]

By the mid twentieth century Helen's mental state had worsened to such a degree that she began suffering violent episodes. More than once she assaulted her own family and soon it became known that should any of the young get too close, they were likely to be thrown down the stairs.

By 1950 Helen's behaviour spiralled and she would regularly be heard alone in her room, screaming. With the Cutbush family in a state of despair they decided that only professional assistance could help. Dr Fenton was called and on his arrival at Burnley Road he was to make a quick and decisive assessment. The doctor concluded that for the safety of all parties Helen needed to be removed. Placed in a waiting car, she was swiftly transported from Lambeth and driven 14 miles to Surrey where she was placed in a local asylum. Like Thomas Cutbush she would never leave, remaining a patient until her death in September 1957.[21]

As for Helen's late father, Supt Charles Henry Cutbush, one can only wonder what the public reaction would have been should the truth of his relationship with Thomas become known. If it had been common knowledge that a potential Ripper suspect was related to a senior police officer, then any confidence once held in the law of London would inevitably have been shattered.

Possibly the police were relieved that the press hadn't taken a greater interest in Thomas Cutbush at the time of his arrest. So it appeared, with Cutbush safely confined in Broadmoor, then any secrets he held, however sinister, were hidden with him, in the dark recesses of Block One.

TWENTY-THREE

Lunatic X32007

There can be no greater thrill for a historian, especially in a case where new information rarely comes to light, to hold in your hands a previously undiscovered piece of evidence. Gaining access to files kept in one of the most secure mental hospitals in the land proved to be as difficult as it sounded. In fact, I was surprised to learn that several other authors and investigators had gone before me, communicating with Broadmoor and asking for access to the Cutbush files, all with no success.

It took me three years of repeated requests and negotiations but finally, in September 2008, I became the first person in over a century to hold the files of Lunatic X32007: Thomas Hayne Cutbush.

Sitting in the Berkshire Records Office, I experienced a rush of excitement as the dossier of papers and reports were brought out to me, the very documents that had been presented to KJ and Tracy during their Broadmoor visit, 118 years before.

I opened the first file and stepped back a century.

Thomas Cutbush was admitted from Holloway Prison on 23 April 1891. His details, including his physical description, were recorded thus:

Registered number of lunatic: X32007
Age: 26
Born: June 29, 1866
Height: Five-Feet-Nine-and-a-half-inches

Hair: Black

Whiskers: Black (Very Short)

Eyes: Dark Blue (Very Sharp)

Complexion: Dark

Build: Slight

Features: Thin

Marks: Slight bruising on left knee. One tooth out in front of upper jaw

Cause of insanity: Temperate habits. Hereditary and over-study.

Education: Good

Religion: Church of England

Occupation: Clerk in Merchants office

Duration of existing attack: Two-and-a-half years

This matched in every way the witness descriptions of men seen just before and after the murders. Witnesses described a young man of twenty-seven or twenty-eight years, about 5 ft 8 in. to 5 ft 10 in. tall, slight of build and of Jewish appearance, his face being thin and sallow; complexion dark; no whiskers; wearing a black diagonal, coat and a collar and tie. Time and again he was described as having a respectable appearance and was thought to resemble a clerk.

Several reliable witnesses, including two policemen who thought they had seen the Ripper, mentioned his distinctive blue eyes. Matthew Packer confirmed that he saw Elizabeth Stride in the company of a man 'of medium height, wearing decent clothes and who bore the appearance of a clerk'. Then there was PC William Smith, who saw Elizabeth with a man in his twenties, approximately 5 ft 7 in., who wore dark clothes, a dark-coloured felt hat and was of a 'respectable appearance'.

Thomas Bowyer had seen a man in his twenties in the company of Mary Kelly. He was also of smart appearance, having a moustache and 'very peculiar eyes'. This was matched by the City Police's description circulated after Catherine Eddowes's murder.

And then there were the two sightings of a man with bloodstained hands almost immediately after Mary's body had been found: one in

Mitre Square, the second near Albert Street in Kennington. He was described as being thin with a 'sallow complexion' and clean-shaven, save for a small moustache.

The attendant also noted that Cutbush's insanity had begun two-and-a-half years before he arrived at Broadmoor. Working back from the date of his admission – April 1891 – would suggest that his illness started in the autumn of 1888, around the time of the first Whitechapel murder.

Inside the first folder were several reports by the Broadmoor staff detailing Cutbush's behaviour, noting that he studied hard and, should attendants remove his books, he would become aggressive. Cutbush was granted access to books despite his tendency for 'over-study'. It's also interesting to note that his mental illness was thought to be hereditary.

Perhaps there was something of the son in the father who abandoned him when he was born, or possibly the mentally troubled Superintendent Charles Cutbush. By May of 1891, the warders working on Cutbush's wing already considered him to be dangerous, believing that he was suffering from a form of degenerative mania. Kate Cutbush's first visit came a month after her son's admittance.

One can only imagine how she must have felt arriving at Broadmoor, walking through the asylum's iron gates, accompanied by attendants for her own safety. She would have known that the in-patients they were there to protect her from had committed unspeakable horrors and that her son lived among them. After going through all that, when she finally arrived in Block One, Cutbush refused to see her.

Five days later, on 20 May 1891, Attendant Kilne reported: 'T. Cutbush told attendant Slater at dinnertime that he would stick a knife into any of us if he had one.' That evening Cutbush attacked another patient:

To Mr Dawson
   At 8.20 I was talking to Gilbert Cooper (a patient) in the Gallery. Cutbush came up and without a word struck Cooper

*a violent blow in the face, the cheek is red and sallow. Cutbush
was put in bed in Room 3.*
   Attendant Kilne

It was followed, three days later, by this observation:

To Mr Gardner.
   *I was listening outside Cutbush's window during the night:
he was using some very disgusting and threatening language:
said that if he had a knife suitable for the job he would rip up
the attendants or anyone else that upset him as soon as look at
them. Said a doctor was trying to do him to death but would
make a mark of one of them if they did not look out: said he
would hang them all with their own rope.*
   Attendant Bailey

Another aspect of Cutbush's paranoia was that he believed someone
was trying to poison him. He ate sparingly at first – just milk, porridge,
tea, water and bread. Eventually he stopped eating and began to starve.

On 28 May 1891, the medical superintendent wrote to Cutbush's
mother informing her that her son's condition had not improved since
his admission, stating that during his time at the asylum he had been
well looked after.

Cutbush's mother and aunt came to visit Thomas again on 7 August
1891. Although, according to the attendant, he acknowledged their
presence, Thomas refused to come in from the recreation area and talk to
them. When the attendants tried to encourage him, he became aggressive.

Unfortunately, the next eighteen month's worth of reports were
missing. The next entry was dated 5 August 1892, consisting of a brief
reference to Cutbush's refusal to eat.

After a few more notes detailing his poor diet, there followed another
lengthy gap, right up until June 1894.

This was after *The Sun*'s story had been published. Almost as if in
response to the article, the attendants now seemed to take great interest

in Cutbush. For a time, they took it in turns to listen outside his door while he talked to himself.

Block 1. June 3, 1894

T. Cutbush making use of the following language to himself between 7 and 8 o'clock.

'You can buy a box of sardines for six pence. If I take my food there is Mercury in it. My coat is not good enough.

I will see Sir Edward Blackall of Scotland Yard and it is all a fraud. If I had the knife from the pawnbrokers I would settle the whole damn Crewe of cutthroats. There is enough men in 4 block to settle it all. If I can't get a bath I will write to get taken to a private asylum. I won't have my body messed about in this manner."

It's quite possible that Cutbush was referring to the Commissioner of the Metropolitan Police, Sir Edward Bradford, and that the attendant, listening through the cell door, misheard. This was the same commissioner who had sent a representative to Cutbush's trial to make sure that only sworn evidence was heard, so its perhaps understandable that Cutbush would hold a grudge against him. Unfortunately, many more documents were missing and the final file, dated 1903, held just three more reports.

February 20, 1903

Sir,

Upon arrival of Mrs Cutbush he refused to speak or take any food whatever for some time. He however asked later about persons they did not know.

Mrs Cutbush remarked he appeared more sullen and bad tempered than on her previous visit and complained of his being more thin. He then uttered sentences which we could not understand, remarked that if he caught her in his house he should knife her. She replied she wouldn't give him the chance. He turned his back on them speaking about people they didn't know.

Kate Cutbush visited her son again on 20 April.

Mrs Cutbush visited T Cutbush from 2.35 to 2.55. Mrs Cutbush tried to kiss her son he tried to bite her face and then commenced to swear at them.

Att. Smith

In June, an urgent telegram was sent to Kate Cutbush informing her that her son was very ill, urging her to visit soon.

This time she didn't come.

At 4.25 p.m. on 5 July 1903, while in the presence of Attendant Brown, Thomas Cutbush died, aged 37.[1]

The few documents contained in the files provided a fascinating, if all too brief, glimpse into Cutbush's twelve years at Broadmoor. As well as giving a detailed physical description that matched so many of the Ripper witness testimonies, the files also confirmed much of what had been written about him in *The Sun* newspaper, particularly in regard to his insanity, paranoia and violent urges. The reports confirmed Cutbush's hatred towards his mother for her 'betrayal' and interestingly show that on more than one occasion he used the murderous phrase 'rip them up', in addition to making reference to his much-missed hunting knives.

As insightful as the files were, as I looked through the scrawled notes and attendant reports, that formed Cutbush's history in the asylum, surprisingly I was unable to find any mention of his burial.

On questioning the staff at Berkshire Records Office, they could only add that in the days following Cutbush's death his remains had been removed from the asylum, presumably by his family. What transpired next and crucially what happened to the body after leaving Broadmoor was unknown and was set to become yet another mystery.

Then, seven years later, I discovered the truth.

TWENTY-FOUR

Jack the Ripper's Grave

By the middle of the 19th century the city of London had been drawn into a new and unsettling battle with mortality. While death itself had remained a constant aspect of Victorian society, with burials taking place in the small parish churchyards that littered the capital, the birth of the industrial revolution had seen London's population sore to almost two million, resulting in an increase in both the living and the dead.[1]

As a consequence of the rising numbers overcrowding of graveyards was soon seen as a major crisis. Illegal burials became common practice with undertakers disguising themselves as clergymen in order to secure a plot. As a means of clearing land for the awaiting corpses quicklime was routinely placed within coffins so as to speed up decomposition.[2] When such chemical options weren't available the gravediggers would resort to more basic measures and often would be found jumping up and down upon the bodies to allow room for the next.[3]

Dignified funerals became a rarity with the dead simply being discarded within graveyards, where they would lay unprotected from the elements, only partially covered with soil. When the corpses started to rot the water supply was affected and very quickly disease began to spread.[5]

To combat the threat to public health Parliament responded and passed what was to become the first in a series of laws that allowed cemeteries to be run as commercial ventures, the hope being that the private companies would solve the issue of congestion with the creation of large sites on the outskirts of the city.

The new concept was immediately seized upon by entrepreneurs and savvy businessmen who from 1832 began the creation of seven magnificent cemeteries in a ring around London. Rather than building larger versions of the local churchyards, those in charge of the scheme decided that a new approach was required and as such created luxurious spaces that would go on to be known as the 'garden cemeteries' of London.

For the middle classes, the new era in cemetery development was greeted with sound applause, with the grand sites and spectacular tombs perceived by many as yet another measure of social status.[6]

By 1833 the first site was opened in Kensal Green. Reputed as the smartest of all public cemeteries it encompassed a mammoth 72 acres and courtesy of John Griffith was set to become a stunning example of the neo-classical, fusing lodges and chapels with sculptured monuments.[7]

Four years later came the unveiling of West Norwood Cemetery in south London while development on the five remaining sites continued. Highgate was to be next, opening in the May of 1839, with its first burial taking place six days later.

The following year would prove a busy period for London's cemetery companies with the opening of three additional sites in Abney Park, Nunhead and Brompton. The last to be established was Tower Hamlets, situated in the East End and opened in 1841.

If Kensal Green and West Norwood were the best known of the seven cemeteries, considered more distinguished and fashionable than the others in their number[8] then the least famous – though the second largest - was All Saints Cemetery in Nunhead, Southwark.[9]

Set atop a hill in a small hamlet bordered by open fields and market gardens, the 50 acre site was a true gem of London's landscape.[10] The sweeping location was a deliberate choice and selected to allow grieving family members and visitors an unhindered view across the capital. It was also set to be the twin of St James Cemetery in Highgate, both owned by the same company and plotted on adjacent hills.[11]

Thanks to the flair of James Bunstone Bunning the cemetery exuded his trademark design, merging neo-classical with gothic and creating a portrait of period imagery. At its entrance cast iron gates were erected, flanked by columns of Portland stone with engravings signifying the extinction of life and the symbol of eternity.

Within its vast lawns magnificent catacombs and vaults were installed as well as an entrance lodge and two chapels, one being Anglican, the other for non-conformists, both designed by Thomas Little.

Such extravagance, though appreciated by all who visited the cemetery, would come at a hefty cost to the London Cemetery Company, landing them an expenditure bill of a staggering £65,000, almost three million in today's money.[12]

One of the most impressive features in the cemetery was the 10 metre granite obelisk built in 1851 and funded through public subscription to honour the 18th century Scottish Martyrs.

Although Nunhead's first plot was sold to George Long Shand, a sailmaker from Bermondsey, the title of first burial would go to the 101-year-old Charles Abbott, a grocer from Ipswich who was interred in the spring of 1899. In the decades that followed Nunhead's reputation blossomed and it soon became a staple burial ground for many of London's deceased.

Today approximately 300,000 dead are buried at Nunhead and though most are individuals whose names are known only to their friends and closest kin, it is estimated that of that number approximately four hundred are persons of interest.[13] Among the buried are world swimming champion Frederick Beckwith and his son William. Songwriter, Augustus Durandeau, whose lyrical observations found a home in the music halls of London, and local celebrity, tailor, acrobat and wrestler - William 'Mutton' Davies.[14]

From sportsmen to actors, tycoons to inventors, Nunhead's roll call of the long departed forms an impressive list of characters who in life left their mark upon the world.

The one name they forgot to mention was Jack the Ripper.

By 1903 Broadmoor Asylum had established an efficient method for dealing with their dead. Once a patient was certified as deceased by the infirmary doctor, within a matter of days an inquest would commence, officiated by a local coroner. Should there be no evidence of foul play then the common verdict of natural causes was to be found. The remains would then be placed in a coffin, hand crafted by the patients of the carpenter's shop, and preparations made for the burial.[15]

As was customary the next of kin would be notified of the death, informed that, unless they wished to remove the body, the patient would be interred into the asylum cemetery or Block Eight as it was otherwise known.

For most patients it would seem that not even death could break their bond with the asylum. As was the case for the majority of men and women residing at her Majesty's Pleasure, any family ties that had once existed were shredded long before their demise.[16] As for the small number of patients who had maintained contact with their family, often the cost of removal for alternative burial would prove too great to consider.

And while this would form the general rule for the majority of Broadmoor's inhabitants, as was the case with all such establishments, there were always exceptions.

After Thomas Cutbush's death on 5 July staff at the asylum immediately alerted the family of his passing and informed them of their options. Perhaps somewhat surprisingly a swift reply was received, instructing the officials that the body was to be removed for private burial elsewhere.

By 9 July, with the inquest complete, the time and date of Cutbush's release was set and in a matter of days his body was dispatched from Broadmoor and transported the forty-five miles to South London.[17]

As was the norm that summer the 13 July was yet another day of swollen rain clouds and downpours that left the streets of Southwark deserted and stole the colour from the usually vibrant All Saints Cemetery.[18]

Cutbush's service would take place inside the small Anglican chapel in the heart of the cemetery, with its arched entrance offering much needed shelter for the hearse and funeral horses.[19]

After the ceremony had concluded the small crowd of mourners, that no doubt included Kate Cutbush and Clara Hayne, gathered outside. Once joined by the pall bearers the cortege began to move, commencing westwards and passing an ensemble of looming monuments and glistening lawns as they straddled the neck of the rising land. Only on reaching the intersection of two lanes did they finally stop, as the grim vision of the Nunhead gravediggers came into view.

Standing under a canopy of trees the silent mourners watched as the coffin was placed upon the sodden ground beneath them, on a small plot of consecrated land that for over a decade had belonged to the Hayne family.[20]

It was then, as whispered prayers began to fill the damp air and rain drops cuffed at the leaves high above, that the final chapter in the story of Thomas Cutbush was written, as his remains slowly descended ten feet below the earth.[21]

In those last moments it is possible that the relatives in attendance felt some small sense of freedom, as the chains that had bound a family to the crimes and violence of a psychopath were finally loosened. Perhaps though, and more likely for those relatives closest to Cutbush, the burial represented merely another moment of grief in what had been a lifetime of despair.

Though several newspapers would carry the stories of other funerals to take place that day, such as that of Colonel Moore at Exmouth.[22] and Mrs Marianne Beal at Exeter,[23] the interment of Cutbush would garner no such interest from the press. Instead and presumably as intended his burial would pass by virtually unnoticed.

In the years that followed Cutbush's funeral two further burials would take place in the family plot at Nunhead, that of Clara Hayne in July 1909 and Kate Cutbush, in November 1922, dying at the age of 74.[24]

As decades passed the cemetery would continue to offer dignified burials to the middle classes and in addition would become a well visited destination by Londoners wishing to stroll beyond the confines of the congested city.

By the mid twentieth century the effects of two world wars and the natural passage of time left Nunhead in a state of deterioration. By 1969, when the owners deciding to abandon the site and cease maintenance, the once elegant cemetery slipped into a neglected wilderness.[25]

With its gates locked Nunhead's neat lawns soon became forests of ash and sycamore, turning open landscapes into tangled webs of trees and plant life. While nature took its toll upon the land Nunhead's grand structures too became victims of damage, with vandals setting fire to the chapel and raiding the catacombs for their jewels.[26]

For six years the cemetery was left to flounder, until in 1975 an act of parliament allowed Southwark Council to purchase the land for a single pound.[27] The result would lead to a slow restoration project to rebuild and rejuvenate Nunhead's fading beauty.

Today the cemetery is again open to the public, having been restored by the Friends of Nunhead Cemetery. At its heart stands the renovated Anglican chapel, set upon the crest of a picturesque avenue, lined with tall trees and bordered by open walkways that snake throughout the site.

While some areas are accessible, accommodating a tableau of imposing monuments and large family vaults, other sections remain off limits, listed as conservation zones, to be viewed only from a series of mudded tracks that skirt their perimeter.

It is in these dark quarters of shrubbery and flora where the secrets of All Saints Cemetery can be found. Where the lost lives of London's past are concealed beyond a wall of bush and bramble and where the answer to one of history's most infamous crimes lay entombed in a woodland grave.

185

TWENTY-FIVE

An Unlikely Monster

Thanks mainly to Melville Macnaghten it would take over a century before Thomas Cutbush would be investigated as a likely suspect. This is quite incredible. If nothing else, the fact that *The Sun*'s investigation was the reason Macnaghten wished to defend Cutbush and thus write his memo makes him the most important suspect in the entire case.

If there had been no memoranda, then there would have been no Druitt, Kosminski or Ostrog. Without these three men, there would have been no books, films or conspiracies, including Stephen Knight's book *The Final Solution*, which caused a sensation with its royal connection to the Ripper.[1]

The Macnaghten Memoranda was discovered when interest in the Ripper case had waned. Nothing new of any real significance had been discovered for decades. The Memo was a gift to investigators but they missed the greatest gift of all – the man Macnaghten dismissed.

It is understandable. As a character Cutbush makes an unlikely monster. He was an odd, quiet, local lad from a middle-class family, who lived at home with his mother and aunt.

At the time of the murders, the press and police were looking for far more exciting suspects: a foreigner, a gentleman, a Jew or a doctor. At the height of the investigation one tabloid alone gave ten possible solutions as to the identity of the killer ranging from religious maniac and fanatical vivisectionist to a policeman.[2]

To most Victorians it was thought that the killer must be a lunatic, an obvious madman, knife in hand, stalking the backstreets of London on the hunt for his next victim. As history tells us, however, serial killers are anything but obvious. Instead they are the ghosts of society, loitering within communities and garnering little fuss or attention — at least for a while — until that moment comes when their mask of normality slips and the real monster is revealed.

Often it is luck, rather than skill, that allows such killers to continue at liberty. Even a brief study of the Ripper case shows that in many instances it was only luck that had prevented his capture. On so many occasions the killer could and should have been caught, but wasn't. If Albert Cadosh had looked over the fence of 29 Hanbury Street on hearing the muted gasps of Annie Chapman, if Louis Diemschutz had glanced behind the gate of Dutfield's Yard instead of running into the working mens club or if PC Thompson had pursued the footsteps heard fleeing from the body of Frances Coles, then Jack the Ripper would have been caught and the world would have known the truth. Instead we are left with a mystery and killer without a name.

And though the number of possible solutions is vast, extending to over one hundred names, when all the evidence pertaining to Thomas Cutbush is considered, he is clearly the best suspect the case has ever seen.

In summary:
- Cutbush was charged with stabbing two young women.
- He attempted to murder a fellow worker in Whitechapel.
- He tried to cut his own mother's throat.
- He violently assaulted a servant girl.
- He had a relationship with a prostitute that ended in a sexual attack, possibly rape.
- He threatened to murder Dr Brooks.
- A respected solicitor believed Cutbush had snuck into his office to murder him.
- When the police raided Cutbush's room, they found pictures of women cut open, their innards exposed.

- Cutbush was obsessed with medicine and surgery and kept several medical textbooks.
- Police officers found blood-stained clothing stuffed up his chimney.
- He was mentally ill.
- He owned several high-quality knives with long blades.
- He worked in Whitechapel and lived nearby.
- He took night-time walks and returned with mud and blood on his clothing.
- He was agile, leaping over fences and high walls to escape pursuers (a strategy employed by the Ripper).
- He was intelligent, persuasive and able to think on his feet and therefore would be able to put any prostitutes he picked up at ease.
- He had a distinctive voice (as heard by George Dixon, the blind boy).
- Cutbush made references to 'laying girls out' on several occasions.
- The onset of his psychotic behaviour came at the start of the murders. After his incarceration in Broadmoor, the attacks and murders in Whitechapel ceased.
- He assaulted a fellow patient in Broadmoor and constantly used threatening language.
- Although he was only tried for two attacks, neither of which ended in murder, Cutbush was classed as a Category One prisoner and placed with the most dangerous lunatics in the country.

When the evidence is stacked up like this the plausibility of Cutbush being the Ripper seems overwhelming. But there is more. In addition to *The Sun* reporters and Inspector Race it also appears that whilst confined behind the walls of Broadmoor Asylum, further suspicions were growing.

In 1929, an article appeared in UK magazine, *John Blunt's Monthly*, about a man who claimed to have known Jack the Ripper during his time as a patient in Broadmoor.

At the time, a serial sex attacker and murderer known as 'The Vampire' was terrorising Düsseldorf and the case had rekindled interest in London's own serial killer.[3]

Of course, there is good reason to question the reliability of the anonymous witness who had been incarcerated in Broadmoor for many years. What made his account so remarkable, however, was what he recalled about this man was so incredibly like Cutbush that it seems hard to put his description down simply to a madman's fantasy.

According to the article the patient was quiet and, for the most part, well-behaved. To those around him, he appeared to be a man of knowledge and was well known for his love of books, specifically those of a scientific nature, as well as a peculiar habit of diagnosing the ailments of other patients.

So the article alleged, the warders working in Broadmoor would often point out similarities between the patient and Jack the Ripper, informing other patients that he had been caught by the police shortly after committing a knife attack on a woman. After his arrest, so claimed the warders, he was found insane by a prison doctor and subsequently sent to Broadmoor without the details of his crimes or capture being made public.

The former patient recalled that throughout his time in Broadmoor, the man who he believed was the Ripper used an alias, going under the name of 'Taylor'.

As I had discovered, it appeared that Cutbush sometimes used aliases, such as Jim or James after the famous American doctor and chemist. When it came to Taylor, he had kept his choice of name closer to home. On researching the Cutbush family I learnt that Thomas's father, who abandoned him when he was only young, was named Thomas Taylor Cutbush.[4]

The former patient then describes how Taylor, who had taken part in some gardening exercise, suddenly made a run for it, claiming that he attempted to escape by vaulting the perimeter wall. Aided by subtle footholds carved in the brick, in no time the patient was halfway up the wall and no doubt would have escaped, had his chisel not fallen out of his pocket and smashed through a pane of glass.

The noise soon attracted the attention of the asylum guards and, as stated by the ex-patient, Taylor was swiftly removed back to his block. Soon after, the patient died.

Apart from describing 'Taylor' as quiet and well behaved, the description offered by *John Blunt's Monthly* precisely matches the known facts pertaining to Cutbush: his obsession with study and his habit of diagnosing the ailments of others, as well as his penchant for leaping over walls and his use of aliases.

Though coincidence can account for much it seems almost illogical to believe that two men could exist in Broadmoor who exhibited such identical traits.

As to whether Thomas Cutbush was the mysterious 'Taylor' or indeed Jack the Ripper, there remains one final and very convincing witness.

TWENTY-SIX

Those Brilliant Eyes

On 27 September 1919 an article appeared in *The People's Journal* that, although being published twenty-eight years after the Ripper murders had ceased, provided perhaps one of the most important statements ever made by an officer involved in the case.

Dubbed one of the 'smartest detectives the Metropolitan Police ever knew', Sergeant Stephen White was recognised as one of the very best. At only twenty-one, in the October of 1875, White realised his ambition and for the first time donned his much-prized police uniform.

Stationed for several years in L Division's Kennington district,[2] White's talents were soon recognised and by 1881 he had earned a promotion to Police Sergeant along with a transfer to Whitechapel CID.[3]

As well as his ability as a thief catcher, White would go on to work on a string of murder cases and on his retirement would be described as having more experience of murder than any other officer in the force. He also had an acute ability to gather intelligence relating to the growing threat of terrorism.

While stationed in Lambeth, White received much praise when, after receiving a tip-off, he interrupted a plot to bomb London, discovering a sizeable arsenal stashed in New Cut.[4]

By 1881 the threat posed by Irish terrorists to Britain was never greater. In an effort to force the British withdrawal from Ireland, Fenians began a series of attacks, planting bombs at Mansion House in London as well as attacking barracks in Salford and Liverpool.[5]

As the years passed so grew the threat and by December 1884 large quantities of explosives were being smuggled into the country to aid the Fenians cause. James Gilbert Cunningham was one such terrorist who, during the winter of 1884, smuggled a brown Saratoga trunk into England, filled with sixty pounds of dynamite.[6]

Within a month terrorists had targeted the London Underground, placing a bomb in Gower Street Station, where a huge explosion rocked the train line and caused extensive damage.[7]

Shortly after, Cunningham, who was lodging at a house in Whitechapel, along with his friend Henry Burton, plotted yet another attack. Twenty-two days after the bombing of the Metropolitan Line, he walked into the Tower of London, concealing a bomb under his overcoat.[8]

Meanwhile Burton and an accomplice, one being dressed as a woman, entered the. Westminster Hall in Parliament, planting bombs in the crypt as well as the Bar room as a diversion to a planned attack on the chamber of the House of Commons.[9]

By 2 p.m. Cunningham's bomb exploded and, though initially believing he had escaped capture, on reaching the entrance gates to the Tower of London he was apprehended by the quick-thinking Stephen White. [10]

By 2.10 p.m. the bomb planted in the crypt of the Palace of Westminster began to smoke, Burton having lit the stacks of dynamite lying within a parcel. A nearby constable attempted to remove the threat, but as he reached a nearby stairwell carrying the parcel in his arms, the bomb exploded.[11]

Though Burton escaped, he too would soon be arrested and in May 1885 the pair, later dubbed the 'Dynamitards', were found guilty and sentenced to life imprisonment. For his efforts, Stephen White would receive a commendation from the Home Office, becoming something of a hero among the populace of London.[12]

As White ascended through his career he garnered yet more praise for his involvement in a string of sensational murder cases, including the notorious crimes of Harry Alt and a man named Karaczewski, who committed murders in Turner Street and Brick Lane, [13] along with the case of 44-year-old Kate Marshall who murdered her sister, Elizabeth Roberts, in

November 1898, during a drunken quarrel. The murder had taken place in Whitechapel, in the very house where the Ripper's fifth victim, Mary Kelly, had lived and died. [14]

By 1894 White had risen to the rank of inspector, a post he would hold for six years until retiring on 15 October 1900.[15]

Although White's career had encompassed a multitude of fine arrests, being hailed as

'having run more dangerous criminals to earth than any other man employed as a police officer in London', one moment would be forever looked upon with much regret.

It came while working undercover in Whitechapel, and saw the experienced sergeant unknowingly allow the most notorious criminal of the nineteenth century to slip through his fingers, earning himself the reputation of being 'the only man engaged in the hunt who met Jack the Ripper'.

The People's Journal reported that, over a decade prior to his retirement, in the autumn of 1888, like many of his colleagues White had been pulled firmly into the hunt for Jack the Ripper, often interviewing witnesses who had encountered the victims prior to their murder, as well as possible suspects.

By the summer of 1889 White was still heavily involved in the investigation and was working on a special operation aimed at catching the killer redhanded. In his report, published for the first time in *The People's Journal*, White wrote that while a sergeant he and a number of his colleagues were sent to Whitechapel in disguise.

One of several operations involving White was centred around a particular alley where, day and night, two plain-clothes officers were stationed, keeping watch on people entering and leaving the alley in the belief that one of them might well be the Ripper.[16]

The *Evening Star* wrote on 18 July 1889 that Castle Alley had, for several weeks, been the subject of an operation, with two detectives posted there to keep watch. In both the magazine and contemporary press reports, the night of 16 July was described as wet and bitterly cold.[17] That night White had been engaged in the operation and was heading to Castle Alley in order to receive updates from his fellow officers. According to him, the location appeared like a cul-de-sac with only one entrance where his two men were stationed in hiding.

On reaching the entrance to the alley he saw a man emerge and begin to walk in the opposite direction as if in a hurry. 'He walked quickly, but noiselessly,' said White, 'apparently wearing rubber shoes. I stood aside to let the man pass.'[18] As the man passed under a lamp, for a moment he became illuminated against the darkness of the street, allowing White to take note of his appearance: 'He was about 5 ft 10 in. in height and was dressed rather shabbily, though it was obvious that the material of his clothes was good. Evidently a man who had seen better days.'

White continued: 'The man's face was long and thin, nostrils rather delicate, and his hair was jet black. His complexion was inclined to be sallow. The most striking thing about him, however, was the extraordinary brilliance of his eyes. They looked like two luminous glow-worms coming through the darkness.'

White would go on to state that the man appeared young and gave him the idea of having been a student or a professional. To the detective, the man's behaviour seemed suspicious and, although wishing to detain him, as White would reiterate in his report, he had no grounds on which to do so.

So eager was the man to leave the area that he stumbled, allowing White the opportunity to engage him in conversation. Although only brief, White was able to make a detailed note of the man's voice, stating that 'it was soft and musical, with just a tinge of melancholy ... a voice of a man of culture – a voice altogether out of keeping with the squalid surroundings of the East End.'

Only as he began to walk away did White make a similar observation to that of *The Sun* journalists who met Cutbush in 1894; that he walked with a stoop, bent at the shoulders, as if his chest was troubled.[19]

As White observed the man slowly walk away one of the officers posted to keep watch emerged onto the street, passing White before walking into Castle Alley. Moments later White heard the officer's cries for assistance and immediately went to his colleague's aid.

In a matter of moments White had joined the constable and in turn discovered, to his horror, the lifeless body of Alice Mckenzie, slumped upon the cobbled ground with her blood running into the nearby gutter.

On realising that the man he had seen was quite possibly her killer White ran back to the street and though only seconds had passed, by the time he had returned the man was nowhere to be seen.[20]

White would remain steadfast in his belief that the man he had witnessed emerging from the alleyway and who had disappeared into the labyrinth of Whitechapel, was none other than Jack the Ripper; a moment that would no doubt haunt the detective for the remainder of his life.

As for the identity of the young man observed by Sergeant White, on that cold July morning, perhaps we will never truly know for certain. It is difficult, however, to imagine that the man whose image became engrained upon the conscience of Stephen White and who, in an instant, vanished into the dark alleyways of London's East End, was anyone other than Thomas Hayne Cutbush: The Man Who Would Be Jack.

Appendix One

THE RIPPERS ASSEMBLE

Since the killing of Mary Nichols on 31 August 1888, countless names have been supplied by historians, reporters and writers as potential candidates for the mantle of Jack the Ripper. While some offer a degree of credibility, other suspects have been named against whom little argument can be made. In this appendix I have covered a small selection of suspects who have come to light since 1888, some well known, as well as others named here for the first time.

JACOB ISENSCHMID

At approximately 7 a.m. on 9 September 1888, an hour after the discovery of Annie Chapman's body in Hanbury Street, a Swiss butcher by the name of Jacob Isenschmid walked into the Prince Albert pub in Brushfield Street and ordered a pint of beer.

His strange appearance caused the landlady, Mrs Fiddymont, to be gravely concerned and she confirmed that Isenschmid's hands were covered in blood, as well as him wearing what she called a 'wild look' about him. After drinking only half his pint, Isenschmid abruptly left and darted out into the street, followed shortly after by Mrs Chappell, a friend of Mrs Fiddymont's. Once outside, Chappell pointed Isenschmid out to a passerby, who proceeded to follow him as far as Bishopsgate.

According to the witness, Isenschmid appeared to be nervous and didn't seem to know where he was going, crossing streets several times as if in some sort of 'trance'. On hearing that another prostitute had been murdered only hours prior to this strange encounter, Mrs Fiddymont went to the police and informed them of the strange man she had seen. Isenschmid's description was given as a man of medium height, around forty years old, with short blond hair and a ginger moustache. At the time he was wearing a long black coat buttoned up to his collar and a brown hat of firm material, pulled low, as if to hide his face.

Three days later, two men walked into Holloway Police Station and informed the officers of a man they suspected as having a connection with the murders. The men, Drs Crabb and Cowan, said that a friend of theirs had informed them of a strange character who lodged at 60 Mitford Road.

This man was Jacob Isenschmid, who had been staying there for the last six days, having recently separated from his wife. It would appear that the landlord had monitored the behaviour of his latest lodger and grew suspicious of Isenschmid due to his keeping peculiar hours, often leaving his residence at one o'clock in the morning.

On being interviewed Isenschmid's wife Mary stated that she hadn't had any communication with her husband for almost two months, as well as confirming that he often carried large knives on him, which he used in his trade as a butcher. The next day Isenschmid was located by several officers and arrested. He was then escorted to Holloway Police Station, but with his mental condition deemed unsound, he was sent to Grove Hall Lunatic Asylum in Bow.

It was thought at the time that the police may well have a strong lead with this man, later nicknamed the 'Mad Butcher'. Indeed, in a paper written by Sir Charles Warren and dated 19 September 1888, it was stated that Isenschmid was one of three men under suspicion of committing the murders.

Inspector Abberline later confirmed his belief that Isenschmid was indeed the strange man that Mrs Fiddymont had encountered in the Prince Albert pub. As this would place Isenschmid in the vicinity of

Hanbury Street on the morning of Annie Chapman's murder, acting in a very odd manner and supposedly with blood on his hands, he was a suspect who seemingly ticked all the relevant boxes.

At one time Isenschmid had been a successful butcher, running his business from 59 Elthorne Road. However, by 1882 the business had begun to fail. As custom dried up, leaving his livelihood in dire straits, Isenschmid began to lose his mind, suffering from severe fits and outbursts of violence.

By 1888 Isenschmid found employment once again, working as a butcher in Marylebone High Street. At the time of the Ripper murders his mind had again given way, seeing him abscond from his employer, leaving his wife gravely concerned for her safety.

In order to survive, Isenschmid would make money by purchasing the feet, kidneys and heads of sheep from the local markets and take them home, where he spent hours dressing them in order to sell them on to restaurants for a high price.

It would seem the police were very keen to confirm whether or not Isenschmid was in fact the man seen by Mrs Fiddymont and Mrs Chappell. It was suggested that the two women, along with Joseph Taylor, be able to see the deranged butcher in order to identify him positively. The doctor in charge of Isenschmid, however, was not happy with this idea and said that due to his ill health he would not permit an identity parade to take place. Therefore, we will never truly know whether or not it was Isenschmid who they had seen.

Although while in Holloway it was discovered that Isenschmid had made a startling confession to several women in the neighbourhood, stating that he was 'Leather Apron' (the name attributed to the Whitechapel Killer prior to that of Jack the Ripper), he would later be found to have no connection to the Ripper murders. As it transpired, while Isenschmid remained in custody, the real Ripper struck, therefore ruling him out as a potential suspect.[1]

In 1996 theorist Bernard Brown wrote of his belief that the Ripper was a Railway Policeman, who used London's Underground as a means of escaping detection. Brown believed that the killer could well have used the Tube tunnels to escape the scenes of the crimes without being spotted.

As the Underground stations were steam operated, 'blowholes' were created in the roadways of Whitechapel so as to allow the sulphurous fumes to escape. Brown believed that these holes may have been seen by the killer as a means of evading capture, allowing him to enter the tunnels unseen.

Brown goes on to support his claims by confirming that each of the murder sites was close to Underground train stations, stating that should the Ripper have been a constable, he could not only have walked to and from the murder sites without attracting attention but elicited the trust of his victims with ease.

As for a motive, Brown provides the names of several officers whose indiscretions with prostitutes had led to their eventual dismissal, thus harbouring a grudge against fallen women. One such officer was named by Brown as Sergeant William New of H division CID, who was demoted to constable on 1 October 1888 and transferred to Paddington after he received a complaint.

The female, whose grievance reached William New's superiors, stated that the sergeant had assaulted her and afterwards destroyed her clothes. Brown concedes, however, that Sergeant New, although fitting his profile of an officer, was far removed from Whitechapel at the time of the killings, with his patrol area encompassing the West End as opposed to the areas of Spitalfields and Whitechapel.

Although Brown's theory is interesting, research indicates that of all the witness statements accumulated throughout the time of the Ripper murders, not one victim was ever seen with a police officer prior to their murder.

To support his claim further, Bernard Brown provides an intriguing story of forty-year-old prostitute, Emily Wood, who was attacked on 7

January 1889. According to him, Wood, who lived on the Commercial Road, had been accosted by a constable, who stabbed her before running off and leaving her for dead. Although after recovering from her injuries the victim stated that she had known the police officer who assaulted her, the man was never traced.[2]

The Brunswick Ripper

A year after the Ripper murders began, newspapers were starting to perpetuate the theory that the Ripper had fled London altogether and had taken up residence in America. The *Atlanta Constitution* was one of them and during the January of 1889 wished to alert their readers to the possibility that the Whitechapel killer was lurking in Georgia. According to the reporters working at the *Constitution* the Ripper had allegedly taken up his pen once again and was now communicating with police officials, taunting them with threats reminiscent of the 'Dear Boss' letters, received in London the previous year.

On 31 January 1889, Marshal Dart of the Brunswick Police Department received a postcard similar to that sent to George Lusk in 1888. According to Dart the letter was stained with what he believed to be blood, with the writer claiming that the Ripper was in the city, a location known for being one of the first ports of entry to the country. According to the author, he planned to resume his work that very evening.

Interestingly, on the night of 31 January a black prostitute was attacked while walking alone in the north of the city. On entering the police headquarters it was noted that her clothes were torn and she had several scratches upon her face.

A further communication was found on the night of Monday 3 February, when a small box wrapped in brown paper was discovered on the Broda Street Bridge simply marked 'For You, City'. Inside was a short note warning the 'dissipated women' of the area that Jack the Ripper was in town.

Only two days later Chief Magruder received a final letter from the would-be Ripper, in which he stated that he had decided to say farewell to Atlanta and was planning to make Rome his next hunting ground. The identity of the writer was never established.[3]

THE SEER

As police forces around the globe discovered, Jack the Ripper had copy-cats, who craved the infamy associated with the Whitechapel murders. One such man was a criminal named 'The Seer', who throughout January 1889 plagued the residents of St. Louis with a torrent of communications, claiming he would destroy them all, as well as doing some 'Jack the Ripper business'.

After receiving fifty threatening letters, the Chief of Police finally located his 'Ripper' in the form of religious lunatic William Breenan. On being interviewed, it was ascertained that Breenan was a disturbed man, who gained a strange satisfaction from spreading fear among the local residents. He was subsequently deemed insane and placed in an asylum.[4]

JAMES GRAY

Two months after the murder of Mary Kelly, stories began to circulate within the press that the Ripper had been arrested in Tunis. Papers reported that a band of robbers and assassins had been captured by French police officers and that one them, a man going by the name of James Gray, was thought to be the 'London murderer'.

Some newspapers speculated that Gray had been charged in Tunis with a murder similar in nature to those committed in Whitechapel, while others indicated that he was in custody merely on a charge of vagrancy. Either way, for a while at least Gray seemed to capture the imagination of the press and appears to have exhibited at least some of the traits believed to be indicative of the Ripper.

According to the newspapers which, by the winter of 1889, were avidly following the story, James Gray hailed from London and had at one time lived in Whitechapel. Upon his left arm he bore a tattoo of his name, along with the image of a naked woman, as well as having the names of several other females tattooed on his right arm. It would appear that, on being questioned, Gray was unable to account for his movements during 1888 or for his time spent in Tunis.

On becoming aware of his apprehension and the suspicions held by the Tunis authorities, the English Consul ordered that a photograph be taken of the suspect. Suspicion was aroused further when, on being photographed, Gray became agitated and started to shake uncontrollably. The general impression from Scotland Yard, however, was that James Gray was nothing more than an English vagrant, who on finding himself on a serious charge in a foreign country was saying all the right things to make the British authorities arrange for him to be brought back to London.

The story of the Ripper's apprehension didn't appear to hold much weight with the Metropolitan Police and it would seem that in fact there was nothing whatsoever to connect James Gray with the murders that had occurred in Whitechapel.[5]

James Maybrick

In 1991 a diary was discovered, allegedly written by Victorian cotton merchant James Maybrick, and for a while it appeared that the mystery of the Ripper had finally been solved. Michael Barrett, a one-time scrap metal dealer, alleged that he had been given the diary by an old friend, Tony Devereux, shortly before Devereux's death. The diary, made up of sixty-three pages of writing, was promoted as being the confessions of Jack the Ripper. It held evidence that its author, James Maybrick, was addicted to arsenic, as well as confirming that he cheated on his wife. The diary also provided a motive for Maybrick killing prostitutes – on discovering his wife had cheated on him with a young cotton broker named Alfred Brierly, so consumed with anger was Maybrick that he killed in an act of revenge.

So, the diary suggested, should Maybrick murder his wife, he would ultimately be under suspicion. Instead he chose to take out his frustrations on the fallen women of Whitechapel. After taking the document to a literary agent in 1992, Michael Barrett soon discovered how great the public interest was in his find. Although causing a sensation at the time of publication in 1994, with many believing the diary to be genuine, concerns were raised from the outset by diligent researchers and historians. One question posed after its publication was why the fifty-year-old James Maybrick, who was believed to be a wealthy man, should choose to make his dramatic confessions not in a diary or a journal but on the pages of an old photograph album.

It was also discovered that the entries allegedly made by Maybrick, although made in ink from the Ripper period, were littered with mistakes in relation to the killings of his victims.

James Maybrick didn't fit eyewitness descriptions of the Ripper, nor did his handwriting match that of the diary's author, yet such was the media hysteria surrounding its discovery that a documentary soon followed, along with talk of a film in which James Maybrick would be depicted as the Ripper. When in the summer of 1994 Michael Barrett confessed to having forged the diary, James Maybrick's candidacy fell apart. Although Barrett would retract hisconfession soon after, the damage was already done. Although many books have been written in connection with the Maybrick diary no clear evidence has been discovered in support of Michael Barrett's claims that James Maybrick was the author and in turn the Whitechapel Killer.[6]

Oswald Puckridge

During the September of 1888, eleven days after the murder of Annie Chapman, Henry Matthews (the then Home Secretary) received a communication from Sir Charles Warren.

The Commissioner of the Metropolitan Police wished to inform Matthews that the Ripper had possibly been identified in the form of Oswald Puckridge, a former surgeon who allegedly owned a long-bladed knife and had made certain threats to rip people up.

On 4 August 1888, Puckridge had been released from a London

asylum and, at the time of his letter, Warren admitted that his whereabouts were unknown. In 1888 Puckridge was fifty years old, and supposedly hailed from Deptford. There, in 1868, he married Ellen Puddle, and at the time gave his occupation as a chemist.

At some point in January 1888, Puckridge was admitted to Hoxton House Lunatic Asylum in Shoreditch. Although Warren was unable to trace him at the time, his name would appear five years later on the admittance register of Bow Infirmary after he had been found wandering aimlessly along Queen Victoria Street in London.

For the next seven years Puckridge, when not working as a labourer, was regularly admitted as a patient to several London infirmaries, as well as an asylum. On 28 May 1900, after a severe deterioration of his mental health, he arrived in Holborn Workhouse, where four days later he died of pneumonia.

At fifty, Puckridge was much older than eyewitness descriptions of the Ripper and although believed by Charles Warren to have trained as a surgeon, no evidence exists to substantiate this claim.[7]

At the time of writing the list of Ripper suspects extends upwards into the hundreds and perhaps, as the years pass, ever more names will take their place in the line-up of men and women suspected of being history's most infamous and elusive serial killer.

Appendix Two

THE LIVES LOST

Much speculation still remains over the exact number of victims who fell at the hands of Jack the Ripper. When the killing of Mary Nichols hit the papers newsmen and reporters soon looked to heighten the sense of unease felt in the capital by suggesting that the Ripper had killed prior to 31 August 1888. Subsequently, after the last Ripper-related murder occurred in February 1891, certain theorists wished to link later victims to the killer's tally.

In this appendix I have provided details of a number of the women suggested as being victims of Jack the Ripper.

ANNIE MILLWOOD

At 5 p.m. on Saturday 25 February 1888, Annie Millwood was admitted into the Whitechapel Workhouse Infirmary. She had been attacked earlier that evening by an unknown male in White's Row. Millwood's legs and lower torso had been savagely cut in what would be seen as a frenzied knife assault.

Annie Millwood was thirty-eight years old at the time of the attacks, a widow and living on her own in a lodging house in White's Row. At some point during the evening of 25 February she had become acquainted with her attacker, more likely a client, who she was leading to a secluded spot somewhere close to her lodgings. All too soon her male companion became deranged, grabbing at a clasp knife hidden in his coat pocket, before violently thrusting a knife into Millwood's lower torso.

Although seriously wounded, Annie would survive the onslaught and went on to make a full recovery from her injuries, discharged on 21 March to the South Grove Workhouse. Unfortunately, only ten days after seemingly recovering, she was found dead at the rear of a nearby building.

During the inquest held on 5 April, Coroner Wynne Baxter stated that the deceased had died from a sudden effusion into the pericardium artery through ulceration, confirming that Millwood had died of natural causes and not as a result of her previous injuries.[1]

Martha Tabram

On the Bank Holiday of Monday 6 August 1888, 39-year-old prostitute Martha Tabram was enjoying drinks in company with a friend, Mary Anne Connelly, or 'Pearly Poll' as she was commonly known.

The pair had spent most of the evening drinking with two guardsmen in the Two Brewers pub on Brick Lane. At some point during the evening the four decided to move on to the White Swan in Whitechapel High Street, where they continued drinking until 11.45 p.m.

By then Martha and Mary had decided to split up, each taking with them one of the soldiers. As Connelly would later confirm, she and her corporal walked to the secluded Angel Alley, while Martha escorted her private into George Yard, a residential property off Wentworth Street and a regular haunt of the local prostitutes. After approximately half an hour, Connelly had left her client and was seen walking in the direction of Aldgate.

At 4.50 a.m. a resident of 37 George Yard Buildings, named John Reeves, came down the stairs and discovered the mutilated remains of Martha Tabram lying in a pool of blood. Immediately he ran to find a policeman, arriving back moments later with Police Constable Barrett.

Coincidently, at 2 a.m. Barrett had seen Mary Connelly's soldier standing outside the George Yard Buildings, allegedly waiting for his pal.

On examination it became apparent that Tabram had been the victim of a most ferocious attack. At least twenty-two stab wounds to her trunk and seventeen to her breast, including a wound to her heart. The lower part of Tabram's body bore a single stab wound, three inches long and one inch deep. Her throat had also been attacked, though unlike the Ripper's victims, it had been stabbed rather than slit. The murder weapon was referred to as being a penknife.

Significantly though, the wound to Tabram's heart had been inflicted with what appeared to be a bayonet. An investigation was immediately launched into Tabram's murder, led by Detective Inspector Reid. Under questioning, Mary Connelly would recount the activities of herself and Martha on the night of the murder, leaving the finger of suspicion pointing firmly at the two guardsmen with whom they had been associating.

PC Barrett, who had seen one of the soldiers on the night of the murder, accompanied DI Reid to the Tower of London in order to view a parade of the Grenadier Guardsman, to see if the man he had observed was one of them. Though scrutinising the line-up several times, Barrett was unable to recognise the soldier he had seen. Connelly eventually came forward to the police and gave them vital information about the two soldiers, making direct reference to the white bands around their caps, inferring that they were in fact Coldstream Guards.

On Wednesday 15 August, Mary Connelly, PC Barrett and DI Reid visited the Wellington Barracks to view a second line-up. Almost instantly Connelly picked out Private George as the man she had entertained. Private George, however, was able to provide a valid alibi. The second man, who escorted Tabram to the George Yard buildings, was identified as Private Skipper, though, like George, he confirmed that he was in his barracks on the night in question.

Martha Tabram's murder remains unsolved, although in recent years her killing has been firmly linked with the Whitechapel series. The evidence, however, would indicate that her killer demonstrated a different MO to that of the Ripper, with her injuries appearing to be stab wounds inflicted with a penknife, rather than the cuts and rips associated with the infamous murderer himself.[2]

LOUISA SMITH

In the early hours of Sunday 10 February 1889, John Cheeseman of Lewisham was walking home along Algernon Road, a long thoroughfare running close to the main railway line,[3] in a district that had made the newspapers the previous year for what was dubbed the carnival of the 'Bonfire Boys', an annual celebration held in honour of Guy Fawkes Night and an event that elsewhere in London saw effigies of Jack the Ripper being symbolically burnt.[4]

Shortly after the bells of the nearby St Mary's Church struck midnight, Cheeseman discovered a heap lying on the ground close to the kerb. The darkness of morning had initially made it difficult to decipher what the object was and only on closer examination did it become clear that the shape was that of a woman, lying upon her back with blood streaming from her face.[5]

In a state of shock, Cheeseman ran in search of help and in no time found Constable Davis, who had been on patrol nearby. On returning to the scene, Davis immediately saw that the woman, lying on the ground, was unconscious and bleeding from the mouth.

After calling for an ambulance, the woman was taken to Lewisham Police Station. There she was seen by Dr Visger who, on examining her injuries, ordered her removal to Lewisham Union Infirmary, where she arrived at 3 a.m.[6]

The victim would be identified as 35-year-old Louisa Smith, who for four days remained insensible and paralysed, with Dr Lewis Robinson doing all he could to save her life. On admittance it was clear that she was bleeding from the mouth as well as from behind her right ear.[7]

On 14 February 1889, Louisa lost her battle and died of a fractured skull. From the evidence provided in her post mortem it appears that an attempt had been made to strangle Smith, with clear signs of bruising and depression behind her right ear, indicating that Louisa's killer had grabbed her from behind, gripping her throat with his right hand and leaving his thumb in its natural position, where the force not only left damage to her skin but also an indentation.

Louisa had put up a struggle and fought against her assailant. Due to this or, more likely, having been disturbed, her killer abandoned his attempt at suffocation and instead struck Smith a huge blow about the head, with an object described by the doctors as having a smooth surface, possibly the butt of a knife. The killer then threw Louisa to the ground, smashing her face upon the cobbled street and cutting open her lip. Then, like the Ripper, the Lewisham killer simply disappeared.

The blow to Smith's head had been made with such force that Louisa's skull was fractured, thus causing her membranes to fill with blood, forming clots. At the subsequent inquest into her death, held at Lewisham Workhouse and presided over by Mr Wood, the deputy coroner for West Kent, the all too familiar verdict was found, that of 'Wilful murder against some person or persons unknown'. The evidence provided showed that Louisa hailed from Deptford, where she had lived with John Luxford, a labourer, at 7 Giffin Street.[8]

The day prior to her murder, Louisa had ventured into Lewisham, where she met a friend named Emily Atkinson in the morning, only parting company at 11 p.m. By this time another woman named Emma Maguire was seen talking to Louisa on a street corner, close to Hilly Fields. It would seem that shortly after this Louisa finished her conversation with Emma and went in search of a client, after which she led him to a secluded location in Lee's Fields, near to a gated entrance.

At this point a resident named John Brown saw the couple and, realising that Louisa was a prostitute, immediately turned the pair away. Due to the timing and location of this incident the man who Brown had seen in company with Louisa was in all likelihood her killer, who then walked with her the short distance to Algernon Road, where he chose to strike. Owing possibly to the poor street lighting, Brown was unable to furnish any description of Louisa's companion.[9]

With her death, Louisa Smith slipped into obscurity, and no

connection was made to the Ripper case. On the surface, it is clear to see why, both the location and the MO seemingly eliminating someone who was, after all, known as the 'Whitechapel' murderer. However, one significant and possibly crucial clue has been overlooked for more than a century.

On 8 January 1889, the Metropolitan Police received a letter through the post enclosed in a small envelope and bearing the postmark W. C. On the piece of yellowing paper found inside were written fourteen lines of text, all in black ink in a forward-sloping style and seemingly from someone who wished to be known as the Whitechapel murderer. It opened with the familiar salutation of 'Dear Boss'. However, the next thirteen lines in this singular correspondence actually predicted a murder.

It read as follows:

Dear Boss

I write these few lines to you just to inform you that
I shall soon be on the job again very shortly near
blackheath.

I have my eye on a few gay women. You have thought you
had me but I have laughed ha ha ha
I Remain
Yours very truly
Jim the Cutter [10]

Within a matter of weeks Louisa Smith was found murdered in the area of Lewisham, very close to Blackheath. And as for the name adopted by its author, could it indicate that the sender was in fact Thomas Cutbush himself ? He, like the writer, often used the aliases of James and Jim, while 'Cutter' is but a short distance from Cutbush.

The paper the letter was written on was stained with a dark substance – not blood, but more likely a dark chemical, perhaps similar to that found on Cutbush's hands and coins as a result of the lotions kept in his pockets. Several droplets were found on the surface of the letter, along with a single, smeared fingerprint. Whether Louisa

Smith was a victim of the Ripper remains debatable. As for the letter, its author has yet to be identified. Further research is needed in order to firmly link this correspondence to Thomas Cutbush or any other suspect named in relation to the Ripper case. The answer, however, may forever remain a mystery.

CARRIE BROWN

On the morning of 24 April 1891, the body of Carrie Brown was discovered in the East River Hotel, situated on the Manhattan waterfront. Described as a squalid drinking den, the hotel was seen as a regular resort for prostitutes and looked upon, by locals, as a place of ill repute.

Due to her love of English literature (especially when drunk), Carrie Brown earned the nickname of 'old Shakespeare' and was well known as a local prostitute.

On the night of 23 April 1891, she had acquired a client and booked into the East River Hotel. Her companion's name was given as 'C. Kniclo'. Carrie was last seen alive when walking to her room at 10.45 p.m. At 9 a.m. on the morning of 24 April, her semi-naked body was found lying on her bed. Like previous Ripper victims, she had been strangled and mutilated, her injuries described as being severe, as if the killer had attempted to gut her. Brown's client was never traced and thus her murder immediately linked to the Ripper series. Although Algerian immigrant Ameer Ben Ali would later be arrested and convicted for her murder, he would be released eleven years later when it became apparent that cross contamination at the scene of the crime had meant blood found in Ali's room (and the only evidence linking him to the crime) had been mistakenly left there by an officer.

A single description was ascertained in relation to the client seen entering the hotel with Brown. A man was described by staff working in the hotel as about thirty-two years of age, 5 ft 8 in. tall, of slim stature, wearing a heavy moustache and appearing foreign – possibly German.

In 1901 a story made the papers that once again ignited the Brown murder case, when it emerged that a Danish farmhand, who was working in New Jersey during 1891, might have been the killer. His employer confirmed that he had been absent from work on the night of the murder. Though he returned on 24 April, the man disappeared soon afterwards. Within days the employer found a key in the farmhand's room that matched those used in the East River Hotel, along with blood-stained clothes. The man was never located.

Why the employer should have waited ten years to make his statement remains a mystery.

Interestingly, one of the officers heavily involved in the case was notable Detective George McClusky, known as 'Gentleman' or 'Chesty George'. In 1888, during the Ripper murders, McClusky was in London and had observed much of the police operation to apprehend the Ripper.

It was at this time that McClusky's mentor, Chief Inspector Thomas Byrnes, condemned the efforts of Scotland Yard as poor, commenting that should the Ripper ever venture to New York, 'he would be under lock and key in under two days.' And though for a while it appeared that Byrnes had lived up to his promise in capturing the man believed by some to be the American Ripper, to this day Carrie Brown's murder remains unsolved.

Appendix Three

Another 'Double Event'

The events of 30 September 1888, which culminated with the death of two prostitutes in the space of an hour, exemplified the shere brutality of the Ripper crimes and in addition highlighted the brazenness of the killer. The two murders also sent a clear and terrifying message to the authorities that, regardless of the risk, the killer had no intention of stopping.

The horror of the double event drew a speedy reaction from both the Metropolitan and City Police who responded by drafting in extra resources and flooding the district with officers. In an effort to squeeze potential clues from the residents of the East End 80,000 leaflets were produced and distributed locally, requesting any information on the murders.[1] In the hope that money might also provide a solution to the crimes a reward of £500 was granted by the Lord Mayor of London.[2]

Sadly such bold tactics would do little to aid the investigation and instead of generating positive leads left the police floundering, battling a faceless killer and a district on the brink of an uprising.

While terror invaded the ghettos of east London and left residents and businesses in a state of constant unease the pressmen of the day cashed in. Whether detailing the gory specifics of the murders or declaring a 'POPULATION IN A STATE OF FEAR',[3] the tabloid prose epitomised the sense of panic being felt throughout the city.

If the killings of Liz Stride and Catherine Eddowes could induce a countrywide hysteria then one can hardly imagine what the public reaction would have been should the Ripper have committed another 'double event' during his spate of murders.

While the written history of the case labels the two murders committed on 30 September as a singular occurrence, taking place only once throughout the entirety of the Ripper killings, today, thanks to a handful of newly discovered press reports, we are now faced with an alternative proposition.

In order to place the new information into its true context we must first revisit the early morning of 17 July 1889 and the discovery of the sixth Ripper victim - Alice McKenzie. As already covered in this book, during the summer of 1889 a surveillance operation was underway in the East End to monitor certain locations of interest. Although being led by the ever impressive Sergeant Stephen White the operation failed to bring the killer to justice.

Like those before her Alice McKenzie would have her life taken in the most brutal manner, in a small pocket of darkness, under the very noses of the police who were there to protect her. As for Stephen White, though his career would garner much praise, to many he would be known only as the man who 'missed' the Ripper.[4]

Looking back one can assume that McKenzie's killer would have been mindful of the likely police reaction to the discovery of another body and as such would have fled the area, away from the intense police activity. Indeed, when assessing the newly discovered evidence this appears to have been the case.

As indicated by contempory press reports from 1889, a male matching the appearance of White's suspect, whom he saw fleeing from Castle Alley moments prior to the discovery of McKenzie's body, was observed in the area of South London where he immediately began to attract attention.[5]

In the hours that followed the murder, with panic spreading throughout the city, across the Thames, the people of South London began to fear that the Ripper was among them. As reported by several newspapers during the 17 and 18 July a stranger had appeared on the 'south side of the River' and was attempting to gain access to lodging houses.[6] His actions appear to have drawn suspicion and he was refused entry.

Although the reason for their suspicion is not given it appears that either the male's demeanour or his conversation had warranted their misgivings, so much so that word soon began to spread to the police.

If the lodging house keepers had suspected that the stranger might be the Ripper then by the evening of 17 July their suspicians were to be compounded.

The story would unfold the next morning at Rodney Road Police Station in Walworth. There the duty officer took an account from a young woman who had arrived at the station in a state of distress. Though no name was given for the female she would confirm her address as Fox Court, Grays Inn Road in Central London.[7]

Like Alice McKenzie the female was a prostitute and on the evening of 17 July she had ventured into the back streets of London to ply her trade. Amid cold conditions the woman had walked the back streets of the East End in search of a client and eventually found her way to Bishopsgate. There, at just prior to midnight, she was approached by a man whom she would later describe as five feet nine, with a dark complexion and dressed in a black suit.[8]

After taking drinks at various public houses the man wished for the prostitute to accompany him away from east London on the pretence of having property across the river. The woman, desperate for funds, obliged and by 2 a.m. the pair had reached the lengthy thoroughfare of East Street in Walworth.[9]

On finding themselves alone and shrouded by the darkness of early morning the man's attitude suddenly changed. As they walked along the deserted street the male seized the woman and began to force her down one of the many narrow passageways nearby.

The woman began to scream and as a consequence the attacker produced a long-bladed knife which until then had been concealed.

He attempted to stab the woman at least once which immediately drew further screams. It was then that the man spoke and threatened that he was going to 'rip her up'.[10]

Aware of the imminent danger the woman continued scream and soon her terrified cries attracted the attention of a passerby, whom the papers would describe as a 'young man'. He had been walking nearby and on hearing the screams had immediately followed their path. On arriving at the short passageway, within the shadows, he found the distraught woman and saw a man fleeing from the area.

On asking the female what had taken place, the young man received a chilling reply: 'Jack the Ripper has attempted to stab me', she said.[11]

With the attacker still in sight the young man gave chase, attempting to close the gap that was growing between them. Despite his valiant efforts the would-be-killer would prove too fast to be caught and before long had vanished from sight.

The story of the woman's encounter with a potential *Ripper* caused an instant reaction from the police, with details of the assault being sent to senior officers who immediately ordered a search of the district. The constabulary saw the incident as being of significance and so much so that every police station in the Metropolis was wired the description of the attacker.[12]

Though the search would prove fruitless, with constables unable to locate the stranger among the teeming streets and lodging houses of the city, on hearing of the assault the Commissioner of the Metropolitan Police ordered that an official report be compiled for the Home Secretary.[13]

Although the victim was only able to provide a partial description of her attacker, that lacked an approximate age, as confirmed by the victim, the assailant was able to outrun the 'young man' who had pursued him, thus indicating that the attacker was himself a man of younger years and importantly was fast.

When comparing the description of the assailant to the known appearance of Thomas Cutbush the similarities are abundantly clear. It is also noteworthy to add that the phrasing used by the attacker is the same expression used by Cutbush while confined in Broadmoor in the spring of 1891.[14]

In choosing Walworth as the site of the attack the assailant had selected an area in the borough of Southwark which runs parallel to Kennington. What makes this location so significant is that in choosing East Street as the setting for his crime the would-be killer had picked a thoroughfare that leads almost directly to the home of Thomas Cutbush, being a mere three streets away from Albert Street.[15]

If the Ripper had wished to commit a second murder after the killing of Alice McKenzie then it seems obvious he would have chosen to do so away from the frenzied police activity in east London, in an area that he knew and from where he could easily escape. East Street in Walworth was perfect and provided the killer with less chance of capture and in addition an all important bolthole only minutes away from the scene of the crime.

When analysing the story of the 'Walworth Outrage' significant details begin to emerge that correspond with the known facts of the Whitechapel murders. Here we have a tale that begins in the heart of Ripper territory, with an attacker who not only matches eye witness descriptions of the Ripper but who demonstrates his cunning in luring his victim out of the area. He chose a prostitute as his target and selects to commit the crime in a dark passageway with a knife similar to the Ripper's murder weapon.

Though one might be inclined to simply dismiss the Walworth incident as an unrelated attack, when compared to the murders in East London and the MO of the killer, the similarities are striking and bring a new significance to a forgotten crime.

Appendix Four

KJ and Tracy

On the publication of *The Sun*'s findings, rival newspapers were understandably excited at the exposure of the first-ever police suspect. As Tracy had promised in order to protect the family *The Sun* declined to publish Cutbush's real name, leaving rival papers sceptical.

Then, as so often happens in the world of journalism, new stories began to grip the imagination of the public. As a terrorist attack on the United Kingdom shocked the world, *The Sun* published its final instalment on Cutbush. Unable to compete with the sensation of a French anarchist bombing at the Royal Observatory in Greenwich, sales of the newspaper began to dwindle.[1]

As the Cutbush story died, so too did *The Sun*. Soon after, T. P. O'Connor decided to throw in the towel leaving KJ desperate. His third child had just been born and with his livelihood in jeopardy, he spotted an opportunity.

The Evening News was for sale. It had large debts[2] but sold well and in 1894 had 100,000 readers.[3] KJ secured a meeting with 29-year-old Alfred Harmsworth (later Lord Northcliffe). Harmsworth had turned a struggling periodical, *Answers*, into a successful venture. He agreed to put up the money if the *News*'s proprietors would sell for £25,000.[4]

Having built up a strong friendship with Louis Tracy, KJ invited him to handle negotiations in return for a share.[5] His decision to include

Tracy in the venture worked well and soon after a deal was struck that gifted KJ the role of editor and Tracy manager,[6] with both men receiving 7½ percent of the income. As expected, the *News* soon turned to profit.[7]

While KJ rejoiced in his new-found success, by the winter of 1894, Louis Tracy was looking for a new cause. So moved was Tracy by his experience while working on the Ripper story, seeing the wicked truth of London's poverty during his many visits to Whitechapel, that he decided to sell his stake in the profitable newspaper and do what he could to help those less fortunate.[8]

By 1894 a recession had led to mass unemployment in the capital and aware that a severe winter (later confirmed as the coldest on record) was likely to take the lives of many of London's poor, Tracy set up twenty-three soup kitchens. At a cost of over £28,000 Tracy saved lives and provided much needed support at a time of crisis. It was, he later wrote, his 'greatest achievement'.[9]

By 1895, KJ had acquired the *Glasgow Daily Record* and the following year founded the *Daily Mail,* the UK's biggest selling newspaper. KJ's accomplishments were considerable. From the sixteen-year-old boy who would pen short articles on life in Glasgow for a local paper, *Scottish Nights,* he now found himself in a position of significant influence.[10]

While KJ remained in the world of journalism, Louis Tracy penned his first novel, *The Final War,* a conspiratorial debut about European powers set to destroy England. This was followed by *An American Emperor,* a tale of an American millionaire who became the Emperor of France. While researching the book in the summer of 1896 Tracy travelled to the United States, immersing himself in the environment within which the book was set.[11]

In the years that followed Tracy would go onto produce a catalogue of written works that would receive much acclaim from the reading public. Tracy's 1903 adventure novel *The Wings of the Morning* would prove one of the most popular books of the day and was described as a 'rattling good' tale and compared to Robert Louis Stevenson's *Treasure Island.*[12]

Two years later Tracy produced yet another mystery novel entitled *A Mysterious Disappearance* in which he would make direct reference to the subject of Jack the Ripper and chose to give a profile of the likely culprit. Tracy would go onto describe the killer as a young athletic lunatic who had a passion for anatomy, a hatred of prostitutes and a penchant for pestering doctors with outrageous theories.[13]

While Tracy continued his career as a writer by 1912 KJ's life took on a new direction. Having helped organise the news services of the *Daily Mail* and assisting in the creation of the *Daily Mirror*, ill health would force an foreseen decision. KJ would turn his back on journalism and seek financial security through the sale of his shares, for which he received a huge profit.[14]

At the age of fifty, in 1914 Tracy chose to assist in the creation of a new branch of the North Riding Volunteer Reserve, where a year later he would become sub-commander. During this time he became a war commentator and successfully presented lectures across America.

So passionate was Tracy in his new-found position that he joined the British Mission in the United States. In 1920 his efforts were eventually rewarded when he was presented with a CBE and a year later received further praise for his work in the restoration of Westminster Abbey.[15]

As for KJ, after two years in the position of chairman at Messrs Waring and Gillow Ltd, a furniture manufacturer, in 1916, he decided that his future lay in politics and became Tory MP for Hornsey.

In the same year Tracy again drew on his experiences in Whitechapel to write a murder novel, *Number Seventeen*, which has striking similarities to the Cutbush case. In addition, Tracy would also weave into his stories the locations that had formed the backdrop to the Cutbush saga, referencing Whitechapel, Kennington and even Broadmoor Asylum.[16]

For KJ, while having little influence at Westminster, he made a positive impact during the war in the Ministry of Food and Transport and in 1917 became the Director-General of the Food Economy Department. Throughout his time working in politics KJ impressed and by 1920 was appointed chairman of the advisory committee on London Traffic, in which he set up the Ministry of Transport. Although Kennedy Jones wished to achieve much in his new appointment, he would only hold the position for a year. At 1.25 p.m. on 20 October 1921, he died of pneumonia. On his death KJ had accumulated an estate worth over £200,000 and a net personal wealth of £86,548.[17]

For five years after the death of his good friend Louis Tracy wrote very little. When, in 1926, at the age of fifty-eight, he again took up his pen, he soon made up for lost time, writing thirteen novels in two years.

In 1928, Tracy began work on his latest novel, *The Fatal Thirteen*, though he would never finish it. On 13 August, Louis Tracy died, having completed only thirteen pages and leaving the world as a true British hero.[18]

Although to many Tracy was viewed as a globetrotter who thrived on adventure, in truth he was never more content than when staying in his rented cottage on the Isles of Scilly. There he remained a man of modesty, often found sitting quietly in his favoured armchair writing poetry.[19]

Louis Tracy and Kennedy Jones achieved much in their lives, creating news and literature that continues to exude their unique talent and enthusiasm. Although they went on to many accomplishments after leaving *The Sun* in 1894, their efforts in researching the life and crimes of Thomas Hayne Cutbush have left the world with an example of what determination and aptitude can achieve and perhaps have provided the answer to the most intriguing mystery the world has ever known.

Notes

PROLOGUE

1. *The Sun,* February 1& *Lloyd's Weekly News,* April 1891.

ONE

1. *Lloyd's Weekly News,* 19 April 1891.

2. This description is based on the photo of Inspector Race (provided by Stewart P. Evans) and also countless newspaper reports that describe his character, including *The Echo,* July 1and *Lloyds Weekly Newspaper,* 28 June 1896.

3. *The Sun,* 14 & 17 February 1894.

4. *The Sun,* 14 February 1894.

5. *The Sun,* 14 & 17 February 1894.

6. *The Sun,* 15 February 1894.

7. *Lloyd's Weekly News,* 19 April 1891.

8. http://www.casebook.org/ - The Macnaghten Memoranda

9. *The Sun,* 14 February 1894.

10. *Ibid.*

11. This is based on the content of Inspector Race's interview with the *Morning Leader* in February 1 and the information provided in the reports published by *The Sun.*

12. *Jack the Ripper and the London Press,* L.Perry Curtis (Yale University Press, 2002), p.51

13. *Jack the Ripper and the London Press,* L.Perry Curtis (Yale University Press, 2002), p.60.

14.   *Ibid.* p.82.

15.   *The Sun*, 13 February 1894 refers to the 'chance clue' that put the newspaper on the tracks of the Ripper that was followed by 'months of investigation,' inferring that they must have received their initial 'clue' in late 1893. Inspector Race was unquestionably *The Sun's* source. After the publication of the Cutbush story Race conducted several interviews with other newspapers. In one in particular he stated that only with the aid of the press could he hope to get the truth out and secure the conviction of Cutbush in relation to the Ripper crimes. Race also stated that he had passed the information, collated on Cutbush, to Scotland Yard and though receiving a bonus for his efforts little had been done. Consistently throughout the *The Sun's* articles they appear to be quoting the Inspector, especially in relation to the search of Cutbush's room and his confession, when arrested, to the 'Mile End Job'. For *The Sun* to have acquired such unique information on Cutbush, which provided a vital lead, their source must have been forthcoming with information. As he later stated, Race was particularly keen to talk in order get the truth of the Cutbush story out into the public domain. Although *The Sun* claimed that they accidentally obtained the clue (i.e. Race's claims) this doesn't detract from the fact that Race was in direct contact with the paper and spoke openly about his findings. We can take *The Sun's* term of an accidental clue to mean a clue or a lead that they hadn't expected. And it is easy to see why. Police Inspectors didn't usually divulge their theories and findings to the press. This was a chance lead for *The Sun* and one that they would seize.

16.   *The Times Law Reports: Volume 12*, G.E.Wright, 1896. p.93.

17.   *The Catholic Press (Sydney NSW)*, 15 June 1916 & *The World of Fashion: 1837-1922*, Ralph Nevill (Methuen & Company, Limited, 1923), p.80.

18.   *The Mirror: A Political History*, Maurice Edelman (H.Hamilton,

1966), p.4.

19.   *Ibid.*

20.   *The Mirror: A Political History* confirms that initially K.J. 'starved in Fleet Street'. In 1 he assisted in starting the *Morning* newspaper, however, this failed to turn a profit. At the same time his wife was pregnant with their daughter who was to be born in 1 when the family was living in Ardville Road, Brixton. *Bouquets of Fleet Street*, Bernard Falk (Hutchinson,1951), p.40, confirms that in his 'poorer days' Jones lived in a small property in Brixton.

21.   *The Sketch,* 11 July 1894.

22.   *The Sun*, 17 February 1894.

TWO

1.   This is taken from a review of Mary Ann Nichols taken from http://www.casebook.org/

2.   *The Jack the Ripper A-Z*, Paul Begg, Martin Fido & Keith Skinner (Headline, 1994), pp.332-333.

3.   http://www.victorianlondon.org/ - The dictionary of Victorian London

4.   Description taken from http://www.casebook.org/ - Flower and Dean Street

5.   The information pertaining to Mary Ann Nichols has been taken from *The Jack the Ripper A-Z,* pp.329-   and *Jack the Ripper: An Encyclopedia,* John J. Eddleston (Metro Publishing Ltd, 2002), pp.12-26.

6.   *Liverpool Echo,* 1 September 1888.

7.   *The Star,* 5 September 1888 & *Lloyd's Weekly Newspaper,* September 1888.

8.   *Jack the Ripper: An Encyclopedia,* pp.12-26.

9.   *The Times,* 4 Sept 1888.

10.   *The Star,* 31 August 1888 & *The History of The Star: In Memory of The Star (1888-1960)* Richard Simms, taken from - http://thestarfictionindex.atwebpages.com/the.htm

11.   *Morning Advertiser,* 4 September 1888.

12.	*The Echo, 6* September 1888.
13.	*The Daily Telegraph,* 3 September 1888.
14.	*Ibid.*
15.	*Woodford Times,* 7 September 1888.

THREE

1.	*Jack the Ripper or When London Walked in Terror*, Edwin T.Woodhall (P & D Riley, 1997), pp.10-13.
2.	*The Sun,* 14 February 1894.
3.	*Jack the Ripper: A Cast of Thousands* (2004) by Christopher Scott http://www.casebook.org/. Cutbush's father, Thomas Taylor Cutbush, bigamously married Agnes Ingles Stoddart on 10 December 1867 in Wellington, New Zealand.
4.	This passage is taken from various sources including the notes in Cutbush's Broadmoor files in which his mother and aunt refer to him as protecting boys from bullies. In addition, *The Sun's* article from February refers to Cutbush's practice of anointing his face with lotions.
5.	*The Sun,* 14 February 1894.
6.	*The Sun,* 15 February 1894.

FOUR

1.	*The Sun* 14 & 15 February 1894. The edition published on February states that in July 1888 Cutbush was using ointments and lotions, no doubt prescribed. In addition, Macnaghten, in his memoranda, stated that in 1888 Cutbush was suffering from Syphilis. As confirmed by *The Sun* in the November of 1890 Dr Brooks had stopped treating Cutbush. In the same year, according to Mr Thatcher, Cutbush was still experiencing pain (his face twisting) and he admitted to self -medication.
2.	*Victorian Diseases: Are They Making A Comeback*, Pat Hagan, an article placed on the website icscotland.co.uk
3.	*Syphilis in Early Modern Europe,* Jamie Whittenberg: http://www. wondersandmarvels.com/2008/11/

syphilis-in-early-modern-europe.html

4. *The Humble Little Condom: A History,* Aine Collier (Prometheus Books, 2007), p.168.

5. *Prostitution and Victorian Society: Women, class and the State,* Judith R. Walkowitz (United States of America: Cambridge University Press, 1980), p. 52 & p. 229 & *The Medico-Chirurgical Review & Journal of Practical Medicine, Volume 33,* edited by James Johnson M.D. and Henry James Johnson Esq. (Richard & George S. Wood, 1840), p.595.

6. *The Sun,* 15 February 1894.

7. *The Medical Profession in Mid-Victorian London,* Jeanne M.Peterson (Berkeley, Los Angeles, London: U of California, 1978), p.5, p. 30 and p.40.

8. *Manchester Guardian,* 12 November 1888 and *The Echo,* 12 November 1888.

9. *Morning Advertiser,* 19 November 1888.

10. *The Daily Telegraph,* 25 September 1888 & *The Star*, 25 September 1888.

11. *The Sun,* 13 February 1894.

12. *Ibid.*

13. *The Sun,* 15, 17 & 19 February 1894.

14. *The Sun,* 14 & 19 February 1894.

15. *The Sun,* 15 February 1894.

16. *Lloyd's Weekly News,* 19 April 1891& http://www.casebook.org/ - The Macnaghten Memoranda

17. *The Sun,* 15 February 1894.

18. *Ibid.*

FIVE

1. *Jack the Ripper: An Encyclopedia.* pp.12-26 & *Daily News,* 10 September 1888.

2. *The Daily Telegraph,* 27 September 1888 & http://www.casebook. org/ – James Hardiman

3. *East London Advertiser,* 15 September 1888 & *Autumn of Terror:*

Jack the Ripper, His Crimes and Times, Tom A.Cullen (Bodley Head, 1965), p.49.& p.72.

4. *Jack the Ripper: An Encyclopedia* pp.26-36 and photo images of Annie Chapman after her removal to the mortuary.

5. *Dickens's Dictionary of London 1888* (Old House Books, 1993), p.102.

6. *The Star,* 10 September 1888.

7. *The Jack the Ripper A-Z,* p.357.

8. *Jack the Ripper: An Encyclopedia,* p.35

9. *Daily Telegraph,* 14 September 1888.

10. *The Jack the Ripper A-Z,* p.9 confirms that on his retirement Abberline had received 84 police commendations and awards. A photograph of Abberline in *Abberline: The Man Who Hunted Jack the Ripper,* Peter Thurgood (The History Press, 2013), p.97, confirms his build and features and shows him to be a smartly attired officer. The book also confirms much of Abberline's character, including his popularity.

11. *Jack the Ripper,* Mark Whitehead and Miriam Rivett (Pocket Essentials, 2012), p.41-42.

12. *The Morning Advertiser,* 11 September 1888.

13. www.mcgonagall-online.org.uk covers Superintendant Hayes's actions in order to save the life of Queen Victoria against an assassin in Windsor.

14. *Jack the Ripper: An Encyclopedia,* pp.26-39 & *Jack the Ripper* (Pocket Essentials, 2012), p.33-34

15. *Evening Standard,* 11 September 1888.

16. *Daily News,* 26 September 1888.

17. *The Star,* 8 September 1888.

18. *El Universal* (Mexico), 1 November 1888.

19. *St. James Gazette,* London 12 September 1888 & *Echo,* 13 September 1888.

20. *Echo,* 13 September 1888.

SIX

1. This is taken from the article entitled 'Whitechapel' by Arthur G. Morrison which appeared in *The Palace Journal*, 24 April 1889. This can be accessed via http://www.casebook.org/

2. http://www.casebook.org/– Weather Conditions

3. For this section I have used accounts published in the following newspapers: *The Times,* 4 October 1888 & 29 September 1888 and *The East London Advertiser,* 6 October 1888, as well as accounts produced in *Jack the Ripper:An Encyclopedia* and *The Jack the Ripper A-Z.*

4. *Jack the Ripper: An Encyclopedia*, pp.4-5.

5. *Ibid.* pp.6-12.

6. *Jack the Ripper: An Encyclopedia,* pp.36-48.

7. *Ibid.*

8. *Morning Advertiser,* 3 October 1888.

9. *The Daily Telegraph,* 6 October 1888.

10. *The Jack the Ripper A-Z* pp.453 & *Jack the Ripper* (Pocket Essentials 2012), p.63.

11. *The Daily Telegraph,* 6 October 1888 & *The Jack the Ripper A-Z.* p. 295 & p.455.

12. *Evening News,* 4 October 1888 and http://www.casebook.org/ - Mathew Packer

13. *Morning Advertiser,* 6 October 1888.

14. *The Jack the Ripper A-Z.* pp.399-400

15. *Times,* 3 October 1888.

16. *Ibid.*

SEVEN

1. *Jack the Ripper: An Encyclopedia,* p.53 *& http://www.casebook. org/ - Catherine Eddowes*

2. *The Daily Telegraph,* 12th Oct 1888.

3. *From Constable to Commissioner,* Sir Henry Smith (Chatto & Windus, 1910), 'Chapter XVI – OF THE RIPPER AND HIS DEEDS AND OF THE CRIMINAL INVESTIGATOR, SIR

ROBERT ANDERSON.'

4.   *The Times,* 5 October 1888, *The Jack the Ripper A-Z,* pp.128-129 & *Jack the Ripper: The Facts,* Paul Begg (Portico Books, 2004), pp.235-236

5.   *The Times,* 3 October 1888.

6.   *The Daily Telegraph,* 3 October 1888.

7.   www.theorwellprize.co.uk– Hop Picking www.genuinelondon pearlykingsandqueens.co.uk– 'Hopping down in Kent'

8.   *The Star,* 3 October 1888.

9.   *East London Observer,* 1st September 1866.

10.   *The Jack the Ripper A-Z,* pp.129-130.

11.   *http://www.casebook.org/ - Catherine Eddowes*

12.   *The Daily Telegraph,* 12 October 1888 & *The Jack the Ripper: A-Z,* pp.168-169 & p.260.

13.   *The Ultimate Jack the Ripper Sourcebook: An Illustrated Encyclopedia,* Keith Skinner & Stewart P.Evans (Robinson, 2001) p.235.

14.   *http://www.casebook.org/ - Catherine Eddowes & Times,* 12 October 1888.

15.   *The Ultimate Jack the Ripper Sourcebook,* p.200 & p.228.

16.   All of the information pertaining to Sir Henry Smith's involvement in the Catherine Eddowes murder investigation has been taken from his autobiography, *From Constable to Commissioner.*

17.   *The Ultimate Jack the Ripper Sourcebook* includes a copy of Fosters work on which, in Fosters handwriting, the time is given.

18.   *Lloyd's Weekly News,* 19 April 1891.

19.   *The Times,* 1 October 1888.

20.   www.alangullette.com/lit/shiel/essays/shiel_tracy.htm John D.Squires A Whiff of Collaboration The Tracy-Shiel Connection (Revised through August 13, 2006)

21.   *East London Advertiser,* 6 October 1888.

EIGHT

1.   It would appear that both KJ and Tracy took it in turns when conducting interviews. Throughout the course of *The Sun's* articles

KJ and Tracy's differing writing styles are evident, whether recounting tales of the lodgers who shared 14 Albert Street with Cutbush or telling the story of Dr Brooks and Cutbush's solicitor.

2.   *East London Observer*, 13 October 1888.

3.   *East London Observer,* 22 September 1888.

4.   *The Sun,* 13 February 1894.

5.   *Evening News,* 11 October 1888.

6.   *The Sun,* 14 February 1894.

7.   *The Sun,* 13 February 1894.

8.   The article in *Lloyd's Weekly News* of 19 April 1891 confirms that Clara Hayne was all too willing to speak to the press about her nephew. In the article she confirms that around two years earlier his personality changed and he had become 'rather strange'. *The Sun* reports confirm that a particular family member (who in all probability was Clara) was willing to speak to Tracy and KJ and no doubt made similar statements to those given to the reporters of the *Lloyds Weekly News*.

9.   *The Sun,* 14 February 1894 & http://www.casebook.org/ - Dr. Thomas Neill Cream

10.   This observation is taken from *Jack the Ripper or When London Walked in Terror,* p.31

11.   *The Sun,* 14 February 1894.

12.   The Admission Notes taken from the Broadmoor Files on Thomas Cutbush.

13.   *The Evening News,* 4 October 1888.

NINE

1.   *East London Advertiser* 13 October 1888 reported that a medium in Bolton had uncovered indisputable proof as to the identity of the killer, being that, according to her connections in the 'other world,' Jack the Ripper was a moustachioed farmer who had peculiar pockets and scars behind his ears.

2.   *Birmingham Daily Gazette,* 8 & 9 October 1888.

3.   *Echo,* 15 October 1888.

4.   *Echo*, 9 October 1888.
5.   *Jack the Ripper: The Forgotten Victims,* Paul Begg & John Bennett (Yale University Press, 2014), p.69
6.   *Evening News*, 19 September 1888.
7.   *The Jack the Ripper A-Z,* pp.269 & 270.
8.   *The Jack the Ripper A-Z,* p.270.
9.   *The Daily Telegraph,* 20 October 1888.
10.   *Lloyds Weekly News,* 21 October1888.
11.   *The Sun,* 17 February 1894.

TEN

1.   *The Jack the Ripper A-Z*, p.58-59
2.   *Ibid.*
3.   *The Jack the Ripper A-Z* p.273 & *The Times* 12 November 1888.
4.   *Penny Illustrated Paper,* 17 November 1888.
5.   *Ibid.*
6.   *The Star*, 12 November 1888 & *Jack the Ripper: An Encyclopedia,* pp.61-72.
7.   *The Star,* 10 November 1888.
8.   *Walter Dew: The Man Who Caught Crippen,* Nicholas Connell, (Sutton Publishing Limited, 2005)
9.   *Evening News,* 12 November 1888.
10.   *The Ultimate Jack the Ripper Sourcebook*, p.417
11.   *Jack the Ripper: An Encyclopedia* & *Jack the Ripper A-Z,* pp.63-70.
12.   *Penny Illustrated Paper*, 17 November 1888.
13.   *The Jack the Ripper A-Z* p.229
14.   *The Daily Telegraph,* 13 November 1888.

ELEVEN

1.   *Evening News,* 12 November 1888.
2.   *Ibid.*
3.   *The Western Mail,* 12 November 1888.
4.   *Illustrated Police News,* 17 November 1888.
5.   *The Ultimate Jack the Ripper Sourcebook*, p.419 & *Penny Illustrated*

Police News, 17 November.

6. The admission notes from Broadmoor along with his case notes provide a description of Thomas Cutbush as taken on 23 April 1891.

7. *Evening News,* 4 October 1888.

8. http://www.casebook.org/– Mary Jane Kelly.

9. *Morning Advertiser,* 20 November 1888 & *Walthamstow and Leyton Guardian,* 24 November 1888.

TWELVE

1. *Evening News,* 10 November 1888.

2. *Jack the Ripper 150 Suspects,* Christopher J.Morley (Ashley Press, 2004) 23: EDWIN BURROWS'

3. *The Ultimate Jack the Ripper Sourcebook,* p.396.

4. *Pall Mall Gazette,* 2 October 1888.

5. *The Daily Telegraph,* 2 October 1888.

6. *Pall Mall Gazette,* 2 October 1888.

7. *Morning Advertiser,* 10 October 1888.

8. http://www.casebook.org/ – Thomas Bond.

9. *New York Herald,* 14 December 1888.

10. *Ibid.*

THIRTEEN

1. *The Sun,* 15 February 1894.

2. A note from Clara Hayne contained within the Broadmoor Files confirms that Thomas was violent and destructive and at times destroyed items and furniture in the house.

3. *Lloyd's Weekly News,* 19 April 1891.

4. *The Sun,* 19 February 1894.

5. This section is taken from three sources: *The Times,* 18 July 1889, *Woodford Times,* 19 July. 1889 & *Decatur Daily Dispatch,* 19 July 1890.

6. *Daily Gleaner,* 26 July 1889.

7. *The Ultimate Jack the Ripper Sourcebook, pp.506-508.*

8.   *Daily Gleaner,* 26 July 1889.

9.   *East End News,* 19 July 1889.

10.   *The Jack the Ripper A-Z,* pp.30-31 & *The Complete Jack the Ripper: A-Z* - ANDREWS, PC WALTER 272H. & *Jack the Ripper: An Encyclopedia,* p.77

11.   *Jack the Ripper: An Encyclopedia,* p.77 & *Decatur Daily Dispatch,* 19 July 1888. At the inquest of Alice McKenzie Constable Allen confirmed that at 12:30a.m. the landlord of the Three Crowns was shutting up.

12.   *The Times,* 18 July 1889.

13.   *Ibid.*

14.   *The Peoples Journal & http://www.casebook.org/victims/ - Alice Mckenzie*

FOURTEEN

1.   *The Times,* 19 July 1889 & *The Ultimate Jack the Ripper Sourcebook* - Chapter 28

2.   *The Times,* 19 July 1889 & 15 August 1889

3.   *Ibid.*

4.   *Ibid.*

5.   *The Times,* 19 July 1889.

6.   *The Ultimate Jack the Ripper Sourcebook,* p.500 & p.503

7.   *Walthamstow & Leyton Guardian,* 20 July 1889 & *Manitoba Daily Free Press,* 20 July 1889.

8.   *Jack the Ripper, 150 Suspects, '18: WILLIAM WALLACE BRODIE'* & *Woodford Times* 26 July 1889.

9.   *The Ultimate Jack the Ripper Sourcebook,* p.517 & *The Sun,* 14 February 1894.

10.   *The Sun,* 19 February 1894.

11.   *James Cutbush: An American Chemist 1788–1823,* Edgar F.Smith (J.B. Lippincott Company,1919). The 1871 Census confirms that Kate Hayne, aged twenty-six, was born in 'Philadelphia, N. America'

12.   *The Sun,* 15 February 1894.

FIFTEEN

1. *http://wiki.casebook.org/index.php/Swallow_Gardens* & *The Eastern Post & City Chronicle*, 14 February 1891.

2. The description of Frances Coles has been taken from *The Jack the Ripper A-Z*, p.88, *Jack the Ripper: The Forgotten Victims*, p.227 & *The Times*, 18 February 1891, as well as contemporary images of Coles that appeared in the press.

3. *East London Advertiser*, 21 February 1891 & *The Times*, 18 February 1891. In addition The Complete History of Jack the Ripper by Philip Sugden (Robinson, 2002)refers to a statement made by the sister of Frances Coles suggesting that she found working at the chemists a very hard and painful experience.

4. Sadler's description comes from a statement made by Mrs Shuttleworth as reported in *The Times* on 21 February 1891.

5. The Macnaghten Memoranda stated that Sadler was a man of 'ungovernable temper' and 'addicted to drink'. Sadler's wife spoke of her husband's personality, describing him as being unpredict-able and when drunk 'irritable' and violent, recounting another incident when Sadler had quarrelled with customers in a public house in Whitechapel. The Times on 21 February 1891 confirms that for around a year he had frequented the Marlborough Head in Brick Lane.

6. *The Ultimate Jack the Ripper Sourcebook*, pp.612- 613 & p.616 & *The Times* 18 February 1891.

7. *The Ultimate Jack the Ripper Sourcebook,* pp.613-614 & *The Times*, 21 February 1891.

8. *The Ultimate Jack the Ripper Sourcebook*, p.614 & *The Times*, 21 February 1891.

9. *East London Advertiser,* 21 February 1891.

10. *The Ultimate Jack the Ripper Sourcebook* p.614 & *The Times*, 21 February 1891.

11. *Ibid.*

12. *The Times*, 21 February 1891.

13. *The Ultimate Jack the Ripper Sourcebook,* p.610.

14.   *The Jack the Ripper A-Z*, p.89.

15.   *East London Observer* 14 February 1891 and *The Jack the Ripper A-Z* p.88 and *Jack the Ripper: An Encyclopedia*, pp.82 & 83.

16.   Many papers of the day perpetuated the theory that Sadler might have been the Ripper including: *Colorado Spring Gazette*, 18 February 1891 & *Manitoba Daily Free Press*, 21 February 1891.

17.   *The Times*, 21 February 1891.

18.   *The Sun*, 17 February 1894.

SIXTEEN

1.   *The Sun*, 17 February 1894.

2.   *Lloyd's Weekly News*, 19 April 1891.

3.   *The Sun*, 17 February 1894, confirms that Cutbush attempted to cut a relatives throat. The 'relative' was terrified of Cutbush but after calling in the authorities she 'became sorry'. It is presumed that the aforementioned 'relative' was his mother based on Cutbush's continued behaviour towards her in the years that followed, including his refusal to see her when she visited him in Broadmoor and his attempt to bite her face.

4.   This narrative is built on the evidence presented in *Lloyd's Weekly News* on 19 April 1891. *South London Press*, 21 March 1891, *The Sun's* articles & notes within Cutbush's Broadmoor files.

5.   *Lloyd's Weekly News* on 19 and 26 April 1891 & South London Press, 21 March 1891

6.   *Lloyd's Weekly News* on 19 and 26 April 1891

7.   *Ibid.*

8.   *Lloyd's Weekly News* on 19 and 26 April 1891 & *The Sun* 17 February 1894

SEVENTEEN

1.   *The Sun*, 17 February 1894 & *Lloyds Weekly News*, of 19 April 1891.

2.   *Lloyd's Weekly News*, 19 April 1891.

3.   *Ibid.*

4.   http://www.threecountiesasylum.co.uk/

5.   *South London Press,* 21 March 1891.

6.   *Ibid.*

7.   *South London Press,* 21 March 1891 & *The Times* 24 March 1891.

8.   *The Standard,* 15 April 1891.

9.   *Lloyd's Weekly News,* 19 April 1891.

10.   *Lloyd's Weekly News,* 19 April 1891 & *The Standard,* 15 April 1891.

11.   *The Sun,* 13 February 1894.

12.   *Jack the Ripper: An Encyclopedia,* p.207 & *Newcastle Chronicle* 2 October 1888 in which Donkin is referred to as 'J.Duncan'.

13.   *Daily News,* 19 September 1888.

EIGHTEEN

1.   *The Sun,* 16 February 1894.

2.   *Ibid.*

3.   *Ibid.*

4.   *Ibid.*

5.   http://www.berkshirerecordoffice.org.uk/

6.   *Doctors of Another Calling: Physicians Who Are Known Best in Fields Other than Medicine,* David K.C. Cooper (University Delaware Press, Newark, 2014), p.178 & 180.

7.   *The secret of Prisoner 1167: Was this man Jack the Ripper?* James Tully (Robinson Publishing,1998)

8.   *The Sun,* 16 February 1894.

9.   *The Secret World of Victorian Broadmoor* by Velma Dinkley found on http://ftfmagazine.lewcock.net/index.php/volume-two-new/january-2009/155-the-secret-world-of-victorian-broadmoor & http://www.dailymail.co.uk/news/article-1088801/Broadmoor-hospital-finally-gives-secrets.html

10.   *The Sun,* 16 February 1894 – This entire section has been taken directly from the findings published in the article.

NINETEEN

1.   This chapter has been created from the details contained in *The Sun's* articles published between 13 and 19 February 1894.

TWENTY

1.   *The Sun* 13 and 15, February 1894.
2.   *The Sun* 19, February 1894.
3.   *Portsmouth Evening News*, 14 February 1891.
4.   *Reynolds's Newspaper*, 18 February1894.
5.   *Dundee Courier*, 19 July 1889.
6.   *The Sun*, 19 February 1894.

TWENTY –ONE

1.   *Western Mail*, 16 February 1894.
2.   *The Man Who Hunted Jack the Ripper: Edmund Reid –Victorian Detective,* Nicholas Connell & Stewart P.Evans (Amberley Publishing, 2012) & *The Complete Jack the Ripper A-Z,* 'RACE, INSPECTOR WILLIAM NIXON (1855-1932).
3.   *Jack the Ripper: The Definitive History,* p.316.
4.   *The Jack the Ripper A-Z* p.116-121and also *Jack the Ripper: An Encyclopedia,* pp.208-211
5.   *The Jack the Ripper A-Z* , p.241-244 & *Jack the Ripper: An Encyclopedia,* pp.218-220 and http://www.casebook.org/
6.   Two of the initial suspects who came under suspicion in 1888 were Joseph Isenschmid, a Swiss Butcher, and John Pizer who was known as 'Leather Apron' and was a Polish Jew.
7.   *The Star*, 27 September 1888 & *Daily News*, 10 September 1888.
8.   *New York Tribune*, 27 September 1888.
9.   *Manchester Guardian*, 8 October 1888.
10.   *Jack the Ripper: An Encyclopedia,* pp.219-220.
11.   *Jack the Ripper: An Encyclopedia,* p.231 & http://www.casebook.org/- Michael Ostrog
12.   *Jack the Ripper 150 Suspects* , '150: MICHAEL OSTROG. 1833-?'
13.   http://www.casebook.org/ - The Macnaghten Memoranda

TWENTY –TWO

1. *The Complete Jack the Ripper A-Z: The ultimate guide to the Ripper mystery,* Paul Begg, Martin Fido, Keith Skinner (John Blake Publishing Ltd, 2010) – 'CUTBUSH, SUPERINTENDENT, CHARLES H.' *Dickens's Dictionary of London 1888,* p.198 confirms that the police station for A Division was located at King Street, Westminster.

2. *The Morning Post,* 24 August 1891 & *Worcestershire Chronicle,* 14 March 1896.

3. *The Complete Jack the Ripper A-Z,'* CUTBUSH, SUPERINTENDENT, CHARLES H.'

4. http://content.met.police.uk/ - 'Timeline 1870-1889' confirms that in 1873 The Metropolitan Police acquired nine new stations in North Woolwich, Rodney Road (Lock's Fields), Chislehurst, Finchley, Isleworth, Putney, South Norwood, Harrow and Enfield Town.

5. http://hansard.millbanksystems.com/commons/1873/jul/28/metropolitan-police-lighting-of-cells

6. *The Morning Post,* 24 August 1891. In addition *Dickens's Dictionary of London 1888,* p.198 confirms that the station designated for 'C or James Street Division' was located at 'Little Vine Street, Piccadilly'.

7. *Dickens's Dictionary of London 1888.* p.151.

8. *York Herald,* 12 February 1875.

9. *Nottingham Evening Post,* 16 August 1878.

10. *The Morning Post,* 24 August 1891.

11. 1891 Census.

12. *Manchester Times,* 28 January 1882 & *The Morning Post,* 24 August 1891.

13. *Reynolds Newspaper,* 27 August 1882.

14. *The Ultimate Jack the Ripper Sourcebook: An Illustrated Encyclopedia,* Keith Skinner & Stewart P.Evans (Robinson, 2001), p.10.& p.13

15. This information was provided by Claire Chevin.

16. *Ipswich Journal,* 14 March 1896 & *South London Press,* 14 March 1896.

17. *South London Press*, 14 March 1896.

18. *Ibid.*

19. *The Morning Post*, 10 March 1896.

20. Claire Chevin.

21. The information pertaining to Helen Cutbush has been provided by Claire Chevin and additionally gleaned from the details contained within her death certificate.

TWENTY –THREE

1. This chapter is made up from the contents of the Broadmoor files on Thomas Cutbush transcribed here courtesy of the Berkshire Records Office in Reading.

TWENTY –FOUR

1. *The Magnificent Seven: London's First Landscaped Cemeteries*, John Turpin & Derrick Knight (Amberley Publishing, 2011), Chapter : 'HOW IT ALL BEGAN…'

2. http://highgatecemetery.org/about/history

3. https://londonparticulars.wordpress.com

4. http://www.bbc.co.uk/london/content/articles/

5. http://www.gracesguide.co.uk/London's_Magnificent_Seven_ Cemeteries

6. http://www.bbc.co.uk/london/content/articles/

7. *City Secrets: London*, Robert Kahn & Tim Adams (The Little Bookroom, New York, 2001), p.175 & *The Magnificent Seven: London's First Landscaped Cemeteries,* Chapter: 'KENSAL GREEN CEMETERY'.

8. http://www.insider-london.co.uk/london-magnificent-seven-victorian-cemeteries-walks-london-marx-highgate-westnorwood/

9. "London's most underappreciated architecture – in pictures". The Guardian, 28 May 2013.

10. http://www.geograph.org.uk/

11. http://hidden-london.com/the-guide/nunhead-cemetery/

12. The Jurist Vol XIV–Part 1(London: S.Sweet, Chancery Lane;

V&R Stevens & G.S.Norton, 26 Bell Yard. Dublin: Hodges & Smith, Grafton Street, 1851), p.519.

13. http://www.bbc.co.uk/london/content/articles/2005/05/10/nunwood_cemetery_feature.shtml

14. http://www.geni.com/projects/People-buried-in-Nunhead-Cemetery/14979

15. *Broadmoor: A History of Criminal Lunacy and Its Problems,* Ralph Partridge (Chatto & Windus; First Edition, 1953), p.147

16. *Ibid.*

17. The inquest took place on 9 July and was presided over by Mr Weedon. Communication with the family must have been quick due to the fact that Cutbush's funeral took place only four days later.

18. *London Daily News*, 13 July 1903.

19. Cutbush's admission notes confirm that he was Church of England.

20. https://www.deceasedonline.com/ confirms that the first interment into the family plot was John Hayne, buried on 15 September 1891.

21. https://www.deceasedonline.com/ - burial register

22. *Western Times*, 14 July 1903.

23. *Exeter and Plymouth Gazette,* 14 July 1903.

24. https://www.deceasedonline.com/ - interment details

25. https://historicengland.org.uk

26. http://hidden-london.com/the-guide/nunhead-cemetery/

27. http://hidden-london.com/the-guide/nunhead-cemetery/

TWENTY –FIVE

1. *Jack the Ripper: The Final Solution* Stephen Knight (HarperCollins Publishers Ltd, 1979). Knight's theory is that the Ripper murders were an elaborate conspiracy between the Monarchy, the Freemasons and celebrated painter, Walter Sickett. Although one of the most widely read titles on the Ripper subject much of Knights evidence has been disproven.

2. *Pall Mall Gazette,* 2 October 1888.

3.   *John Blunts Monthly*, 16 December 1929.

4.   http://www.findmypast.co.uk/ - Register of Births 1865

TWENTY –SIX

1.   "The cop who missed the greatest collar of all time" John Rennie, February 2011 - http://www.towerhamlets.gov.uk/news/east_end_life

2.   *News of the World*, 14 October 1900.

3.   http://wiki.casebook.org/index.php/Stephen_White

4.   *News of the World*, 14 October 1900.

5.   *The origins of the vigilant state: the London Metropolitan Police Special Branch before the First World War*, Bernard Porter (Boydell & Brewer, 1991), p.27.

6.   *The American Slave Narrative and the Victorian Novel*, Julia Sun-Joo Lee (Oxford University Press, 2010), p.139.

7.   The first terrorist attack on London's Underground - http://www.historyhouse.co.uk/articles/terrorism_on_the_underground.html

8.   *The Irish-American Dynamite Campaign: A History, 1881-1896*, Joseph McKenna (McFarland, 2012), p.99.

9.   *The American Slave Narrative and the Victorian Novel. p.139* & *Irish Political Prisoners, 1848-1922: Theatres of War*, Seán McConville (Routledge, 2003), p.354.

10.   *The American Slave Narrative and the Victorian Novel.* p.139 & East London Observer 16 October 1900.

11.   *he American Slave Narrative and the Victorian Novel.* p.140

12.   *News of the World*, 14 October 1900.

13.   *Ibid.*

14.   *The Times*, November   1898.

15.   http://wiki.casebook.org/index.php/Stephen_White

16.   *The People's Journal*, 27 September 1919.

17.   *The Times*, 15 August 1889.

18.   *The People's Journal.*

19.   *Ibid.*

20.   *Ibid.*

APPENDIX ONE

1.   *The Star*, 10 September 1888 & *The Jack the Ripper A-Z* p.141 & 203, *Manchester Guardian* 10 September 1888, *The Complete History of Jack the Ripper* Philip Sugden, p.158 & *Jack the Ripper Sourcebook*, p.131.

2.   *Jack the Ripper 150 Suspects*, '112: THE RAILWAY POLICEMAN' & *Murder Most Foul*, True Crime Magazine (Forum Press, 1996), pp.38-42

3.   *Atlanta Constitution*, 31 January 1889 & 5 February 1889.

4.   *Newark Daily Advocate* 17 January 1889 & *Brooklyn Daily Eagle* 20 January 1889.

5.   The details relating to James Gray have been taken from several newspaper reports including: *Croydon Advertiser* 19 January 1889, *The Times* 18 January 1889, *Evening Star* 15 January 1889 & *Newark Daily Advocate* 16 January 1889.

6.   *Jack the Ripper 150 Suspects*, '97: JAMES MAYBRICK. 1838-1889' & *Jack the Ripper: An Encyclopedia*, pp.225-230

7.   *Jack the Ripper 150 Suspects*, '114: OSWALD PUCKRIDGE. 1838-1900'. *Jack the Ripper: An Encyclopedia*, p.234 & *The Ultimate Jack the Ripper Sourcebook*, p.132

APPENDIX TWO

1.   *The Eastern Post & City Chronicle*, 7 April 1888 & *East London Advertiser* 7 April 1888.

2.   *The Jack the Ripper A-Z*, p.465-466, *The Times* 10 August 1888 & *The Eastern Post and City Chronicle* 18 Aug 1888. In addition, I have also used details included in Dr Killeen's examination as found on http://www.casebook.org/ and within *The Ultimate Jack the Ripper Sourcebook* Evans & Skinner

3.   *The Times*, 20 February 1889.

4.   *Daily News*, 6 November 1888.

5.   *The Times*, 20 February 1889.

6.   *Ibid.*

7.   *Ibid.*

8.   *Ibid.*

9.   *Ibid.*

10.   *MEPO 3/142*

11.   *The New York Affair, Part II* by Wolf Vanderlinden on http://
www.casebook.org & *The New York Affair, Part Three* by Wolf
Vanderlinden published in *Ripper Notes: The American Journal
for Ripper Studies,* edited by Dan Norder (July 2004), pp.8-25. In
addition I have also used details published in *Qu'Appelle Vidette*
(Canada), 7 May 1891.

APPENDIX THREE

1.   *Jack the Ripper*, Miriam Rivett & Mark Whitehead (Pocket
Essentials, 2012), p.78

2.   *Jack the Ripper: The Definitive History*, Paul Begg (Pearson
Education Limited, 2005), p.250.

3.   *The Freeman's Journal and Daily Commercial Advertiser*, 1 October
1888.

4.   *East London Advertiser,* 27 September 1919 ran the headline:
'DEATH OF FAMOUS EAST-END DETECTIVE. OFFICER
WHO JUST MISSED CATCHING THE MYSTERIOUS
"JACK THE RIPPER"'.

5.   *Derby Daily Telegraph,* 19 July 1889.

6.   *Ibid.*

7.   *Daily Gazette for Middlesbrough,* 19 July 1889.

8.   *Derby Daily Telegraph,* 19 July 1889.

9.   *The Maryborough Chronicle,* 21 August 1889.

10.   *Ibid.*

11.   *The Evening News* (Australia) 23 August 1889.

12.   *Ibid.*

13.   *The Maryborough Chronicle,* 21 August 1889.

14.   In the Broadmoor report dated 23 May 1891 Attendant Bailey
noted that Cutbush had stated he would 'Rip up' the attendants
or anyone else that upset him.

15.   East Street is a long thoroughfare in the district of Walworth and

in 1889 was abutted by a maze of courts and alleyways. It is known for its bustling market and as the birthplace of Charlie Chaplin. At its junction with Walworth Road, virtually opposite, is the entrance to Penrose Street which leads to Penton Place from where access can be gained to Albert Street.

APPENDIX FOUR

1. The Observatory underwent an attempted bombing in 1894. This was possibly the first 'international terrorist' incident in Britain. The bomb was detonated by a 26-year-old French anarchist named Martial Bourdin.

2. *The History of the Times: The twentieth century test, 1884-1912*, (The Times Office, 1951), p.103.

3. *Northcliffe: Press Baron in Politics, 1865–1922,* J. Lee Thompson (London: John Murray, 2000), pp.22-23.

4. *Lords of Fleet Street: The Harmsworth Dynasty,* Richard Bourne (Routledge, 2016), p.24.

5. *Northcliffe: Napoleon of Fleet Street*, Harry James Greenwall, (A.Wingate, 1957), p.45.

6. *Politicians, the Press, & Propaganda: Lord Northcliffe & the Great War*, 1914-1919, J.Lee Thompson (The Kent State University Press, 2000), p.7.

7. *Northcliffe: Press Baron in Politics, 1865–1922,* J. Lee Thompson (London: John Murray, 2000), pp.22-23.

8. www.alangullette.com/lit/shiel/essays/shiel_tracy.htm John D.Squires A Whiff of Collaboration The Tracy-Shiel Connection (Revised through August 13, 2006)

9. *Ibid.*

10. *Fleet Street: Five Hundred Years of Press,* Dennis Griffiths (British Library, 2006), p.129.

11. www.alangullette.com/lit/shiel/essays/shiel_tracy.htm John D.Squires A Whiff of Collaboration The Tracy-Shiel Connection (Revised through August 13, 2006)

12. *The Sunday Times* (Australia) 26 June 1904

13. *A Mysterious Disappearance,* Louis Tracy (Gordon Holmes), (Edward J.Clode, 1905), p.196.

14. *History of the Times*, vol. IV, *The 150th Anniversary and Beyond, 1912–1948* (London: Printing House Square, 1952), pp.124-126

15. www.alangullette.com/lit/shiel/essays/shiel_tracy.htm
John.D.Squires, *A Whiff of Collaboration The Tracy-Shiel Connection* (Revised through August 13, 2006)

16. The books include: *The King of Diamonds: A Tale of Mystery and Adventure* (Grosset & Dunlap, 1904) *The Stowmarket Mystery,* (Booklassic, 2015) and *The Postmaster's Daughter* (1st World Library – Literary Society, 2005)

17. *Hull Daily Mail,* 20 October 1921 & 27 January 1922.

18. www.alangullette.com/lit/shiel/essays/shiel_tracy.htm
John D.Squires A Whiff of Collaboration The Tracy-Shiel Connection (Revised through August 13, 2006)

19. *Ibid.*

Select Bibliography

Books

Begg, Paul, Fido, Martin & Skinner, Keith. *Jack the Ripper A-Z* (Headline, 1994)

Begg, Paul, Fido, Martin & Skinner, Keith. *The Complete Jack the Ripper A-Z: The ultimate guide to the Ripper mystery* (John Blake Publishing Ltd, 2010)

Begg, Paul. *Jack the Ripper: The Definitive History*, (Pearson Education Limited, 2005)

Begg, Paul & Bennett, John. *Jack the Ripper: The Forgotten Victims* (Yale University Press, 2014)

Bourne, Richard. *Lords of Fleet Street: The Harmsworth Dynasty*, (Routledge, 2016)

Collier, Aine. T*he Humble Little Condom: A History* (Prometheus Books, 2007)

Connell, Nicholas. *Walter Dew: The Man Who Caught Crippen* (Sutton Publishing Limited, 2005)

Connell, Nicholas & Evans, Stewart P. *The Man Who Hunted Jack the Ripper: Edmund Reid – Victorian Detective* (Amberley Publishing, 2012*)*

Cooper, David K.C. *Doctors of Another Calling: Physicians Who Are Known Best in Fields Other than Medicine* (University Delaware Press, Newark, 2014)

Eddleston, John J. *Jack the Ripper: An Encyclopedia* (Metro Publishing

Ltd, 2002)

Edelman, Maurice. *The Mirror: A Political History* (H.Hamilton, 1966)

Ferris, Paul. *The House of Northcliffe: A Biography of an Empire* (World Pub; First American Edition, 1972)

Greenwall, Harry, James. *Northcliffe: Napoleon of Fleet Street*, (A.Wingate, 1957)

Griffiths, Dennis. *Fleet Street: Five Hundred Years of Press,* (British Library, 2006)

Hodgson, Peter. *Jack the Ripper: Through the Mists of Time* (Minerva Press, 2002)

Kahn, Robert & Adams, Tim. *City Secrets: London* (The Little Bookroom, New York, 2001)

Morley, Christopher J. *Jack the Ripper 150 Suspects* (Ashley Press, 2004)

Partridge, Ralph. *Broadmoor: A History of Criminal Lunacy and Its Problems* (Chatto & Windus; First Edition, 1953)

Perry Curtis, L. *Jack the Ripper and the London Press* (Yale University Press, 2002)

Peterson, Jeanne, M. *The Medical Profession in Mid-Victorian London.* (Berkeley, Los Angeles, London: U of California, 1978)

Pfeiffer, Carl J. *The Art and Practice of Western Medicine in the Early Nineteenth Century.* (Jefferson, NC, and London: McFarland ,1985)

Porter, Bernard. *The origins of the vigilant state: the London Metropolitan Police Special Branch before the First World War* (Boydell & Brewer, 1991)

Skinner, Keith & Evans, Stewart P. *The Ultimate Jack the Ripper Sourcebook* (Robinson, 2001)

Sugden, Philip. *The Complete History of Jack the Ripper* (Robinson, 2002)

Thurgood, Peter. *Abberline: The Man Who Hunted Jack The Ripper* (The History Press, 2013)

Thompson, J.Lee. *Northcliffe: Press Baron in Politics, 1865–1922,* (London: John Murray, 2000)

Thompson, J.Lee. *Politicians, the Press, & Propaganda: Lord Northcliffe & the Great War,* (The Kent State University Press, 2000)

Tracy, Louis. *A Mysterious Disappearance* (Gordon Holmes), (Edward J.Clode, 1905)

Tully, James. *The secret of Prisoner 1167: Was this man Jack the Ripper?* (Robinson Publishing,1998)

Turpin, John & Knight, Derrick. *The Magnificent Seven: London's First Landscaped Cemeteries*, (Amberley Publishing, 2011)

Whitehead, Mark & Rivett, Miriam. *Jack the Ripper* (Pocket Essentials ,2012)

Wolf, A.P. *Jack the Myth: A New Look at the Ripper* (Robert Hale- London,1993)

Websites

http://www.casebook.org/
https://www.deceasedonline.com/
http://www.threecountiesasylum.co.uk/
http://www.berkshirerecordoffice.org.uk/
www.alangullette.com/lit/shiel/essays/shiel_tracy.htm
http://www.gracesguide.co.uk/
London's_Magnificent_Seven_Cemeteries
http://www.insider-london.co.uk/london-magnificent-seven-victorian-cemeteries-walks-london-marx-highgate-westnorwood/
http://www.geni.com/projects/
People-buried-in-Nunhead-Cemetery/14979

Newspapers

Birmingham Daily Gazette
Daily Commercial Advertiser
Daily Gazette for Middlesbrough
Derby Daily Telegraph
East London Advertiser
El Universal (Mexico)
Evening News
Hull Daily Mail

Liverpool Echo
Lloyd's Weekly News
Manchester Guardian
Morning Advertiser
Newark Daily Advocate
Newcastle Chronicle
Penny Illustrated Paper
St. James Gazette
The Catholic Press (Sydney NSW)
The Eastern Post & City Chronicle
The Evening News (Australia)
The Echo
The Evening News
The Freeman's Journal
The Daily Telegraph
The Maryborough Chronicle
The Pall Mall Gazette
The Weekly Standard and Express
The Star
The Sun
The Times
Woodford Times
York Herald

Magazines

*John Blunts Monthly (*16 December 1929)
*Murder Most Foul (*1996)
Ripper Notes: The American Journal for Ripper Studies (July 2004)
The People's Journal (27 September 1919)

Acknowledgements

I would like to extend my gratitude to the following people who have helped me throughout the preparation of this book: Mark Stevens, the curator of Berkshire Records Office, for allowing me to view the files on Thomas Cutbush in 2008, and John D. Squires for his fascinating research into the life of one of Britain's best novelists.

A huge thank you goes to my agent Andrew Lownie for his passion and unwavering belief. Thanks also to Kris Hollington for his input and advice over the years and to Stephen P. Ryder for use of material from the research website www.casebook.org.

To Sam Carter, Hollie Teague and all at Biteback Publishing and The Robson Press, I would like to extend my sincere appreciation for having faith in me with the first publication of this book. Thank you also to Claire Chevin for providing a fantastic insight into the life of the Cutbush family and shining a new light on the life and death of Charles Henry Cutbush.

For their support I would like to say a big thank you to the following people: Jeff and Jacquie Clarke; Sarah, Helen, James and Bob Reed, Charlene Bourg, Louise Crichton Bullock, Dave Wright and Nick Knowles.

Thanks also go to my brother —the very talented Steven Bullock — for bringing Thomas Cutbush to life in creating a fantastic portrait. I would also like to express my heartfelt appreciation and love to Richard and Sherryl Bullock for buying me my first book and for being the very best parents a son could ever wish for.

To my boys, Benjamin and Samuel, and to my beautiful wife Beccy, thank you for everything. I love you with all my heart.

To all at The Whitechapel Society, Waterstones Windsor and the staff at Windsor Library I am truly grateful for the support that you have shown me along the way. Thanks also to the wonderful author Peter Hodgson for his kind words and encouragement over the years. My appreciation also goes to Paul Begg, Essie Fox, Tessa Harris and Linda Stratmann for their very generous reviews.

I would also like to acknowledge a number of authors whose work I have referred to or summarised in this book: Bernard Brown, Stewart Evans, A. P. Wolf, H. Simonis, L. Perry Curtis, Paul Ferris, Keith Skinner, Martin Fido, John J. Eddleston, Richard Simms, Christopher Scott, Edwin T. Woodhall, Horatio Bottomley, Pata Hagan, Jamie Whittenberg, Aine Collier, J. Walkowitz, Jeanne M. Peterson, Carl J. Pfeiffer, Trevor Marriott, Mark Whitehead, Miriam Rivett, Christopher J. Morley, Edgar F. Smith, Philip Sugden, James Tully, John Rennie, Julia Sun-Joo Lee, Wolf Vanderlinden and J. Lee Thompson.

To all my friends and colleagues at Thames Valley Police, thank you all for the support you have shown me over the years. I appreciate it immensely.

I would also like to express my sincere appreciation to my friend and unofficial publicist, Lou Turner. Thank you for all that you have done.

Finally, thank you to you the reader. I hope you enjoyed the book.